Passage to Torres Strait

Also by Miles Hordern

Voyaging the Pacific

Passage to Torres Strait

Four Centuries in the Wake of
Great Navigators, Mutineers,
Castaways and Beachcombers

MILES HORDERN

JOHN MURRAY

© Miles Hordern 2005

First published in Great Britain in 2005 by John Murray (Publishers)
A division of Hodder Headline

The right of Miles Hordern to be identified as the Author of the Work has been asserted by him
in accordance with the Copyright, Designs and Patents Act 1988.

1 3 5 7 9 10 8 6 4 2

A CIP catalogue record for this title is available from the British Library

ISBN 0 7195 6496 4
Trade paperback ISBN 0 7195 6498 0

Typeset in 12.25/15 Monotype Bembo by Servis Filmsetting Ltd, Manchester

Printed and bound by Clays Ltd, St Ives plc

Hodder Headline policy is to use papers that are natural, renewable and recyclable products and
made from wood grown in sustainable forests. The logging and manufacturing processes are
expected to conform to the environmental regulations of the country of origin.

John Murray (Publishers)
338 Euston Road
London NW1 3BH

Contents

Illustrations

All photographs were taken by the author.

Illustrations in the text

Maps

Hawaii

PARTS OF THE
NORTH AND SOUTH
PACIFIC OCEANS

Kiribati

Equator

Tuvalu   .Starbuck

POLYNESIA   Rakahanga .Penrhyn   Marquesas
                      Manihiki
Rotuma   Alofi   .Samoa   .Suvarov
.Sandalwood Coast
         .Lau   Cook Islands
Fiji   .Vava'u   Raiatea
Levuka   .Ha'apai   Tahiti
                 .Tongatapu
     Ata   Rarotonga

                                    Tuamotu Archipelago

SOUTH   PACIFIC OCEAN

Bay of Islands (Russell)
Waiheke

New Zealand

                              W140°   S40°

Lambert Azimuthal Equal Area Projection

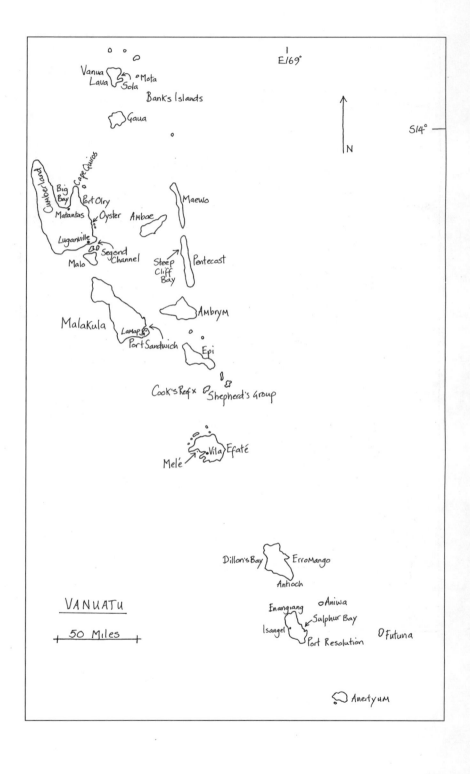

E 169°

S 14°

N

Vanua Lava
o Mota
Sola
Banks Islands

Gaua

Cape Quiros
Cumberland
Big Bay
Port Olry
Matantas
Oyster
Luganville
Malo
Second Channel
Ambae
Maewo
Steep Cliff Bay
Pentecost

Malakula
Lamap
Port Sandwich
Ambrym
Epi

Cook's Reef ×
Shepherd's Group

Melé
Vila
Efaté

Dillon's Bay
ErroMango
Antioch

VANUATU

50 Miles

Enanguang
o Aniwa
Sulphur Bay
Isangel
Port Resolution
o Futuna

Aneityum

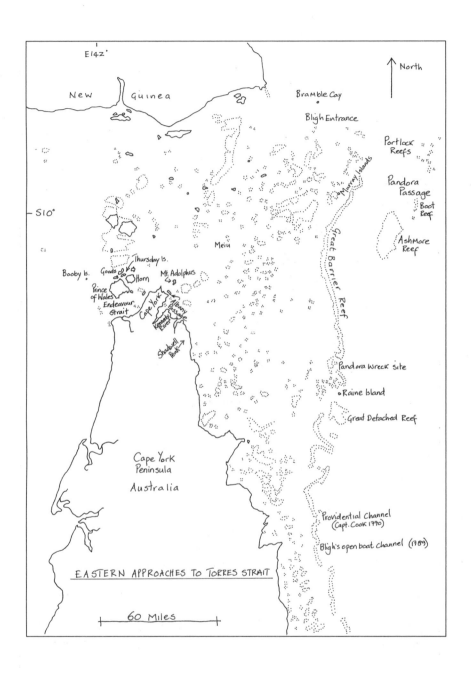

E 142°

North

New Guinea

Bramble Cay

Bligh Entrance

Portlock Reefs

Pandora Passage

S 10°

Murray Islands

Boot Reef

Ashmore Reef

Meiu

Great Barrier Reef

Thursday Is.

Goods

Booby Is.

Horn

Mt. Adolphus

Prince of Wales

Endeavour Strait

Cape York

Kennedy River

Adolphus

Shadwell Peak

Pandora Wreck Site

Raine Island

Great Detached Reef

Cape York Peninsula

Australia

Providential Channel (Capt. Cook 1770)

Bligh's open boat channel (1789)

EASTERN APPROACHES TO TORRES STRAIT

60 Miles

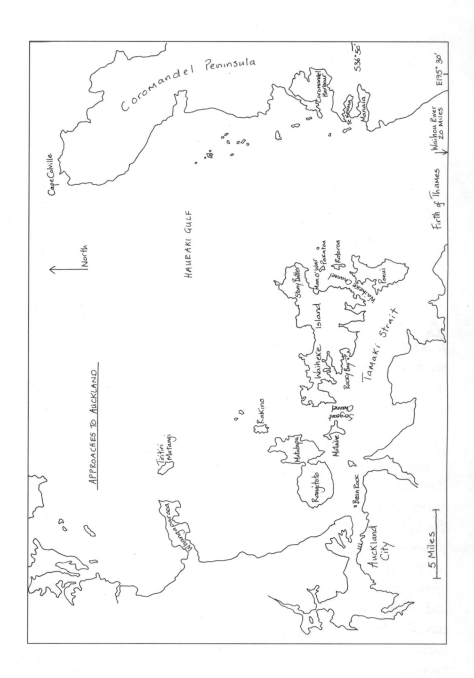

APPROACHES TO AUCKLAND

North

Coromandel Peninsula

Cape Colville

HAURAKI GULF

Coromandel Harbour

536° 50'

Te Kouma

Manaia

E175° 30'

Waihou River
20 Miles

Firth of Thames

Stony Batter

Chamo'War

Pakatoa

Island

Waiheke Channel

Kaharoa

Ponui

Tamaki Strait

Waiheke

Rocky Bay

Tiritiri Matangi

Rakino

Sergeant Channel

Motutapu

Motuihe

Rangitoto

× Bean Rock

Whangaparaoa

Auckland City

5 Miles

PROLOGUE

Flotsam and Beaches

'It is the common sailors and the lowest order of them, the very vilest of the whole, who will leave their ship and go to live amongst the savages and take with them all their habits and all their vices.'

Reverend John Williams, 1838

AT LUNCHTIME I finished a bottle of rum. The wind was steady for the first time on the passage and the sails were pregnant with purpose, pressed tight and swollen without a crinkle in their weave. In the afternoon I hid from the tropical sun, wrote a short message, sealed it inside the empty rum bottle, then threw the bottle over the side of the boat. After that I forgot all about it. Perhaps it was the rum.

Ten months later, to the day, a letter arrived at home in New Zealand postmarked Cairns, Australia. It read as follows (the punctuation is unaltered): 'We found your message in a bottle on the 24/10/03. at a sand cay named Meiu (fisherman name for it is Aeroplane as the cay has a wreck from WWII on it. Its position is 10° 19. 77S 143° 14. 28E where we were at anchor. The Aus crew paddled ashore to have a look at the wreck have a walk swim and found bottle and brought it back to the boat. Obviously it travelled fast on the South Easterlies your position according to message was 19° 40' S 168° 16' E 20/5/03. Gotta go – meet mothership. All the Best, crew of F.V. Aquarius 6, Cairns, Peter Simon Andrew. P.S. Melbourne Cup Day Today.'

I

When I received the fishermen's letter I studied the chart of the waters north of Australia. Meiu Cay lies 47 nautical miles north-east of Cape York, in the heart of Torres Strait. The reef is one-and-a-half miles long, with a tiny disk of compacted sand at its centre. Meiu is just one of the hundreds of uninhabited coral and sand formations that litter Torres Strait and stretch south down the coast of tropical Queensland, a saltwater maze of shoals and reefs which Captain Cook named the Labyrinth. At its eastern extremity the Labyrinth is defined by the Great Barrier Reef beyond which the shallow seabed plunges down to form deep ocean. After looking at the chart I checked the sloop's logbook. The bottle had drifted 1,500 miles and I had sailed a similar course, across the Coral Sea and up the Cape York Peninsula. A few weeks before the crew of FV *Aquarius 6* found my bottle I'd anchored overnight at Mt Adolphus Island, only 40 miles from Meiu Cay.

I sent a copy of the fishermen's letter to Dr Curtis C. Ebbesmeyer in Seattle, publisher of *The Beachcombers' Alert*. For modern-day beachcombers, messages in bottles – or 'MIBs' in beachcomber jargon – are one of the most valued items to find washed up among the kelp and shells. Maurice Jacobs, an officer with the shipping line P&O Nedlloyd, has thrown more than 350 MIBs overboard and received 16 replies, a return of 5 per cent which is considered good for oceanic drift. Despite this seemingly poor rate of return, MIBs are still sometimes used as a means of communication. In the early 1980s Taiwan released more than 100,000 MIBs – or 'propaganda drifters' – off the coast of China all advertising Taiwanese freedom and prosperity. Dr Ebbesmeyer wrote a short article for his newsletter about my own MIB being found in Torres Strait, which he titled 'Bottle Shadows Lone Sailor'. The fact that I anchored 40 miles from Meiu Cay after a passage of 1,500 miles is unusual, but not exceptional. The fate of some MIBs is freakish. Thirteen-year-old Alexi Hall threw a MIB from his parents' yacht near Guadeloupe Island in the Caribbean which then drifted 5,000 miles and was found on a beach near Lydd, Kent, 10 miles from Alexi's home. Barbara Read's MIB shadowed her voyage even more tenaciously. Barbara was sailing the tri-maran *Cream* from the Galapagos to Tahiti in June 1993 when she drank a two-litre bottle of Stoli vodka, put a message inside and tossed it over the side. Thirteen months later *Cream* arrived at the small Pacific island of Alofi. The following day, 17 July, a local fisherman at Alofi found Barbara's Stoli bottle on the beach.

Today, beachcombers are a thriving community and stage regular fairs including Washington's 'Grayland Driftwood Show' and Alaska's 'Paths Across the Pacific'. Beachcombers experience sea travel at one remove: prowling the ocean's periphery they hunt for flotsam, then stare out to sea and wonder about its source. Beachcombing has become a homage to ocean drifts and beach debris, the interaction of system and chance, currents and coast-lines, and the cargoes to be found wherever surf hits the sand. Curtis Ebbesmeyer monitors 'flotsam events' such as the 29,000 children's bath toys (blue turtles, yellow ducks, red beavers, green frogs) that fell from a ship in the Pacific in 1992 and have been turning up on beaches around the world ever since. Ebbesmeyer is a popular ring-in for radio stations on both sides of the Atlantic. His tales of beach debris and epic toy-beaver voyages epitomize the quirkiness of modern-day beachcombing. Today, combing the beach has become a whim, a harmless pastime to which few of us would object.

But it hasn't always been this way. In earlier times beachcomb-ers were despised.

It was only when I sailed into the Pacific that I discovered beachcombing had once meant something else. I left England alone in *Gordian*, a 28-foot sloop, in 1990 and early the next year cleared the Panama Canal. My first landfall in Polynesia was in the Marquesas Islands where I read the story of the beachcomber Edward Robarts. After deserting from the whaler *Euphrates* in December 1798, Robarts lived on the beach for nine years, married into a family of chiefs and became a man of rank. He had never been that on board ship.

I sailed south-west through the coral atolls of the Tuamotus and reached Tahiti, an island once overrun by beachcombers. At Matavai Bay I stood beneath the palms where a group of beachcombers led by James Morrison had built an 18-ton schooner. The little ship was an ensemble of improvisation and enterprise, but still the beachcombers were not always easy men to like. The beach could be a violent and bloody arena. When a Tahitian stole a pair of trousers Brown cut off a man's ears 'tho he Could not be sure that he had stolen [them]'.

Seven hundred miles to the north-west I anchored in the lagoon at Penrhyn Atoll where the brig *Chatham* had smashed onto the reef at night 138 years earlier. The *Chatham*'s owner, E.H. Lamont, came ashore with his band of drunken, illiterate sailors at a ribbon of land, densely populated, where no white man had ever been spoken to before. 'This was their world,' Lamont wrote, '. . . though they knew another land must exist where these great ships came from, one that they called "Te Tera range," or "the Land beyond the Sky".' The castaways spent a year ashore, negotiating for their lives.

In September of that year I reached Vava'u, a northern archipelago in the Kingdom of Tonga. The cyclone season was imminent, so I anchored the sloop here for six months and worked as a teacher in island schools. The children asked me whether I had heard of the beachcomber George Vason. Then they sniggered. It turned out that for George Vason the beach had been an erotic adventure. He arrived in the islands in 1796 proudly clad in a missionary's frock coat, intent on claiming the Tongans for God. But the converter became a convert. In no time at all he had submitted to having his backside tattooed and dressed in a loincloth. Vason described his first Tongan wife as 'a handsome girl of the age of eighteen'; his second was 'a fair pretty girl, only fourteen years of age . . . I lament to say, that I now entered, with the utmost eagerness, into every pleasure and entertainment of the natives.'

Today, 'going native' is a cliché, but in the age of sail it represented a stain on a man's moral character. In North America those pioneers who crossed the cultural divide and lived among the native tribes were known as 'Indian-traders'; in Australia they were 'white-blackfellows'; in the tropical Pacific anthropologists and historians have long referred to these men as the original 'beachcombers'. At best, they were seen as men with feckless, roving dispositions. At worst, beachcombers were considered to be shameless degenerates who had abandoned every notion of civilization and propriety. The beachcombers and the missionaries were sworn enemies.

Beachcombing has always been a part of voyaging. Beachcombers came into the Pacific on the first European voyage of discovery. When Ferdinand Magellan's *Trinidad* reached the Mariana Islands in 1521 three of the crew deserted. Two were killed but a third man, a Galician named Gonçalo de Vigo, lived ashore in the islands for four years before being picked up by another Spanish ship. Two hundred years later, when the Dutch navigator Rogeveen was wrecked in the Tuamotus, his quartermaster and four seamen elected to live among the islanders. None were ever seen again by Europeans.

But beachcombers only arrived in force with the coming of the trading ships that sailed in the explorers' wakes. The traders represent the grimy, lawless underbelly of Pacific voyaging and their stories have seldom been chronicled. They came for sandalwood, bêche-de-mer, and cargoes of human labourers to work on the plantations. As the schooners sailed and fought their way between the islands, the crewmen started to come ashore. Some were the victims of shipwreck; many deserted; a few were mutineers. Beachcombers' stories narrate the course of a difficult and dangerous journey from ship to shore. Others still were convicts on the run from the penal colonies of Australia who stole frail open boats and made desperate voyages of escape into the Pacific vastness.

I found beachcomber history at almost every island group I visited. Sometimes scores of beachcombers had once inhabited the shores of a single island. Beachcombers lived through a bewildering array of experiences far broader than those described in most sea narratives. Collectively, they were castaways and drift voyagers, torture victims and slaves, ship's pilots and trading agents, interpreters and mediators, armourers and innovators, mercenaries and executioners. Some were elevated to the ranks of chiefs and deities. Others peddled religion and quack medicines. A few led 'sailor cults' with thousands of followers. Their stories began on the decks of ships, yet have been ignored by maritime historians. Beachcombers were the ordinary sailors who found themselves living in extraordinary circumstances. No general history of beachcombing has been published that I've been able to find. But there still remains a substantial body of beach literature, written by the beachcombers themselves. In Tonga, two of these beachcomber narratives are still in print. The accounts of George Vason and William Mariner rattle off local printing presses in dilapidated warehouses that still stink of copra. Beachcombers left the first written accounts of indigenous culture in the Pacific Islands. They were the first unwitting anthropologists who bridged the gap between ship and shore and caught a glimpse of European voyaging from the other side of the beach.

I have two small bookcases in my sloop, one above each bunk on either side of the cabin. From the outset, pride of place had been given to the great explorers: I carried the journals of Pedro Fernandez de Quiros, Louis Antoine de Bougainville and Captain James Cook. But as time went by I added a different kind of tome to my shelves, mostly written by people with shorter names. I collected the beachcomber texts of Edward Robarts, James Morrison, E.H. Lamont, George Vason, William Mariner, William Cary, William Lockerby, Samuel Patterson, Peter Dillon and Benjamin Morrell. With the addition of their stories, my library better reflected the totality of European voyaging in this sea. I slid the beachcomber accounts between those of the great navigators as if this were somehow a subversive act. Beachcombing has always been a subtext awash between the lines of received history.

When I arrived in Tonga at the beginning of the cyclone season in 1991 I had no intention of living in the Pacific permanently.

This was only to be a pit stop on a longer voyage around the world, so I found employment as a temporary schoolteacher. In April or May of the following year, when the threat of storms had lifted, I planned to sail north-west to Torres Strait and so through into the Indian Ocean and ports further west.

But six months later, when the time came to leave Tonga, I put off the passage to Torres Strait. Instead, I sailed south-west to New Zealand. Island schoolteachers aren't well paid and I needed to earn some money. I didn't know it at the time but modern New Zealand's origins lie partly in a beachcomber society. In the early 1800s thousands of runaway sailors had thronged these shores having made a permanent landfall in the ocean. And as I too have now made my home in New Zealand, these men are, for better or worse, my forebears.

Twelve years passed before I began making preparations for that often postponed passage out of the Pacific Ocean. The journey would take me north from New Zealand to the Melanesian islands, then west across the Coral Sea to the Great Barrier Reef and Torres Strait, the treacherous, reef-strewn channel that separates New Guinea and Australia. I wanted to make this Pacific voyage a quest for origins, my own origins in the Pacific as a sailor turned settler. I would sail in the wakes of my forebears as they ran before the south-east trade winds into the first racing tides and coral waters of Torres Strait. But I would also follow them up the beach, the melting pot where the world of ships both fought and merged with the world pre-existing behind the tree line. It had been on the beach that some sailors found themselves out of their depth for the first time in a life spent at sea.

I

Sandalwood and the Cross

'For popular effect, for the reputation of Reverend Williams,
and for the purposes of history, he died in the proper manner,
at the proper place, and at the proper time.'
  Dr John Campbell, historian of the maritime missions, 1842

MY HOME ISLAND of Waiheke is 15 miles from downtown Auckland, New Zealand. Helen and I drove through the twisting lanes to Rocky Bay in near silence, the car's headlights an extension of our shared empty gaze into the breaking dawn. Helen had been the reason I had stayed in New Zealand. When I'd first arrived here 12 years earlier I had gone to work in a school in the city. Her desk had been opposite mine in the teachers' room. I'd made several voyages since then, always alone, first eastwards across the Southern Ocean to Chile, and later north to the tropical islands. When we had started going out together, almost the first thing she said to me was 'I know you will always go away to sea.' I hadn't known this until she'd said it, but she gave me licence and I wanted to repay her generosity by making her understand why. I tried to explain the process of passage making, the allure of voyaging beyond the horizon, the cycle of squalls and calms, war and peace on the ocean, but could never make it stick. Helen was not a sailor and saw only emptiness in the seascape. She crossed the water every day on the ferry to work in the city and saw the 35-minute journey as a void to be filled with books or chatting to friends. I think that in Helen's mind, when I went to sea, I disappeared out into this same emptiness, an unknown non-place beyond the ferry's rail.

'Have you got your passport?' she asked.

'Yes.'

It was a good question. Amid the other preparations it was easy to forget you still needed documents at sea.

I parked the car on the slipway at Rocky Bay and started untying the kayak from the roof rack. Helen carried the last couple of bags down to the water's edge. I kissed her wet cheeks and lips as a pasty sun seeped over the ridgeline. She told me to be careful. 'I'll see you in a few weeks,' I said. Helen had booked a flight to Port Vila in Vanuatu and would come for a holiday once I reached the islands. By the time I'd reached the sloop on its mooring and pulled the kayak onto the deck, the car had gone.

At least the wind was fresh. A woolly, easterly flow was rushing in from the Pacific, thick and heavy with the promise of rain. White caps, littered with leaves and twigs torn from the bush, cut the surface of the bay. I got up the mainsail and headed south into the waters of the Tamaki Strait, then poled out the genoa and ran west beside the tumbling vineyards and ochre crags of Waiheke's southern shore. Ahead, in the distance, Auckland's skyline appeared as a dome of broken teeth, nestled among the volcanic cones. In the Sergeant Channel I saw the Waiheke commuter ferry, two miles to the north, steaming towards town. It was a muggy morning, Helen would be sitting somewhere on the after-deck. I fingered my mobile phone for a moment, thinking of one last call, then turned the phone off and threw it down onto the bunk. There was nothing else to say.

I was early, so furled the genoa at Bean Rock and ran the last miles into the city at an easy gait. A car-carrier was berthed at the container port, the vast, dimpled slab of its hull obscuring the whole of downtown Auckland. Beyond the bulbous bow, Marsden Wharf lurched out into the harbour, crooked with age. I dropped the mainsail and motored towards the customs pontoon.

An 80-foot trawler yacht, the MV *Galleria*, already occupied the berth. I could see the white shirts and gold lapels of customs officers in the wheelhouse. At the stern a crewman was leaning over the rail, a cigarette pinched in clawed hands.

'Where are you bound?' I asked.

'Rarotonga, then back though the islands.'

It was mid-May, autumn in the Southern Hemisphere, the season of migration.

Customs were busy clearing boats heading for the tropics before the onset of winter. A white-haired officer stuck his head from the trawler's wheelhouse and shouted to me: 'You *Gordian*? You're early. Give us ten minutes.'

'So what about you?' the crewman asked. I told him I was going to Erromango, an island in the southern part of Vanuatu. He nodded, at the boat, not me. 'I used to go up and down to the islands in little boats like that. She's thirty foot is she?'

'Twenty-eight,' I said.

'It was my knees that went in the end.'

I motored to the more sheltered waters at the base of the wharf. Two blocks inland, the glass and steel towers of the central business district climbed high above the sloop's rig, bearing the legends of the new age on the Pacific Rim: KPMG; Citibank; Qantas; PriceWaterhouse Coopers. But crouching at the feet of these towers, Auckland's Victorian waterfront was still largely intact, now defunct brand names permanently embossed on the stonework: Union Fish Co.; The Northern Steamship Company Ltd.; Quay Buildings; Seafarers' Centre. Most of these buildings were abandoned. Net curtains the colour of dust filled rows of arched windows. Attic dormers were boarded up. Even the sex workers had deserted the waterfront while the developers lined up, ready to storm these urban beaches.

The MV *Galleria* sounded a blast on its klaxon and pulled away from the dock. A customs officer beckoned that I should now come alongside. It was an uncomfortable berth that day. The east wind was sending swell the length of the harbour, while in the lee of Marsden Wharf there was a sharp joggle on the water. Once tied to the pontoon, the sloop was thrown hard against its fenders.

There were two customs officers on duty, a young woman and an older man. They stared uneasily at the bucking boat, and then at me. My boat is a Twister 28, a marvel of elegant simplicity designed on the east coast of England by the wonderfully camp Kim Holman in 1963. The Twister is sometimes said to be based on the Scandinavian Folkboat, but although only three feet (0.9m) longer, it displaces twice as much. The epitome of mid-1960s boat design and named partly after the 'Twist' dance rage of that era, it is the product of inspiration rather than perspiration. By Holman's own admission, the plans were 'roughly thrown together in a matter of hours, a sort of knockabout cruising boat for the summer with some racing for fun . . . one of my best ever and I still don't know how I did it!' My own Twister was built out of glass fibre in 1972 and completed at the famous yard of J.W.&A. Upham in Brixham by Holman's brother Jack. I found the Twister's unique blend of elegance and function irresistible: almost perfectly balanced, sure-footed in big seas, to my mind this was the perfect boat for single-handed ocean cruising.

The customs officers in Auckland didn't seem so certain. After the solidity of the *Galleria*, they were both wary of this fidgety little craft and neither came on board. The man passed me a four-page form to complete. As I sat at the chart table they were leaning over the edge of the pontoon, peering down the companionway into the cabin, speaking softly. 'What about this one then?' the man said with a chuckle, 'how would you like this? He's got everything though, just in miniature.'

Handing back the forms I realized the young woman was a trainee. She was grinning at the novelty of it all. The wharf must have made a pleasant change from the airport arrivals hall. The man took the forms from me and began talking her through the layout. 'So they put all their personal details here. Next of kin go in this section – always check they've completed that. Then details about the boat.' He spoke in a hushed, conspiratorial tone though

I was standing an arm's length from them. They both gave a little wobble each time the sloop crunched into the pontoon.

'They give their destination here,' the man said.

'You're going to Vanuatu?' the woman beamed. 'Wow that's so cool! My sister had two weeks at the Castaway Resort last year.'

The man frowned. He took a step backwards, drawing her with him. He tapped the paperwork with his pen, bringing her back to the matter in hand. The message was clear: *Be professional. Don't get conversational with them.* He said, 'You carry on by yourself. Look through the rest of the information while I check his immigration card. Ask me if there's anything you don't understand.'

He studied my immigration card, then asked to see my passport. Where was I going after Vanuatu? How long would I be away?

'You've got a *parachute!*' the woman blurted. She was obviously impressed. The man walked over to her and glanced irritably at the form. Then he adopted his patient voice. 'No. Look. That comes under the heading, EMERGENCY EQUIPMENT. Then there's the subheading, 'Types of Flares'. And he's ticked 'Parachute', 'Hand-held Smoke' and 'Collision Avoidance'.

'Oh,' she said, with an unrepentant smile.

I love the process of clearance. The passage begins with the rustle of paper. There's a perverse intimacy with these uniformed strangers: it's there in their eyes as they check you have properly recorded your next of kin on the form. The threshold of the ocean is the signing-off of forms, the final human interactions, the unknown officers who linger in the mind over the weeks ahead.

The clearance document itself is very simple. It shows the place of departure and the destination that the boat must reach. The clearance is a memo between the customs departments of two countries that the sailor must, in effect, deliver. The final act on leaving land, and the first act when the sailor returns, is bureaucratic. In this respect the document is inflexible. But between these two the land relinquishes its responsibilities; the clearance is a big and breezy page. The route the boat must take is not stipulated. Nor is a time limit for the passage set. The clearance has boundaries, hard edges, but nothing much in between. It is a true document of the ocean.

Everything was in order and my clearance to sail was granted. As I released the warps the senior officer began a final, well-rehearsed speech. 'Now remember, you've cleared customs and must directly leave New Zealand waters. If you do need to stop anywhere before you leave the coast, either for the well-being of the ship or your own personal safety, you should anchor and then immediately call Customs on the 0800 number, or call Russell Radio.' I had cast off by now and was gunning the engine to push the sloop away from the still bucking pontoon. 'But if you anchor for more than 24 hours they'll make you come back to Opua and clear customs all over again.' When the sloop was safely away from the dock I turned back to acknowledge them. The woman was waving happily. 'HAVE AN AWESOME TIME!' she shouted. The man visibly stiffened.

I got up the sails in the prickling waters off the end of Marsden Wharf. A wrack of cloud was splitting the blue sky from the east as I hardened the sheets and got underway for Erromango.

Before dark the wind backed into the frozen south and rose to 25 knots. Lighthouses, settlements and ships dotted the horizon, then faded into the black. After midnight I passed Moko Hinau light, the traditional point of departure for vessels bound for the tropics.

It was a chill south wind, and the promised companionship of history, that combined to carry me into the waters of Melanesia.

The *Brigand* cleared from the wharves at Auckland in October 1843, bound for the island of Erromango. The ship's company had not made a favourable impression on the stalwart settlers of the young township, as is evident from an article in Auckland's *Southern Cross* newspaper dated 7 October. 'The *Brigand* sailed on Thursday last, for the New Hebrides, with the most extraordinary and promiscuous set of passengers that ever sailed from a port. The passengers consisted of Chinamen, Malays, Maories, English, Scotch, Irish and Americans, of various characters and descriptions, together with a lot of old sailors, surveyors, runaway convicts from New South Wales and Van Diemen's Land . . . We are glad to get rid of the motley crew who have departed in the *Brigand*; may they prosper in their adopted country. They are a happy riddance.'

The captain was a 30-year-old Englishman named James Paddon. Born in Portsmouth, Paddon learned his craft in the Royal Navy before cutting loose and running opium to the coast of China. In 1840 he won his first command, the brig *Brigand*.

On the Chinese coast Paddon observed a European ship unloading aromatic timber and made discreet enquiries as to its origin. He learned that the timber was sandalwood, and that there were plentiful stands on the South Sea island of Erromango. Moreover the Chinese demand for the wood was almost insatiable on account of its hard, reddish-brown core called *natora*, which could be burnt as incense. He recognized an opportunity for a lucrative trade and persuaded his owner, a Parsee merchant based at Canton, to finance a new venture harvesting sandalwood in Melanesia. The *Brigand* sailed for New Zealand to execute the plan.

It was the English taste for drinking tea that first motivated the trade in sandalwood. By the 1830s demand at home for tea was so high that duty on imported leaf provided 10 per cent of the revenue for the British Exchequer. China accounted for the majority of tea production at this time and ordinarily there should have been no difficulty procuring an infinite supply. The problem, however, was finding a commodity for which the Chinese were interested in trading their tea; other than opium, there were few products that the insular Chinese claimed to need. Aromatic timber proved to be an exception and the discovery of sandalwood in the Marquesas, Fiji, and later in the New Hebrides, heralded something akin to a seaborne gold rush as trading ships flocked to the South Pacific.

At a public meeting in Wellington, Paddon proposed an unprecedented undertaking. He intended to establish a settlement in the southern New Hebrides from where his ships would have easy access to Erromango. Nothing similar had been attempted before. Indeed, Paddon's contemporaries, at least those familiar with the western Pacific, could have been forgiven for thinking his plan was insane. From the time of the very first European voyages into the Pacific, sailors had recognized that the ocean's peoples could be divided into two distinct groups. In the east, among the islands around Tahiti, were the Polynesians. The ships commanded by Wallis, Bougainville and Cook were given an ecstatic welcome at Tahiti by canoe-loads of cheering islanders, many of them naked women offering sexual favours. Greater contact with the Polynesians proved that the welcome might not always be this warm; even in the east the islanders sometimes attacked ships and shore parties. But in general the islands within the Polynesian Triangle – Hawaii in the north, Easter Island in the east, and New Zealand in the south – were culturally extrovert, and also homogenous, sharing similar languages and beliefs.

In the western isles of Melanesia, however, it was quite different. The Spanish came first in 1528. Their ship had not closed within five miles of the coast before the islanders waged war, attacking from a handful of flimsy canoes. Later navigators expressed amazement at the mix of resourcefulness and sheer aggression shown by the Melanesians, who were experts at ambush. Gomez Catoira recorded one such attack. As the sailors came ashore the islanders let loose a barrage of poisoned arrows. When their supply of arrows was exhausted they threw stones. When they could find no more stones they threw earth. After that they hurled their bows. 'And when they had thrown everything they had they spat at us and jeered at us, turning their hinder parts.' The islands of Melanesia – New Guinea, the Solomon Islands, the New Hebrides (Vanuatu), and New Caledonia – were culturally and linguistically fragmented, and so insular that out-siders were invariably greeted with violence. By 1843, the year of James Paddon's proposed voyage, the New Hebrides were still a group of islands barely known to Europeans, and much feared, with Erromango considered to be 'the darkest spot in the whole

Pacific'. Only four years earlier the Reverend John Williams had been beaten to death on the beach there. By taking the brig to the same island, Paddon and every man he addressed at the public meeting in Wellington must have known that they were likely to be attacked.

Undeterred, he set about recruiting settlers for his island station and evidently met with considerable success. Among those departing Wellington on the *Brigand* were Mr Murphy, a former police magistrate, Mr Sutton, who had been employed in the colonial secretary's office, as well as Messrs Johnston, Brewster and Prentice. At least thirty woodcutters of various nationalities made up the bulk of the remainder of the emigrants.

The *Brigand* got no further north than Auckland before the first of her crew were killed. The *Southern Cross* newspaper was in no doubt as to where blame lay. 'LOSS OF LIFE – Four persons have been drowned on Sunday last, by the upsetting of an open boat belonging to the brig *Brigand*. This unhappy circumstance is the first of the kind which has occurred in our harbour, and has been the result of much carelessness on the part of those who sailed the boat.'

Paddon sailed north at the wrong time of year since he would arrive in the islands at the beginning of the cyclone season. But over the years he would weather all of the destructive storms that the ocean threw at him. Instead, it was the process of contact across the beach that changed James Paddon and other trading sailors like him.

I had shaped my own course to the islands in order to trace his story. He left Auckland as a committed colonist, the union flag flying proudly from the *Brigand's* stern. Nine years later James Paddon was married to an island woman and living on the beach; many of those who had sailed with him on the *Brigand* were dead.

He made two further stops on the passage north to the islands. The first was a short call at Norfolk Island, where most of the crew went ashore. A few days later the *Brigand* anchored again, this time at a little known island called Maré.

*

Eleven days out of Auckland I was beating north up the weather coast of Ile Maré. It was a miserable day. A trough of low pressure was going through and conditions had been deteriorating since before dawn. The wind first backed into the north, then rose to gale force for a short time, but soon melted away into an afternoon of shifting breezes and torrential rain. Ile Maré was five miles to the west, hidden beneath a pall of gluey cloud stuck to the surface of the ocean. Once the wind had died the sea fell into disarray, as shapeless as an unmade bed. The sloop staggered between patternless swells, making little way. I was beginning to regret ever making the detour to Ile Maré. I'd never intended to stop there; I'd simply use the island as a waypoint, sight the coast where James Paddon's crew had been massacred, then sail on to the north. Now I couldn't even see the island. It wasn't long, though, before I had other things to worry about.

In the mid-afternoon, as I was climbing to the deck to put up more sail, I saw the chainplate was broken. This is part of the rigging: a strong point on deck to which the wire rope that supports the mast is attached. At worst, a chainplate failure could cause dismasting. One side of the steel V-bolt had fractured and bent upwards from the deck. Now the weather cap shroud had lost tension and the top portion of the mast was bent out of shape.

I sat on the coachroof for a moment and watched my bloodless fingers curling round the steel fitting, seeking some sort of reassurance. Alone at sea, the sight of broken steel is horribly final, almost as sickening as a fractured bone. I couldn't continue beating to windward with the rig damaged in this way, so I pushed the helm over and ran off before the wind, seeking sheltered water under the lee of Ile Maré.

I had no chart of the island, but as the sloop ran west through the rain I held the pilot book under the sprayhood and studied the written description. A mile offshore, in failing light, the cliffs at Cap Boyer finally loomed through the murk overhead. Colonial pines stood in a rank along the cliff top, bent double before the prevailing wind, ghostly in the drizzle and tearing cloud.

Beyond the cape the seas eased and night fell. Wavelets slapped harmlessly against the sloop's transom. The north-east wind brought spitting rain. I dropped the sails and allowed the sloop to drift parallel to the coast, towards Cap Wabao. The glow of a small settlement was visible ashore. Once or twice, headlights flashed along the coast road. Otherwise the island was in darkness. I sat up until midnight when the sloop drifted round Cap Wabao and wholly into the island's lee, then catnapped in the cockpit till first light.

At dawn a heavy dew coated the deck and rigging. The sea was calm. A layer of high, hard-looking cloud filled the sky, pressed by the lightest trade. It was Sunday, and soon the sound of a distant bell came across the water from Ile Maré. Through binoculars I watched the small settlement at Tadine: a wharf and storage sheds, houses tucked up the hillside behind, an occasional truck climbing the switchback road to the plateau.

As the boat shifted and settled on the calm, I unbolted the broken chainplate and replaced it with a heavy stainless-steel eyebolt. From the masthead I saw a speedboat leave Tadine and plane south past Cap Wabao, not seeing or not interested in, the yacht drifting offshore. There were no other signs of damage to the rig and I climbed back to the deck. The trade wind was rising with the sun. White caps were already forming here in the island's lee.

Ile Maré is a raised coral island, uplifted from the ocean as a uniform slab of rock, the plateau densely wooded with palms. Colonial pines line every cliff and escarpment. Along much of the coast golden sand plunges into deep, black water. I hardened the sheets gingerly as a load came on the new chainplate for the first time, then beat in towards the breakwater at Tadine. Half a mile offshore I furled away the genoa and, with no chart to guide me, motored cautiously towards the coast. The rising sun was in my eyes making the water ahead an impenetrable silver-black mass. Just off the breakwater the seabed shoaled rapidly and soon the sloop was floating in only a few metres of water.

Ahead, looking into the sun, the water was still a black sheet giving no sign of its depths. But when I turned around and looked behind the boat I saw a band of turquoise shallows fringing the island as far as Cap Wabao. The first sight of that colour hit me as an almost physical force. After the tensions of the previous day, the sight of cool, blue-green coral shoals felt as soothing as an icepack on a burn. I could almost smell the vanilla and feel the sticky juice of pawpaw running down my chin. These are the things that today bring sailors to the South Pacific: the contrasting colours in the lagoons and on the lush hillsides, the vast ocean skies without a cloud. But what struck me when I read the journals of the traders who sailed between the islands 150 years ago was how very modern this was. The traders seldom noticed any beauty in the islands. A sandalwood trader named William Lockerby kept a journal of his extensive trading voyages in Fiji, a group of islands renowned for their natural beauty that today attract sailors from around the world. Yet for Lockerby the coral islands among which he sailed were no more than '. . . a simply dismal corner of the Globe'. The seascape of the traders was invariably black and white.

Behind the small breakwater at Tadine there was a fine sheltered anchorage. I landed the kayak on a coral beach, but hadn't walked far along the coast road when a car stopped to pick me up. We drove up the switchback road and came out at the plateau where all the villages were located. Coral churches glinted in palm-speckled shade and steady trade winds cooled the air. It was to one of these villages on the plateau that a group of men from the *Brigand* had come in 1843.

It has never been entirely clear why James Paddon made this unscheduled stop at Ile Maré on his passage north to the New Hebrides. But Maré was also known to have sandalwood and presumably the captain wanted to reconnoitre the possibilities for trade. Judging by later events, his crew and passengers were also clamouring for contact with the island's women.

As soon as the *Brigand* anchored here on 7 November 1843 two

Samoan teachers came off in a canoe. The Samoans had been landed by missionaries some years earlier and knew the island well. They warned Paddon that the entire crew of the brig *Star* had been killed in this same anchorage the previous year. Paddon was cautious: no crewmen from the *Brigand* went ashore that day, but neither was the anchor raised.

Next morning another canoe came alongside and several Melanesians boarded the brig. Seemingly friendly relations were established and the Europeans dropped their guard. That afternoon Mr Sutton and one of the other gentlemen went ashore, looking for entertainment. In the evening a group of ten wood-cutters also rowed to the beach. They climbed a steep path through the bush, intent on visiting one of the villages on the plateau.

There are two accounts describing what happened next. The first is a report given to the *Sydney Morning Herald* by an unnamed crewman from the *Brigand*. The second is contained in the narrative of Reverend George Turner, who arrived at Maré two years later and talked to the Samoan teachers who had witnessed much of the episode.

By dawn on the third day none of the *Brigand*'s shore party had returned to the ship. Soon Melanesian men came off in canoes and told Paddon that his sailors were still asleep in the village, having enjoyed many festivities the night before. The islanders produced tomahawks and sought permission to sharpen them on the ship's grinding wheel. Paddon ruled that only one axe was to be brought aboard the brig at a time, after which it should be placed back in the canoe. Then the next man could take his turn at the grinding wheel. This was done, but when the captain's back was turned the tomahawks were surreptitiously passed back up to the deck. Sensing trouble, Paddon armed six seamen with a cutlass and pistol each. However, on sandalwood ships the weapons were all too often old and poorly maintained. When the Melanesians already on deck seized their tomahawks and others swarmed up from the canoes, four Europeans and five Chinese were killed in the initial assault. Paddon was armed with a sword and pistol, but finding his gun useless he dived down a hatchway to escape along with the remaining crew. Three of the sailors fired through the cabin skylight killing several Melanesians. The second mate shot two more through the fore hatch, at which the remainder jumped overboard.

Paddon immediately slipped the cable and made sail. But as the brig was clearing the bay the lookout saw two crewmen on the beach, waving frantically. The boat was lowered and Mr Sutton, together with one of the woodcutters, was brought off. Sutton described how the shore party had been attacked late the previous night as they walked back through the bush towards the ship. Most had been speared or clubbed to death; a handful had escaped and scattered into the darkness.

Throughout that night the brig stood off and on, several miles under the lee of Ile Maré. Next morning a canoe paddled out bringing one more of the woodcutters who had managed to escape the ambush. Later that day a chief came to the brig and told Paddon there were no further survivors.

Some crewmen demanded that Paddon take revenge. No successful trade could ever develop in these islands, they argued, unless the Melanesians learned to fear the arrival of a European ship. The chief should be killed and a punitive raid mounted against the village.

Paddon would have none of it. He made several gifts to the chief, then set a course back to the south. At Norfolk Island the most seriously wounded men were put ashore, before the *Brigand* sailed south-west for Newcastle on the coast of New South Wales.

It had been a disastrous first foray into Melanesian waters. Eighteen of the intended new colonists were dead, several others had been abandoned owing to the severity of their wounds, and this was before the brig had even made landfall in the New Hebrides.

But James Paddon made only a short stay at Newcastle before sailing back east into the Pacific later the same month. By January 1844 the *Brigand* was in the waters south of Erromango. Captain

Paddon was still intent on setting up the first sandalwood station in this part of the South Seas.

I woke at midnight in the anchorage behind the breakwater at Tadine, disturbed by the eerie stillness and silence after twelve nights at sea. The seabed six metres down was clearly visible in the moonlight as a creamy sheet of sand.

At dawn I was woken again by birdsong. The air was perfectly still and the sloop's deck lacquered with a chill film of dew. I motored north up the coast of the island as the sun rose in an empty sky. Maré was a brilliant green slab rising from the ocean, edged by the shortest skirt of flooded turquoise. Off the north cape the surface of the sea was crazed with white scars and stretch marks where the waters met and swirled. As I came out onto the open sea the trade wind began to fill in from the south-east. It had been a mixed passage up from Auckland so far, during which I'd never found the trades. Each day's run had been halting and uncertain, broken by shifting winds, light variables, electrical storms, squalls and calms. But as Ile Maré fell away behind the boat, the sails were pressed evenly into shape and the sheets gently creaked before a steady flow of air. With the coming of the trade wind a single, simple governance spread over the ocean. The trade wind conjures its own strange magic: the ability to dissolve memory and erase the truth that the sea hasn't always been this way. Puffball clouds in the sky and bright white caps across the water each mirrored the progress of the other as they scattered across the seascape into the north-west. In the afternoon I crammed on all three sails and ran out across the New Hebrides Trench where the seabed fell away from 1,000 to 5,000 metres. In the dense tropical darkness after sunset I heard dolphins blowing around the boat, a wet puff-and-gasp just audible beyond the rustling bow wave.

After lunch the next day I threw my message in a bottle from the boat. Shortly afterwards I saw the greying husks of several coconuts bobbing on the swells, a sure sign of the islands beneath the horizon to windward. The three main islands of southern Vanuatu formed a line across the ocean out of sight to the east. All three were associated with the sandalwood trader James Paddon. On Aneityum, with the only tolerable all-weather anchorage, he made his first base; on Tanna he ended up living on the beach; and on Erromango was the reason he came – the hillsides clothed in valuable stands of sandalwood.

Paddon arrived in the islands 50 years before the first colonial administration was established and could come and go as he chose. But I was obliged to first sail north to the capital Port Vila to clear customs and then to beat back south into the trade wind to reach Erromango.

Late that afternoon, as I ran towards the capital across a long, loose and lazy swell, I caught sight of Erromango, 35 miles away to the east. The island's mountainous backbone appeared as a smoky green shadow fading and reforming in the sky. It was the Irish trader and beachcomber Peter Dillon who first noted the rich forests of sandalwood on Erromango in 1825. I would cross Dillon's wake again later in the voyage. As a trader he lacked neither courage nor entrepreneurial zeal; indeed, he would do almost anything to make a quid and proved as much many times. But Dillon would have nothing to do with Erromango. He described the islanders as being 'in such a barbarous state of ignorance as not to attach the least value to any of our goods'. Furthermore, he judged them so hostile as to preclude any possibility of a profitable trade. Despite the wealthy forests, Dillon left Erromango without a cargo and never returned, though the principal anchorage still bears his name.

As was typical among the traders, Dillon was nonetheless highly secretive about what he had seen on the island. But he does seem to have told his friend Captain Samuel P. Henry, the Tahitian-born son of an English missionary, because four years later Henry chartered the *Sophia* for a sandalwood voyage to Erromango. Henry clearly knew he could expect trouble from the Erromangans as the *Sophia* landed a crew of more than one hundred Tongan warriors at Dillon's Bay with instructions to cut timber and wait for the ship's return. Like Dillon, the captain of the *Sophia* was also highly secretive and told none of the crew the coordinates of this potentially lucrative island. However, two shadowy figures travelling as steerage passengers, Blaxesly, a watchmaker, and Cox, a silversmith, contrived to manufacture a crude sextant and so identified Erromango's position – information they sold in Hawaii where the value of sandalwood was already well known. Within a month two more ships had sailed for Erromango. The *Becket*, navigated by Blaxesly who like numerous other beachcombers sold his services to the Hawaiian chief Kamehameha, carried a force of 179 Polynesians armed with muskets and cannon, while a further 130 sailed on the schooner *Dhaule*.

Among the Hawaiians was the self-styled 'Governor Boki' who intended to rule Erromango once the indigenous population had been killed or enslaved. When these ships arrived at the island, they were joined by the *Sophia* who returned on her second voyage carrying a further 200 Polynesian woodcutters. There were now on Erromango competing gangs of more than 600 Polynesians, together with a smattering of European beachcombers and mercenaries. Soon, a three-way war was commenced between the Hawaiians, the other Polynesians, and the native population that only lost pace when fever broke out. What began as a trickle of deaths soon escalated into a full-blown epidemic. Most of the 600 Polynesians were either killed in warfare or died of malaria. Of the 179 Hawaiians, only 20 lived to beat a final retreat to the *Becket*.

For the next decade trading ships avoided Erromango. The southern islands of the New Hebrides were considered to be a death trap, a breeding ground for inescapable fevers and home to 'savages of the most invincible ferocity' according to one missionary writer. Dillon's Bay, Erromango, acquired a reputation as the most dangerous anchorage in the Pacific.

*

Erromango was visible before first light as a series of rugged black mounds in the greying sky to windward. One hour later, an orange dawn was spreading from behind watery, broken cloud. As I short-tacked into the anchorage the sun cleared the mountains and filled Dillon's Bay with light. Mist was burning off the Williams River. Ground swell sent a slight surf onto the pebble beach. The bellow of cockerels drifted out on the wind, but the village itself was out of sight behind the tree line. Fields of silvery grasses climbed steeply towards Erromango's vertiginous core. There was good anchorage on a sandy seabed to the south of the river, 100 metres off the beach.

I pushed the kayak into the water and paddled towards the notorious killing grounds at Dillon's Bay. The beach was steep, formed of black pebbles and stones, shaped into terraces by wet season gales. The kayak grounded hard, and I struggled to drag it up the first slippery incline where the stones were the size of eggs and just as smooth. Behind the beach hundreds of swallows fluttered and darted above a wall of bush so thick it allowed no entrance.

After the first disastrous sandalwood voyages to Dillon's Bay in 1829 ten years passed before the mission ship *Camden* cautiously approached this shore and anchored some distance off the beach. No missionary had ever been in this part of the ocean before, and the churchmen knew their reception was uncertain. Captain Morgan ordered that the longboat be put in the water and took his station at the tiller. With him was Mr Cunningham, HM vice-consul at Samoa. Both men would write accounts of what happened that day, 20 November 1839, on Erromango. There were two other passengers in the boat. The first was John Williams, the most prominent missionary in the South Seas, a man who had spent 22 years evangelizing in the islands. When the *Camden* had sailed from London thousands of well-wishers lined the Thames. His companion was Mr Harris, a novice who had only recently determined to devote his life to the London Missionary Society. Four seamen took the oars.

As they rowed in towards the pebble beach Captain Morgan watched an outrigger canoe approach. He called to the three paddlers, who made no reply. Morgan observed them to be wild looking, different from any other race he had encountered in the Pacific. Several more islanders were standing on the beach. As

'The Rev. John Williams on board ship with native implements, in the South Sea Islands.' Watercolour by Henry Anelay, c. 1838

Morgan put it: 'We made signs to them to come towards us, but they made signs for us to go away.' He ordered the oars to be shipped while his party took stock.

John Williams announced himself satisfied with the islanders. They were shy certainly, but he could see young boys playing on the beach nearby – surely a good sign? Captain Morgan was not sure. Where were the women? 'Because when the natives resolve on mischief they send the women out of the way.' Mr Harris was the first of the *Camden* men to wade ashore.

Harris was killed beside the river with an ironwood war club when the islanders came tearing out of the bushes. John Williams could not outrun his pursuers so crashed down the stony terraces straight into the sea, hoping to swim to the retreating longboat. It's slippery and uneven where the surf breaks and Williams lost his balance, tumbling forwards into the water. According to the accounts, he was then passive, not attempting to fight back as club blows landed on his head and shoulders and his body was pierced with arrows.

'The massacre of the lamented missionary the Rev. J. Williams and Mr Harris at Erromango, 1839.' Oil print by G. Baxter, London, 1841

Cunningham and Morgan only just made it back to the longboat. As the seamen heaved at the oars, heading for the *Camden*, a hail of arrows landed in and around the boat, one splitting the planking.

I pushed the kayak back through the surf and paddled north along the beach. Safely aboard the *Camden*, Captain Morgan had watched through a spyglass as the Erromangans stripped John Williams's lifeless body of its mid-Victorian dissenter clothing. As I paddled beside the beach I pictured these garments lying wet and bloody on the stones, surrounded by hunks of driftwood and flotsam: a broad-brimmed felt hat, rather flat; a black topcoat with high collar; a high-buttoned waistcoat and a white stock.

After a few minutes I came to the entrance to the stream – known today as the Williams River. Two domed spits strewn with more flotsam marked the extent of the bar. Once through the muddy shallows the river narrowed and deepened to form a peaty trench that meandered inland round rocky promontories. I beached the kayak beneath the casuarina trees on the north shore and followed a flinty track through the village.

An old man hurried from a gateway and hailed me as if he had seen a cab. He was Chief William Meté, the headman of the village. I was very lucky, he told me bluntly, because I was shaking the hand of the most important fellow in these parts. Over the coming days I heard Chief Meté called a number of things, with 'crook', 'hustler' and 'impostor' being the most frequent. But given a few more weeks in Vanuatu I learned such descriptors were commonplace here, most of all 'impostor'. At independence in 1980 the planters had been booted out and all land reverted to the customary owner, with the consequence that many chiefly titles, and the land that went with them, were now in dispute.

Chief Meté hustled me for ten litres of diesel. The supply ship was late, he said, months late. No one knew when it would now come. They had no fuel for the generator, no flour for bread, no tobacco, rice, sugar, soap, oil or kerosene. He needed to go to Vila to sort it all out. The flight left in two hours but he couldn't get to the airstrip. He had a truck, the only one in the village because, as he told me again, he was the most important man here, whereas I had just arrived. But the truck had no fuel. Chief Meté thrust a small jerrycan into my ribs. I paddled back out to the sloop and filled the can with diesel.

'My sons will look after you while I'm away,' the chief told me as he piled bundles into the back of the truck. His eldest son was in Port Vila standing for parliament. The other three were standing round the truck. 'We have a guest house here for visitors. You can use it as long as you are here. I'll be away for two weeks.' It was hard to say which of the three boys was smiling more broadly.

The eldest was named Joe, a short, powerful man in his early twenties. He wore a gangster hat, wrap-around shades and a 'Crazy Love' T-shirt. Joe offered to take me to Williams Rock and as we walked he talked fondly of his time at a Christian boarding school in Auckland. At the riverbank the chief's son called for a dugout canoe, then settled himself imperiously in the bows. A bare-chested boatman named Thomas paddled him across the stream while I followed behind in my kayak.

We landed a short distance upstream on the far bank. Joe pushed a path through bush and tall grasses until we reached the Martyrs' Cemetery. No one had been here for months. The shape of a once-pretty glade, overhung with poinsettias, was only just discernable in the regenerating bush. The cemetery contained the graves of later missionaries who had been killed in this bay, but not that of John Williams. His body was eaten and Williams had no grave. The notoriety of Williams's death still hung over Dillon's Bay. His name was everywhere and the islanders, today devout Christians, had long struggled with the reputation as the killers of God's man in the South Seas. Joe told me he was a direct descendant of Worris Nematangi, the chief of this settlement when Williams landed here in 1839. He referred to that period of history as 'the darkness' or 'before the coming of the light'. 'They were savages then,' he said, 'bad sort of people.'

'But Williams was killed in revenge,' I protested. 'Sandalwood traders had committed earlier atrocities here.'

Joe Meté looked at me coldly. 'They were savages,' he said.

'You could see their balls and arses.' I could think of no reply to this and followed him silently along the trail.

At a bend in the river we reached a distinctive, flat-topped rock jutting out into deep water. This was a traditional meeting place, named Punnilai, but Joe Meté called it Williams Rock. The missionary's body had been carried up from the beach, laid out and divided.

Joe swept away the leaves and moss to expose two holes, each the size of a clenched fist. The boatman was instructed to lie down between the two marks. 'They put John Williams here, stretched him out and measured him. These two holes show how long he was.' I asked if taking such measurements had been common. 'It's the same as when you catch a big fish, you want to weigh it to record your success.'

Later I came back with a tape measure. The distance between the two holes was 6 feet 1 inch. Williams's body had then been carried far inland to a village in the hills. This was the custom, Joe told me. When the coastal people caught a large fish they took it to a landlocked tribe and traded it for game. As Williams had come from the sea, his body was subject to this customary exchange.

John Williams had been a sailor for the 22 years he had spent in the Pacific. He was an accomplished shipwright and navigator as well as a missionary. On the beach at Rarotonga Williams built an 80-ton schooner, the *Messenger of Peace*, taking just three months to complete the work. In his sermons the church was always 'an anchor' and his congregation 'tempest-tossed souls'. For Williams, the Pacific was an azure firmament and he spread the gospel with the south-east trade wind at his back.

It would be difficult to think of a European sailor in the Pacific, with the sole exception of Captain James Cook, whose influence has been greater than that of John Williams. His voyages changed the lives of millions of people beyond recognition. Yet most of the Europeans I know who live here have never heard of him. And while new books are published almost every year detailing Captain Cook's magnificent voyages of discovery, John Williams has largely been forgotten. A slim biography was published in 1974; otherwise the only sources are his own published writings and his journals. In the post-colonial, post-nuclear Pacific, the missionaries are about as fashionable as enriched uranium.

One consequence of John Williams's numerous Pacific voyages was that he inevitably came into contact with beachcombers, a group of sailors for whom he only had contempt. When Williams sailed to Samoa in 1832, six years before his death at Erromango, he found one runaway sailor staging religious services on the beach and performing 'miracles', including raising a 'dead' cow. The missionary questioned the man and recorded the conversation in his journal.

'You baptize them do you? How do you do that?'

'Why Sir,' he exclaimed, 'I takes water, and dips my hands in it, and crosses them on their foreheads and in their breasts, and then I reads a bit of a prayer to 'em in English.'

'Of course,' I said, 'they understand you.'

'No,' he rejoined, 'but they says they knows it does 'em good.'

This beachcomber had more than 300 followers and lived in fine style. Williams was outraged and remonstrated with the man for the 'fearful wickedness of his conduct'.

John Williams, like most missionaries, was appalled by the beachcombers. They represented precisely that side of European culture that missionaries didn't want the islanders to see. It was a constant source of irritation to Williams that the ships which allowed him to save the Pacific peoples for God had also introduced these delinquents into the islands. It was John Williams more than any other commentator who did everything in his power to blacken the name of beachcombers. In his lectures and published writing Williams branded the beachcombers as 'a noisesome pestilence . . . low life worthless men, the vilest of the vile . . . the scum of the crew . . . Ratcliffe highway runaways.' This latter reference is to the London street that became notorious in 1811 after the brutal murders of seven people in twelve days.

An irony of John Williams's life – one not pointed out by his biographer – is that some of his own activities fulfilled what were also classic beachcomber roles. The 80-ton schooner he built on the beach at Rarotonga was a masterly blend of western technology and local resources. The shipwright missionary used ironwood pins for want of iron proper; tapa cloth served as oakum; a pickaxe was fashioned into rudder pintles; rigging was plaited from hibiscus bark. The construction of improvised escape boats, often with few suitable tools, was almost a rite of passage for beachcombers. James Morrison and the *Bounty* beachcombers famously built an escape boat on Tahiti. Castaway crews on Penrhyn and Vanikoro Islands similarly fashioned boats beneath the palms. A group of beachcombers led by David Whippy in Levuka, Fiji, made a business out of boatbuilding, constructing small vessels especially suited to sailing among the islands which served as scouts and tenders to trading ships from Salem harvesting bêche-de-mer and tortoise shell.

Williams was also similar to the beachcombers in that he probably traded in alcohol – or 'grog' as it is still known in the islands. I found one description of John Williams's home station on the island of Raiatea by chance while reading about a quite different matter. When the American ship *Independence* was wrecked on Starbuck Island in December 1835, most of the crew embarked in three of the ship's open boats. One was commanded by a crewman named Milo Calkin who made landfall at Rarotonga after a voyage of 1,000 miles. Calkin then shipped in a Yankee whaler which subsequently lay at anchor for two weeks off Raiatea, the small island that had been John Williams's home mission for the last 18 years. Calkin was shocked by the lawlessness he found at Raiatea, noting that 'several vessels owned by the Mission were engaged in traffic among the different islands and to Sydney. Spiritous liquors formed a large and profitable portion of the trade . . .' The beach was haunted by tattooed deserters and their mixed-race children; 'the calaboose was often filled with the victims of a night's debauch'. Like boat building, trading in grog was one of the stock beachcomber roles in many of the island groups. Many beachcomber grog-sellers dealt in raw alcohol, usually received as payment in kind from the ships on which they served as pilots or interpreters. Others applied western technology to local products, distilling from the *ti* and other tropical plants the lethal brews sold to both visiting sailors and islanders. One beachcomber in Hawaii, Harry Zupplien, made a small fortune from selling grog. If Calkin was correct, John Williams's mission station supplemented its income in a similar way.

In his heart at least, Williams seems to have recognized that his own world and that of the beachcombers were not so far removed. Just three years after he arrived in the Pacific, Williams wrote to the London Missionary Society requesting a transfer. 'There is no prospect whatever of our dear children becoming useful members either in religious or in civil life [here on Raiatea], but on the contrary they will become a disgrace to their country and to the religion of their fathers.' Williams recognized the role of the beach as a staging ground for contact between two profoundly opposed cultures, and he didn't like what he saw. He believed that white men might lose their souls once they trod the tidal margins. But John Williams was a proud man; his fears were for his children. He had no doubts about his own safety on the beach.

When Williams was killed on the beach at Erromango there were those within the London Missionary Society who were, frankly, relieved. Dr John Campbell for one could not disguise his satisfaction that things had worked out so neatly. Williams's personal popularity with the English public, coupled with persistent rumours that he engaged in trade in the islands, had made him a liability. In death, he was anointed the 'Martyr of Polynesia', and all was forgiven. The London Missionary Society even acknowledged his seafaring by giving his name to successive mission ships. The last, the *John Williams VII*, was decommissioned in 1972.

*

In Auckland I met Tom Ludvigson, a broad-shouldered, square-jawed Scandinavian who looked most like a marine colonel. He was well known as a jazz musician around the town, but I had looked him up because in the 1980s he lived for a year in a Ni-Vanuatu village conducting anthropological fieldwork.

We met in a café in the city and I pulled out a list of questions I planned to ask him about Melanesia. 'Whose questions are these?' he said. 'Europeans have always defined Melanesia in terms of its absences. They compared it to Europe and described what it didn't have. Supposedly there were no chiefs. Supposedly they killed people in cold blood. Some anthropologists are still doing the same thing today. What you end up with is how different Melanesia is, how Other. You won't understand Melanesia until you start asking *their* questions.'

'What are their questions?'

He didn't reply for a long time. Perhaps I was supposed to find out for myself. Then he said, 'One question they asked me was this: "When the Americans come back, will they kill all the women?" That was more than 35 years after the Pacific War had ended.'

'I don't get it,' I said. 'Why would the Americans kill the women? They were fighting the Japanese. And why would they come back?'

'Jesus came back. But you're right, it's a very Melanesian question.'

We talked about my voyage through the islands. I boasted that even today, in this age of jet travel, sailing your own boat was still the only true way to make journeys among the Pacific Islands. Ludvigson wasn't so sure. 'You think you have the right to go wherever you like, don't you?' he said. But the thing was, I did think that. For me, even the mention of boats had always triggered a host of mental images as a reflex: exploration, adventure, an unbridled liberty to escape into a sea of a thousand islands. I had inherited these notions; they are deeply entrenched in western thought. The 'freedom of the seas'; the 'right to free passage': these associations of sea travel with liberty were hinted at in the Magna Carta, explicitly described by the Dutch jurist Hugo Grotius in his treatise *Mare Liberum* of 1609, and best expressed by the eighteenth-century English jurist Sir William Blackstone who wrote that 'water is a moveable, wandering thing and must of necessity continue common by the law of nature'. This was the tradition of sea travel I took for granted: ocean is qualitatively different from land in that it cannot be owned or controlled, and is free to all. That is its beauty.

'A lot of sailors got themselves killed in Melanesia,' Tom Ludvigson told me. 'Have you ever wondered why? In Melanesia, a man is measured by what he doesn't have. What's important is generosity and how much you give away. If you want to be accepted in a Melanesian village, first give away everything you have. Then they will look after you until the day you leave. That's hard in a boat. Boats are so standoffish. All that wealth hidden inside. In a Melanesian village, it's unmanly not to share.'

Ludvigson's words echoed the narratives of some castaways and beachcombers in the Pacific who found that safety lay in possessing nothing material that the islanders wanted. Ironically, it was the beachcombers' poverty that sometimes extended their lives. This was the experience of the ill-fated crew of the Nantucket whaler *Oeno* which voyaged north up to the islands from New Zealand in 1825. One of the sailors aboard the *Oeno*, William Cary, recorded the wreck and its aftermath in his journal. While sailing through the Melanesian Fiji Islands between 2 and 3 o'clock in the morning on the night of 5 April the helmsman saw white water ahead and 'sung out lustily to the officer, who sprang to the deck, but before a general alarm could be sounded, the ship struck on a coral reef. All hands were immediately called and the topsails clewd down. By this time the sea was making a clean breach over the vessel.' Before dawn the *Oeno* had been given up as lost and the crew had taken to the boats, though several men had broken bones in the process. The castaways headed for nearby Turtle Island having 'decided it was better to land and take our chances with the natives than starve in open boats'. The crewmen were initially treated well by the Fijians. They were given the use of several houses, their wounds were dressed and they were provided with ample food and drink. Each day, the Fijians went out to the wreck in the canoes and plundered rusty muskets, tools and provisions until the ship finally broke up. The sticking point became the few muskets and other possessions the twenty-one sailors had brought ashore in the boats. 'Capt. Riddell took every opportunity to advise us not to use force and let them take everything they wanted,' Cary wrote. Yet some of the sailors ignored this, and when one Fijian tried to take some clothes a whaleman 'helped him from the house. This treatment he did not relish. He took his club and beat the ground most furiously, and expressed his displeasure by every possible gesture.' After twelve days of an increasingly tense standoff, the Fijians clubbed twenty of the sailors to death. Cary was the only survivor. He hid in a cave for three days until hunger and thirst forced him out into the open where he fully expected to share the fate of his shipmates. 'I sat down on the path with my back towards them [the Fijians], expecting to have the hatchet driven into my head, and not wishing to see the blow.' However, Cary was taken in by the chief and lived in the group for nine years as a beachcomber, enjoying chiefly patronage. 'It is my belief,' he wrote, 'that if the captain's advice had been strictly followed and we had let them take whatever they chose without resistance, they would have left without molesting us.'

Life on the beach often began with a shipwreck, and castaways played a role in the process of first contact between Europeans and Pacific Islanders that is rarely recognized. The classic image of first contact depicts an orderly scene in which a Polynesian chief and a uniformed ship's officer are exchanging gifts. An alternative image, one relevant in some of the outer islands especially, would show white sailors in the dead of night, terrified and exhausted, struggling ashore over the coral reefs from a crippled ship. This was what happened early one morning in 1853 when the trading brig *Chatham* was wrecked on Penrhyn Island. The ship's owner,

E.H. Lamont, described the events as follows: 'A white crested wave, raining us on its top, bore us onwards with impetuous force, and dashed us amidst the boiling foam on the rugged walls of coral.' Even before the sailors had gathered their wits the islanders were on the scene: '. . . a wild yell from shore sent the blood thrilling to my heart'. No ship had previously anchored at Penryhn and as the islanders swarmed down on to the coral, Lamont seized his sword but 'The captain begged me, for God's sake, to lay aside the weapon, or we should all be murdered . . . I had scarcely touched dry land, when, as if to prove that their conduct was not prompted by humanity, my pockets were rifled of their contents.' Utterly dejected, Lamont 'passed on into the interior [of the tiny atoll] to discover what kind of place we were doomed to spend it might be the remainder of our lives in'. When he returned to the beach he found the crew were employed carrying all the supplies from the ship ashore, 'which they were bearing inland under the direction of the natives, who were already employing them as slaves'.

Coral reef navigation became synonymous with castaways and beachcombers. What Cary and Lamont learned was that being washed ashore with no possessions at all was sometimes the safest way to approach the beach.

Compared to these nineteenth-century trading ships laden with trade goods and weaponry, I thought of my own sloop as being relatively modest. Now more than 30 years old, it was 28 feet long with a maximum width of 8 feet. There were few frills: a cabin in which I couldn't stand up containing two simple bunks and a two-burner cooker, and no refrigeration. I'd sailed it out from England in the 1990s and later across the Southern Ocean to Patagonia. Now it showed signs of its age and travels.

But still I was conscious of the boat as it shifted on the ground swell that first evening anchored in Dillon's Bay, Erromango. A boat doesn't blend in with its surroundings; there's no anonymity when anchored in the shallows.

I was late getting back to the boat that evening. I spent the afternoon with Joe Meté and then took up his offer of using the shower in the family guesthouse. So it was dark by the time I paddled back down the river and out into the empty waters of the anchorage. I turned on only one cabin light and kept the stereo volume low in an effort to be unobtrusive. It was a black night, the sky full of cloud. No lights showed from the village. As I'd been told many times that day, the ship was late, they had no kerosene, no supplies. But the sloop's kerosene tank was full, and the kerosene cooker now hissed as the water boiled for pasta. Beneath the bunks the lockers were jammed with 300 tins of food in readiness for the four-month voyage to Torres Strait.

I heard a splash in the water nearby. A moment later someone coughed. The islanders often announced themselves like this. They could circle the boat in their canoes in perfect silence, levering the paddle against the outrigger's cross-beam so the hull slipped noiselessly through the water. When ready, they made a deliberate noise, slapping the paddle against the surface or clearing their throats. Then they waited for an invitation to come alongside. After dark it was impossible to know how long they had been out there, paddling round and round, watching.

'Who's there?' I called.

'It's Christopher. I want to ask you something.' Christopher was the youngest of the chief's sons, about 17 years old. I told him to bring the outrigger alongside. It was the usual thing, expressed directly for want of polished English. 'I want to ask you something. I want tobacco. My friends are drinking kava. But no tobacco.' Kava is the Pacific drug, a narcotic drink made by mixing water with the crushed roots of the pepper plant (*Piper methysticum*).

I asked Christopher if I could drink kava too.

This equally direct response surprised him. For a moment he was stuck for an answer. 'But only small kava – "smol kava" – and too many men. I only want tobacco.'

I gave him a fistful of tobacco and he paddled off, promising to take me to the Caves of the Ancestors next morning, which he didn't do, claiming he was sick having drunk so much kava.

Fifteen minutes later the same moves were repeated: the slap of a paddle, a cough. 'Who's there?'

'George.' He pronounced his English name 'Sauce'. He was going to the same party. I gave him a fistful of tobacco. Then he asked for papers, so I gave him half a dozen papers. He paddled off.

William arrived next. I hoped I would be left alone now, but half an hour later there was another slap of paddle, more muted coughing from the darkness. 'It's Johnson.'

I was short with Johnson. This business of 'sharing' possessions was all very well but I was tired, having been up on watch for most of the windward passage from Port Vila the previous night. Wordlessly I thrust a mean amount of tobacco into Johnson's out-stretched hands. No, I had no papers left. I went below, hoping this might staunch the flow of scroungers.

I was almost asleep when I heard movement alongside the boat for the final time. I climbed wearily to the deck just as Johnson started heaving things over the rail. I shone a torch and saw three woven *pandanus* baskets piled on the transom. One contained oranges, another limes, and the third pamplemousse. Later I counted. There were more than sixty pieces of fruit. I turned on the cockpit light so that Johnson and I could see each other's faces. He said, 'This is for you, friend.'

Overnight, heavy ground swell crept into the anchorage as the trade wind freshened. By dawn the sound of cocks crowing in the village was drowned out by breaking surf. Gusts of warm, cloying wind fell from the cliffs sending fingers of ruffled water scattering across the bay. The sloop rode back hard against its anchor in submission to each blast. In a lull I launched the kayak and paddled towards the beach. It would have been difficult to land here today. Surf was crashing with an almost continuous roar onto the pebbled shoreline.

Today, there was no other boat in the anchorage, but by the 1840s sandalwood ships had again started calling regularly at Dillon's Bay. No trading ship was more unlucky here than the schooner *Elizabeth*. In 1845, under the captaincy of W. E. Jones, four of her crew were killed off the beach when their longboat was ambushed in the shallows. Jones was still in command a year later when the *Elizabeth* was back in Dillon's Bay, and two more crew were killed trying to procure sandalwood.

So long as the trade wind is blowing the anchorage at Dillon's Bay is well sheltered. But when the *Elizabeth* returned in 1848, she was caught in a wet-season gale that blew directly onshore. The schooner's anchor dragged and the ship struck the fringing reef beneath the southern cliffs. Many of the crew were killed when the *Elizabeth* broke up in heavy seas, but some managed to scramble from a yard onto a rocky ledge in the precipice while a few succeeded in getting ashore through the surf. All were killed when they reached the beach where the Erromangans were waiting with tomahawks. But the trading ships kept coming. By 1840 supplies of sandalwood elsewhere in the ocean were all but exhausted and whatever the risks of trading in the New Hebrides, they were deemed to be worth it.

When Reverend Turner cruised through the islands in the 1840s, he found a Sydney sandalwood schooner anchored here in Dillon's Bay. The ship had ridden fruitlessly out in the anchorage for a week, conducting little trade while the islanders played cat and mouse with the crew. The tone taken in some books on exploration, of hapless native peoples selling their birthright for a handful of baubles and trinkets, would have been a dangerous condescension here in Dillon's Bay. The Erromangans were cut-throat traders who drove a hard bargain; bloody hard. They learned quickly that they had all the time in the world, unlike the sailors. The first sandalwood ships brought beads, fish-hooks and hoop iron, but the islanders soon demanded more. So the traders brought saws, tomahawks, carving knives and butchers' cleavers; they handed over the very weapons that would be turned against them. In time, the islanders would accept nothing but muskets, powder and tobacco. Reverend Turner records how the Sydney sandalwood skipper was too terrified to land on the beach.

Instead, he spent each day in the longboat, rowing up and down outside the surf line. Occasionally an Erromangan came with a scrap of sandalwood. Tense and lengthy negotiations followed, shouted over the crash of breaking waves, while the captain tried to broker a deal, 'With the pistol in one hand and his fishhooks in the other. What will man not do for money?'

I paddled along the beach, outside the line of breakers, then into the eddies and dark pools of the Williams River. Village men were walking the riverside track, bush knives swinging jauntily in their hands as they strolled towards the gardens. Boys had brought down parrots with slingshots and were plucking them as they walked, a litter of green feathers falling in their wake.

Above Williams Rock the river strayed to cover most of the valley floor. Cattle waded up to their bellies in a waterlogged pastureland. Dogs panted in the shallows as the sun was now high. At a stepping-stone ford the village women were gathered, pounding laundry against smooth river stones. I tethered the kayak to a branch at the top of the last navigable stretch of water and followed a path inland.

Ten minutes beyond the ford the bush gave way to cultivated gardens. Nut and fruit trees lined the path. Several growing sheds with shade-cloth roofs and walls occupied a clearing. Behind the cloth I could see the outline of a man watering pot plants. The whole set-up might have passed for a dope-growing operation camouflaged in the bush. I hoped I was in the right place.

The man in the shed was indeed Sempet Naritantop, the gardener I'd been hoping to meet. And the seedlings were sandalwood trees, hundreds of them in plastic sleeves stacked on the floor or on rough trestles. He had spent three decades raising sandalwood trees on Erromango, engaging in a trade that had been more or less continuous here since the 1820s. Compared with the mid-1800s, however, today's trade in sandalwood is small. The timber is mostly exported to Europe and used in the production of soaps and cosmetics.

Sempet Naritantop led me proudly through his garden. There

41

were orange trees from Aniwa, *navele* nuts from the Banks Islands, vanilla from Futuna, breadfruit trees, avocados, mangoes, sugar cane, pineapples, pawpaw, passion fruit and pamplemousse. On the hillside above the house we came to a grove of sandalwood trees. He pointed out one planted 18 years earlier. Even at a relatively old age, this specimen was an inauspicious and unimposing plant with its crooked trunk, twisted limbs, and small, pale leaves. It seemed an improbable cause of so much bloodshed.

A sandalwood tree requires ten years, or better fifteen, to produce *natora*, the dark, aromatic core with its rich, crumbly consistency. He cut off a small branch and dug around with the tip of his bush knife to expose it, the only valuable part of the tree, and then remarked, in his characteristically circuitous, sometimes lyrical, style of discourse: 'Only when the tree begins to look very old, like an old man, like me, with deep wrinkles in the bark, and fewer leaves, like a man going bald – only then does the *natora* come.'

In one decade, the 1840s, more than 150 sandalwood voyages were made to the southern New Hebrides. And the principal player in this trade was James Paddon. After the *Brigand*'s ill-fated call at Ile Maré, the brig finally reached the New Hebrides early in 1844. Paddon established his station on Aneityum, 80 miles to the south of Erromango, largely because the island boasted a tolerable all-weather anchorage. Paddon himself left no journal, but one man who visited Aneityum was Captain Erskine of the Royal Navy. He anchored off Paddon's station six years after its foundation and was impressed by what he found. From offshore a flag was seen, 'indicating the headquarters of a British establishment'. Erskine records a thriving settlement of about fifty traders, commanded by Paddon whom he described as 'an enterprising Englishman, known in these seas as one of the most active and honourable masters of the [sandalwood] trade'. Paddon's unique gift, according to Erskine, was the ability to establish peaceful relations with the islanders.

Nonetheless, the Melanesians were not to be taken lightly. As soon as a longboat came inshore to trade, it was vulnerable. One of James Paddon's long-term employees, a notorious drunk named Edward Rodd, was just one of many victims. While serving as mate of the schooner *Avon*, Rodd's longboat was ambushed in shallow water off the beach and capsized. The sailors and their muskets were tipped into the surf, which the islanders well knew rendered the guns useless. Edward Rodd lost a hand and an eye in the tomahawk attack that followed. A blow to his side cut a rib through to the spine. Somehow he got back to the ship where he faced a 42-day voyage to Sydney before he could receive medical attention. Edward Rodd was still sandalwooding in the New Hebrides 15 years later. And although Paddon complained of his drinking binges in Nouméa and debilitating fits of delirium tremens, Rodd was eventually given his own command, the schooner *Bluebell*.

That afternoon Sempet Naritantop led me up the hill that rises to the south of Dillon's Bay. The path was ill-formed and steep, twisting through scrubby bush. After an hour's work we came out at a tableland 300 metres above the sea.

I followed Sempet off the path where he showed me a line of stone remains set in crumbling mortar. Pushing aside the undergrowth we traced what were the foundations of an old house, about ten paces long and eight wide. This had been the first European house on Erromango, built in 1857. It was the home of George and Ellen Gordon, the first missionaries to venture into Dillon's Bay since John Williams's death on the beach 18 years earlier. The Gordons built their house up here on the tableland to escape the malaria – 'fever and ague' – that was so prevalent beside the river. Both were killed in 1861. George was ambushed with axes on the path we had just climbed. Ellen was decapitated in the stone mission house. They died in the aftermath of a measles epidemic that reduced Erromango's population by one-third. The disease was introduced to Dillon's Bay by the sandalwood schooner *Bluebell*.

I sat with Sempet on a promontory overlooking the valley. By now the sun was high and the view superb. The Williams River was a black lace threaded through the ravine below, overhung by palms and tropical bush. To the east were the mountains above Port Navarin, a full day's march across the island. To the west there was only ocean, smooth and glossy close under the island's lee, riven by white caps offshore. A fresh wind was blowing across the tableland. A whole hillside of yellow grasses was bending in the trade.

Throughout the mid-nineteenth century the missionaries and sandalwood traders had fought a war for control of Dillon's Bay. The missionaries made no secret of their disgust for the traders, calling them 'sailing profligates' and 'the most Godless and abandoned men'. George and Ellen Gordon's deaths were incited by the sandalwooders because the missionaries had started giving away the very trade goods the sailors wished to exchange for timber.

As we sat on the hillside I wondered if Sempet Naritantop identified with the Gordons. Like them, he was an outsider preaching a foreign creed. Sempet was from the Polynesian island of Futuna and had spent 30 years in Melanesian Dillon's Bay trying to teach the simple process of sandalwood propagation. His goal had been to create a sustainable forestry enterprise here, but he had met with only limited success. 'The Erromangans will never change,' he told me. 'They live only for the minute. They want everything now. It takes 15 years for a sandalwood tree to grow, but they are only interested in cutting them down.'

Meanwhile a Queensland timber company was courting the chiefs. Joe Meté had shown me the proposal for this venture when I'd visited the guesthouse. 'What do you think of this?' he asked, handing over a spiral-bound document as we'd been sitting in the garden drinking sweet tea. I flicked through the proposal: a 50:50 partnership to harvest Erromango's remaining timber; a $2 million investment in infrastructure; local jobs; full training; health and safety paramount. 'So what do you think?' Joe asked eagerly.

'I'm a teacher,' I said. 'I honestly don't know. But I really think you should get some professional advice about this before you sign anything. Maybe you could find a lawyer in Port Vila.'

Joe threw me a scornful look. 'Yeah. Yeah. We've got plenty of lawyers on it.'

I now repeated this exchange to Sempet Naritantop and told him what I'd seen in the proposal. 'It's the Queenslanders who'll need the lawyers,' he said with a grin. 'They don't know what they're getting themselves into. The chiefs had a Malaysian timber company here a few years ago. They left with their tails between their legs.' It seemed that little had changed: those who would trade for timber at Dillon's Bay still took their chances. 'It could be worse,' Sempet went on. 'The chiefs will sign, of course they will. But it would be better if we managed the trees ourselves.'

As we walked back down into the valley Sempet told me about his daughter. It was something of a sob story and I braced myself for the inevitable. She attended a secondary school on the neighbouring island of Tanna but had been thrown out because he was in arrears with the fees. The sum owing was 500 Vatu (approximately $4.50*). I assumed Sempet was going to touch me for the 500 vatu. Everyone else in Dillon's Bay would have. But Sempet Naritantop had something else in mind. He told me he had been trying for months to ship some sandalwood seedlings to Port Vila and so raise some money. But the supply ship was months late, no one knew when it would now come. He asked if I could take the seedlings to Vila in the sloop. My next stop was Tanna, in the opposite direction, to see where James Paddon had set up home after he fled Aneityum. But I told Sempet I would pick up the plants on my way back to Port Vila in a few days' time.

That evening, shortly after sunset, I got the anchor up and put to sea.

*At the time of writing US $1 bought 114 Vanuatu Vatu.

2

Cargo and Kings

'They called us "the men of the sky" because, observing that the sky appeared to touch the ocean . . . and knowing that we came from an immense distance, they concluded that we must have come through the sky to arrive at Tongataboo.'

George Vason, beachcomber, 1810

B Y MIDNIGHT THE worst of the squall had gone through. At first a crack of paler sky was visible to the south-east. Then a crevice of moonlight seeped through a right-angled slot in the rain cloud, like a door ajar in the heavens. As the squall moved away to the west, lightning flickered behind cloud towers in the sky. In one flash I caught sight of Erromango, the great cliffs at Antioch rising from a green sea, as bold and monstrous as a gothic tomb. In the aftermath of gale force winds, the seas in the Tanna Channel were belligerent. The power that had given them life had already passed through and they fell about in disorder, short and concave in chaotic death throes. The sloop laboured to windward, wallowing in the troughs, stumbling over the crests, making only a halting way. I lit the stove as it hung crazily from its gimbals, clamped the kettle in place over the paraffin burner, then climbed to the deck to shake out the reef in the mainsail. By the time I got back the kettle was intermittently whistling, omitting a plaintive peep each time the boat crunched into a trough. I drank the tea governed by this same pattern. At the top of each wave there was a moment of suspended animation, a window of stillness in which to take another scalding gulp.

At dawn I was four miles off Tanna's northern coastline. Dark cliffs rose from the sea and climbed into the smothering, sodden cloud. Sheets of rock flowed with a film of gunmetal moisture. Deep ravines fell down from the tableland, choked with tumbled boulders. As the rising wind tore the cloud from the land, the bush looked frigid in the first light, a frosty blue. The ocean was black, marbled with braids of foam. In the grey, sunless early morning I beat for two hours along the island's north coast before finally clearing Cape Enangiang and reaching the longer, undulating swells of the open ocean.

It was a slow day spent beating south down Tanna's windward shore. The wind fell ever lighter; in the troughs between the swells the air was almost still. To the west the island was mostly lost in cloud, but once or twice on the inshore tacks I caught a glimpse of patchwork gardens and plains of volcanic debris. Shortly before the onset of night I finally slipped through the reef entrance to Port Resolution and anchored at the head of the bay.

Sandalwood ships had routinely made this 50-mile passage between Erromango and Tanna: one ship took two days to beat through the Tanna Channel. Both islands were thick with timber, though Tanna's was of inferior quality. Captain Erskine lists the names of several ships employed in procuring sandalwood: *Phantom, Terror, Spy, Vulture,* and of course *Brigand.* The schooner *Terror* mounted swivel guns on the bulwarks and lived up to her name: a chief on the beach was once used for target practice. At the completion of its final voyage the *Terror* ran down the weather coast of Erromango firing on every settlement that had proved uncooperative so as to 'spoil the trade' for competitors.

I woke at Port Resolution the next morning when a further squall buffeted the anchored boat and bands of rain smattered through the hatches. As the squall cleared, fruit bats winged across the anchorage and spitting trade. On the craggy western shore, balls of steam puffed with locomotive regularity from a volcanic vent among the palms. It was a secure bay, but a long swell crept incessantly round the reefs, sending any anchored boat into a heavy roll.

The first European ship to heave on the swells here was Captain Cook's HMS *Resolution* in August 1774. Cook was first, too, to record the hostility ashore: '. . . one fellow shewed us his back side in such a manner that it was not necessary to have an interpreter to explain his meaning.' Many of those who came later reported something similar, or worse. The first missionaries sank to their knees on the beach and read the 46th psalm, convinced the Tannese were about to kill them. Turner, Murray and Nesbitt then climbed into a 30-foot open boat to escape to the southern island of Aneityum, 'our dear wives wrapped up as well they could'. None ever returned to Tanna.

For Europeans, Tanna came to epitomize the islands of Melanesia, a term coined from the Greek words *melas* 'black' and *nēsos* 'island'. These were the Dark Isles; the Tannese were 'fiends of black skins and blacker souls'. Sixteen years passed before another missionary ventured into Port Resolution. Around the head of the horseshoe bay a beach of blond sand sweeps in a cambered arc as if it had been poured from a pot of molten honey. Reverend John Paton landed here from the *Hirondelle* in November 1858 with his wife Mary Anne, her grand piano, a silver cutlery service, a bound set of the *Penny Cyclopaedia* and two longboats. Of Port Resolution he wrote, 'I have never seen such a lovely spot . . . Only man is vile'. Within a year his wife and infant son were dead from malaria and buried in a grave lined with coral blocks to preserve their remains from cannibals. Paton fled for his life and was eventually rescued by the sandalwood schooner *Bluebell*. Much to his disgust the mate and many of the crew were wearing his own clothes, looted from the ransacked mission house.

Even in the twentieth century, few Europeans revelled in the experience of living on this island. The colonial era was marked by a series of bizarre accidents and tragedies. James Nichol was run over and killed by his own driverless jeep on a bush track in 1944 when he got out to open a gate. His replacement, Gordon White, went mad and had to be removed. White was succeeded by Basil Neven-Spence, whose suicide in the official residence mystified both his colleagues and family, while future occupants of the house complained that his bloodstains could never be removed from the floorboards. A final death occurred in 1970 when the district agent's wife was asphyxiated in the bath by a faulty gas water heater. One district agent in the 1950s wrote simply that Tanna was 'a heavy place, there was something terribly ominous . . . I don't know what it was'.

Tanna was a posting: a place to which missionaries and colonial agents were sent. No one chose to come here. No one, that is, except the sandalwooder James Paddon, whose course in the *Brigand* I had traced from Auckland. When Paddon's world fell apart, he beat a path direct to Tanna.

In a lull between squalls I slid the kayak into the water to find the place where James Paddon had lived. Scores of outrigger canoes were berthed in a mass of vines and mauve flowers behind the beach. A group of women were squatting beside a volcanic spring in the sands, cooking plantains and reef fish in a pool of bubbling water. Others were steaming *pandanus* fronds to soften them for weaving. Behind the beach a trail led inland through an orchard of lime, orange, guava and soursop trees. Kingfishers perched in the beach hibiscus. A clearing led out onto a land-locked lagoon lined with tall grasses where men were standing chest deep in the water casting for bait fish with bamboo rods. It was here at the water's edge that James Paddon had built his house in the 1850s.

Paddon's original station on the island of Aneityum, 40 miles south-east of Port Resolution, had initially prospered, despite numerous mishaps among his fleet of trading ships. The *Harriet* foundered in a cyclone off Maré with the loss of nine crew. The *Rosetta, Alfred and Avenger* were all wrecked, and the *Rover's Bride* was badly damaged. However, in 1848 a storm in human form approached Aneityum that would shake Paddon's world to the core. After dawn on the morning of 13 July the new mission ship *John Williams* closed the shore. The principal passenger, the Reverend John Geddie, wrote, 'Observing the coastline with spyglasses, we saw long shadows dressed in black robes marching up and down in front of the shacks. At that moment we recognized the sign of the beast . . . The battle would take place not only against Paganism, but against Paganism and Popery together.'

Contemporaries called John Geddie 'Little Johnnie'. He was 'Gentle as a girl, guileless as a child' with a smooth chin and a 'peeping' high-pitched voice. In the event, the Presbyterian Geddie overestimated the challenge posed by the newly arrived Catholic missionaries. The eight brothers were removed a matter of months later. Geddie's greatest battle on Aneityum would be with neither Paganism nor Popery, but with Paddon. Little Johnnie and his pious wife Charlotte would reduce the phlegmatic sailor to a trembling hysteric.

Geddie, like most missionaries, was scandalized by the treatment of women in the New Hebrides. In some islands women had lower status than pigs and were forced to suckle piglets. Women were sometimes kept on a leash, often given no personal names and widows were habitually strangled to accompany husbands on their final journey. Geddie was outraged but the Aneityumese ignored his protests.

But if John Geddie was unable to change the islanders' customs, hell would freeze over before he tolerated anything similar from the Europeans. 'All the sandalwood vessels that I know are floating brothels,' he wrote and resolved to save the native women from ruin. 'I made up my mind to speak to Capt. Paddon on the subject. I called on him but before I could introduce the object of my visit he broke out into a torrent of abuse, such as it has not been my misfortune to hear before. He called me a liar, hypocrite, and every thing bad, and said that Mrs. Geddie was a great deal worse than myself. She has perhaps been more directly instrumental than I have in saving some of the poor females.'

Thereafter relations deteriorated sharply. By November of 1851 Paddon was 'an avowed and bitter enemy'. The Geddies were convinced that Paddon and his odious sidekick, the beastly one-eyed, one-handed skipper of the schooner *Bluebell*, 'a wicked man named Rodd', were inciting the islanders to burn down the mission. Two days later the mission house was set alight a little after midnight. The thatch caught fire but Little Johnnie managed to extinguish the flames 'as the night was calm and the dew heavy'.

Within a week 'Captain Paddon came to me trembling with rage and carrying a large pistol. He spoke to me in the most boisterous manner and his language to Mrs Geddie was vile . . . He told me that he would not live on the same island with me and said he would leave Aneityum in a few weeks . . . [The boat-builder] Underwood assisted his employer in the abuse of Mrs Geddie and myself, and it is hard to say which of them excelled in it. They were both at home in the language of Billingsgate and they added to this much Botany Bay slang which I have not heard elsewhere.'

When Paddon quit Aneityum in January 1852, Geddie concluded, 'It is hard to say whether these savages are most degraded or the white men who encourage their revolting deeds'. Paddon boarded the *Rover's Bride* and sailed north 40 miles to Tanna. It was a short passage but a considered decision. More than any other island in the Pacific, Tanna has stubbornly, sometimes violently, most often colourfully, resisted missionary influence.

Paddon's new settlement was a far cry from the colony he had first proposed establishing at the public meeting in Wellington 11 years earlier. There was no union flag flying outside his house at Port Resolution and the captain's new mode of life shared some of the characteristics of beachcombing. Pacific beachcombers were different from other Europeans in the islands. Whereas the missionaries tried to change the islanders and the settlers maintained satellite European communities, the beachcombers had largely abandoned their former cultures and crossed the sand to live among the islanders where they conformed to local norms, adhered to the taboos and obeyed the chiefs. At Tanna, James Paddon married a Tannese woman, who did have a personal name, Naitani, and four daughters were born. The Geddies may have been exposed to Paddon's 'rage', but even they agreed that the Melanesians warmed to his rough affection.

Among sandalwooders, Paddon had an enviable reputation for honesty and fair treatment.

In the afternoon I joined three of the crew from an American yacht to hike over to the John Frum village. We met on the beach and spent an hour waiting for our guide to arrive. No one knew what was going on. We'd heard that the John Frum people held a celebration every Friday night but, depending on the source, the walk to the village would take between one and four hours. We had little food, no idea where we would spend the night, and it was threatening to rain. Like beachcombers, we had given up our boats and would be dependent on the islanders, if only for a day or two.

The western technologies introduced to Tanna by traders like James Paddon left a legacy that endures to the present day. The John Frum village is a 'cargo cult', a product of the beach, that shifting strip between land and sea where cultures meet and merge. In most Pacific island groups sailors were associated with the supernatural. Sandalwood ships were believed to be transports from the spirit world loaded with a divine cargo of knives, tomahawks, saws and muskets sent by the ancestors. The Frum Cult is an amalgam of Tannese means and western ends: through their own supernatural processes, the Frum followers attempt to acquire very real western products: originally tools and weapons, today washing machines and hair dryers.

Our guide that afternoon, a teenager in a Brazilian soccer shirt named Joel, set a cracking pace up the hillside to the west of Port Resolution. We climbed for an hour through a forest of banyans and tree ferns before reaching the plateau. Here, beside the path, we came to a burnt-out hut. Only the blackened frame was still standing. Around the corner were the remains of many more grass houses, all burnt to the ground. I asked Joel why this village had been burnt down, but he only offered something unintelligible about a 'great flood' and 'a fire from heaven'. Presumably it was something to do with the John Frum Cult but none of the people we met on the plateau could, or would, tell me what had happened. And there was little time to investigate. Joel was jogging ahead along the path, worried that darkness would fall before we reached the village.

At the lip of the plateau we got our first view down into Sulphur Bay, home to the John Frum Cult. It was a forbidding scene. To our south the summit of the Yasur Volcano was lost in the gathering rain-clouds. Lava flows and ash fields cut swathes through the bush, feeding a grey river that swept down onto the coastal plain. Directly below us a few grass huts were just visible in the surrounding bush.

We reached the village perimeter as heavy rain started to fall. Joel gestured that we should wait at the tree line while he sought permission from the headman to bring visitors into the settlement. Soon after we were waved ahead.

An hour later we four sailors were sitting alone in a longhouse at the centre of the village. From the darkness outside we heard the dull, muffled thudding of numerous bare feet in the sand as a crowd gathered. A length of bamboo was struck hard, then deep male voices broke into song. Guitars joined in, followed by women and girls, as the singers pushed inside and sat in a tight huddle in the centre of the floor. From all around the building, wet black faces and pink eyes peered in from the dripping night. Heavy handclapping now echoed beneath the thatch roof. The 'song' was a kind of screeching. The performers appeared to be in a trance.

When the rain eased I went outside. At least a hundred villagers were gathered on the sand. The women danced in line, dressed in ankle-length grass skirts over vibrantly coloured dresses. A beanpole of a man, wearing a top hat and tails, danced eccentrically, his body shaking and hands clutching at the air. I shared some tobacco with a man named Daniel who came here every Friday night from his village of Ipeukel, and asked him what on earth was going on. 'John Frum did not want us to build a church or have a priest. He chose Friday as his special day. Every Friday night we don't sleep. All night we sing seven new songs, one for each day of the week. Every day is John's day.' So that was as clear as mud.

The trade wind was strong that night, coming off the ocean at 40 knots. The combined noise in the village was deafening: the guitars, the singers, the clapping crowd, overhead thunder, tropical rain, the wind tearing at the grass thatch. I divided the night between lying shivering on the damp and draughty floor of a hut we'd been given use of, and shuffling around with the dancers in an effort to warm up. At 5 a.m. I went back outside for the last time. The crowd had thinned only slightly. Stiff with cold I joined the ranks of villagers dancing in the rain. Then, as the first light of dawn filtered through the trees, the singing abruptly stopped. The villagers filed away and I was left surrounded by footprints in the sand.

On the far side of the square there was a figure dressed in US army fatigues. He introduced himself as Nikiau Ianimoli, the village chief. 'Come up to Headquarters,' he said.

Three bamboo flagstaffs and a grass hut stood on a spur overlooking the square. Chief Nikiau Ianimoli pushed open the door and I followed him inside. On the wall were two painted memorials to John Frum (or Brum). 'Belif In John Brum Brophercy. John Promise America. One Day He'll Be Returning'. An American flag and plastic bald eagle stood on a desk. 'My grandfather was first to see John Frum,' Chief Nikau Ianimou told me. 'It was right here, outside Headquarters. John landed his airplane on the Yasur Volcano and came down into the village. He had hurt his leg and came with a big walking stick, like Moses. He told us he was John from America, so we called him John From.'

The 'From', or 'Frum' – sometimes 'Brum' – Cult has been an embarrassment to Port Vila since its inception in 1940 as a pagan revival. John Frum was a mythical figure, possibly inspired by a downed American wartime pilot, who started 'appearing' to groups of kava drinkers all around Tanna. In 1943 the colonial authorities ordered a clampdown and enlisted help from the US Navy ship *Echo*. Forty-six suspected cult leaders were arrested and charged with 'dreaming' and 'spreading rumours'. Many were imprisoned including Nelawiyang who died in a mental institution in Nouméa several years later. The role played by the ship *Echo* was celebrated in the 1950s television series *The Wackiest Ship in the Army*.

This repression was wholly ineffective. It transpired that John Frum had three sons: Isaac, Jacob and Lastuan ('Last One' – kava drinking can cause memory loss). With three new figureheads the movement endlessly morphed and splintered. The authorities could never squash the cult because they could never pin down exactly what it was. Today, depending on to whom you talk, Frum is variously a reincarnation of the early trading sailors bearing exotic cargoes of western goods, a Christian messiah, or a nationalist hero urging a return to the pre-Christian animist belief system. The last two are obviously contradictory, but that wouldn't worry the Frum people one bit.

Later that morning a larger group of villagers had assembled for the walk back to Port Resolution. As we filed up the hillside above Sulphur Bay a column of about twenty people formed. The path was slippery after so much heavy rain and the trade wind was still at gale force. To our east the sea was white with driven spume. The crashing bush overhead was so noisy we had to shout.

The women were all wearing the Mother Hubbard dresses introduced by the missionaries. The originals had been drab calico tunics, but the contemporary model comes in bright prints with various tassel and bow options. These dresses are virtually a uniform worn by all married Ni-Vanuatu women. The women called us '*Masta*' and, when we passed them on the track, fussily pulled their skirts in around their knees so the fabric wouldn't brush our legs. The men were mostly old and stooped, with long, wiry grey beards. They had no pockets, so used their beards as a repository: a piece of straw for use as a toothpick was pushed into the tight curls, or a short knife. Their chests and legs were bare and scarred, their shorts torn. They had the splayed feet of those who habitually walk barefoot, a pad of thick, white skin extending up from the soles like a frill. These elderly villagers weren't our guides, but there was a sense of shared identity as we walked the same track. When we slipped on the treacherous mud they didn't help us but stopped and waited, making a cooing or clucking noise in empathy. When we halted to rest they squatted nearby. They asked for nothing, but if we offered tobacco or water or biscuits they took it with a nod and quietly smoked or drank or ate. The villagers were a warm presence on the trail.

When we reached the plateau the others went ahead. I wanted to have a better look around the burnt-out village we had passed the previous day. I counted the remains of 135 huts, all destroyed by fire. Fresh weeds were just breaking through the blackened earth. After several enquiries I found a woman working in the gardens nearby who told me the village had been destroyed by the VMF – the Vanuatu Military Force – along with the police, but she could not explain why.

In the centre of the village at Port Resolution there was a solar-powered telephone surrounded by grass huts. I wanted to know more about the burnt-out village so the next work day I called the Commissioner of Police, whose name was Robert Deniro (truly). Deniro confirmed that the village had been destroyed in a joint operation between the police and VMF because it had been the base for a breakaway cargo cult established by a man named Fred. However, Fred was now in custody so I should call Fake Rakau, the Superintendent of Prisons. Rakau said Fred was not in custody and I should talk to Commander Pierre Carlot. Carlot had no idea why I'd called him when Inspector Kensie at the Isangel police station was the obvious man to talk to. Kensie was out, but when I got hold of him later that day he proved frank and forthcoming.

Fred Nasse – or 'Prophet Fred' as he preferred to be known – was the most recent manifestation of John Frum. Ships and sea travel are still associated with the supernatural in Tanna and Fred's voyages as a deckhand working on cargo ships in Africa, Europe and America had supposedly granted him divine powers. When he returned from the sea Fred challenged the leadership of the

John Frum Cult with an apocalyptic new prophecy – all the usual Tannese mumbo-jumbo about a fire in the sky and a flood from heaven, or so it seemed. But then the Yasur Volcano on Tanna really did erupt and a destructive mudslide known as a *lahar* swept down through the Frum village at Sulphur Bay. Fred quickly attracted a following of more than 3,000 supporters and led this faction onto the plateau where a new village was built, until the police and army had moved in two months before my visit. The village was burnt and 108 suspects, including Fred, arrested.

Inspector Kensie rejected my suggestion that the cult had been suppressed. The issue, he said, was trespass. The site where Fred's followers had built the village, called Yanekahi, was private land. No, it would not be possible for me to interview Fred until after his trial, a date for which was yet to be set.

These Melanesian cargo cults are usually described as twentieth-century phenomena, the result of the islanders' sudden exposure to US military might when massive bases were established in the New Hebrides during the Pacific War. But John Frum and Prophet Fred can trace their origins back to the first sailing ships that penetrated the islands and the 'sailor cults' established by beachcombers. The best record of the sailor cults was left by W.T. Pritchard, British consular agent in Samoa in the 1850s. Pritchard describes Samoa as being overrun with beachcombers in the early 1800s, many of whom claimed to be members of the English royal family. 'In no group of the Pacific,' Pritchard wrote, 'have our erratic countrymen, in the pursuit of their vagabondism, lived what they termed such "jolly lives" as in Samoa in its days anterior to the introduction of Christianity and intercourse with a better class of whitemen . . .'

One group of runaway sailors founded their own religion under the leadership of Big-legged Jimmy. They announced the existence of a Supreme Being and described his 'grand doctrines'. These were that polygamy was good and proper and the most acceptable service to the Great Spirit was maintaining Big-legged Jimmy with regular feasts, kava, and young women. Services of devotion began with the singing of a sea shanty, usually 'Tom Bowline', and concluded with another, typically 'Black-eyed Susan'. Big-legged Jimmy lived in fine style for more than 40 years and left hundreds of grandchildren.

But the most successful of all the sailor religions was the Siovili Cult. Siovili was a Samoan who, like many Pacific Islanders, worked as a deckhand aboard European trading ships. In the 1820s Siovili voyaged on the sandalwood schooner *Samuel Henry* to Tonga, Tahiti and New South Wales. According to Siovili, the *Samuel Henry* then ran before a gale under full canvas through the night sky and at dawn made landfall on the shores of Heaven. Joe's cult began as a small movement in the Samoan village of Eva in 1830 and had thousands of followers 30 years later.

Beachcombers were pragmatists who exploited the trauma caused by the arrival of European ships. Throughout many of the island groups at the time of first contact, white sailors were assumed to be spirits or supernatural beings. The generic name for white people still in use today across much of Polynesia translates as 'men from the sky' or something similar. The beachcomber Edward Robarts records how the Marquesans were 'afraid to come near me, [and] said I was a ghost. Others said I was from the sky. I endeavoured to undeceive them. Some of the fair sex would come and feel my hands, arms and feet. Others more rude would pinch me to see if I had feelings.' Robarts, and many other beachcombers, took advantage of this. As 'spirits' the sailors saw an opportunity to act as cultural go-betweens, guiding the islanders through the magical new world of western technologies that had arrived on ships.

After the wreck of the whaler *Oeno* in Fiji in 1825, William Cary survived the massacre of the other twenty crewmen by hiding in a cave. When he was discovered by the Fijians Cary's life hung in the balance. Initially, he was little more than a captive. But the beachcomber won friends and prestige by working as an armourer. In the aftermath of the wreck the Fijians had dived on the crippled *Oeno* many times before she broke up and salvaged seven rusty muskets among other valuable cargo. He serviced and repaired these muskets, then instructed the chief on how to use them. 'While I was taking the locks apart and putting them together the old man watched me with the keenest interest . . . he expressed his satisfaction as well as he could by signs, frequently repeating the word caloo.' The Fijian word *kalou* translates as 'spirit' or 'ghost'. 'When I had finished he said: "Are you a spirit?"'

Joshua Newborn, a beachcomber in New Zealand, who stated that his Maori name translated as 'the tattooed spirit'. Cartoon from the *Illustrated London News*, 1842

Another beachcomber who played a similar role was an American named Leonard Shaw, one member of a group numbering nearly two dozen seamen who went ashore in Melanesia from the schooner *Antarctic* to gather and cure bêche-de-mer. Shaw was the only survivor when the seamen were attacked and subsequently found himself a castaway when the *Antarctic* fled to sea assuming that all of the sailors ashore were dead. His 'scull was broken to the extent of two or three inches each way' following a blow from a war club. He was stripped of all possessions and kept naked, fully exposed to the sun, until 'I was covered from head to foot with smarting blisters'. For many weeks Shaw assumed he was going to be killed and his sufferings were such that he welcomed the prospect. In the end, however, he preserved his life and even gained some slight status in the tribe by working as a smith. He set up the forge and using the hoop iron stored in the sailors' workshop ashore 'I commenced the manufacture of knives. Being better acquainted with the duties of . . . Neptune than of Vulcan, my progress was slow, and my productions not remarkably well finished; but I did the best I could.' Shaw's skills at the forge were sufficient to prolong his life for nearly four months until the *Antarctic* returned and picked him up.

Thus the beachcombers sold themselves ashore as both priests and artisans. In the Pacific Islands this wasn't an unusual combination of roles. Indeed, the missionaries themselves were eminently practical men. The Reverend John Williams, the missionary killed on the beach at Dillon's Bay, had been apprenticed as a 13-year-old to the ironmonger Enoch Tonkin on London's City Road where he had learned to use a hammer and anvil. In the Pacific, Williams did not simply establish his church and teach the gospel; he also set up a forge and taught carpentry. The islanders built chests in which to store their new calico tunics, beds, stools and tables, his goal being to reproduce the physical trappings of the Victorian world as well as its religion. In the early 1800s missionaries were working class: 'Godly men who understand the mechanic arts'. Among the missionaries on the *Duff*, the first mission ship to sail to the Pacific, there was a shoemaker, brazier, joiner, surgeon, Indian weaver, wheelwright, tailor, hatter, linen draper, cabinet maker, stonemason and bricklayer. These men brought their tools to the islands as well as their bibles. In the process they sowed the seeds of confusion regarding the relationship between Christianity and material goods that endures to the present day in the John Frum Cult on Tanna.

Muskets, adzes or Christianity: all were viewed by the islanders as 'technologies'. So the beachcombers set themselves up as armourers, blacksmiths and priests. Sometimes they adopted multiple roles. A beachcomber named Old Tom Franklin, a deserter from an English man of war, first sold himself to the Samoans as a 'priest', then a 'teacher', and finally a 'doctor', administering breadfruit pills laced with vinegar. Tom's endless supply of quack medicines earned him a chiefly rank, many wives, and as much pork and fish as his cult-like entourage could eat. The islanders also considered western medicine to be a technology so doctoring was another of those roles popular with the beachcombers. In the Marquesas, Edward Robarts curried favour with both the islanders and visiting ships by establishing himself as a physician, though some of his practices were pretty frightening. When a crewman from a passing whaler was brought ashore with a serious case of scurvy 'I buryd him in the ground nearly up to the heart several times . . . thank God, I had the satisfaction in a few days to see my patient walk about'. In the course of his nine years on the beach Robarts also worked as a ship's pilot, priest, midwife, moonshiner, builder, mercenary and tailor: on the beach, even a humble deckhand became a wise man.

Some beachcombers were certainly little more than slaves and captives in the islands. But others prospered by peddling a parcel of skills and technologies, both practical and spiritual. With their numerous wives, chiefly status and cult following, these sailors were the forebears of John Frum and the deckhand Prophet Fred. Today, being 'on the beach' conjures an image of somehow being down on one's luck. But in the original context of beachcombing, it was sometimes the opposite that transpired. Sailors who had been nobodies aboard ship lived as kings on the beach.

Behind a line of wash-worn laundry strung between the grass huts at Port Resolution I met Sampson Meake, the Presbyterian minister. Sampson led me down one of the paths to his Sagiem Memorial Church. This building was the legacy left by the first missionaries on Tanna, Murray, Nesbitt, Turner and Paton, who had all fled the island in fear of their lives. It was a simple, wall-less structure with a thatch roof and an old table for an altar.

Sampson told me that for 15 years he had worked as a deckhand on the *Sofrana Alliance*, running cargoes of cement and sugar between Nouméa, Suva, Santo and Port Vila. He had picked up some English from the Canadian first engineer – 'Mr Bob 'im teach me plenty gud'. Sampson spoke in loud, explosive bursts with many wild gesticulations. At the end of an utterance he had the habit of throwing his arms across his bare chest and squeezing his own shoulders as if this were the only way he could bring his limbs to rest. When he quit the trading ship Sampson had returned home to Port Resolution and become an elder of the Presbyterian church, his experiences at sea seemingly all the qualifications that were required.

As the sun set we walked through the village. Sampson had offered to take me onto the *nakamal*, the place where the island-ers drink kava, Vanuatu's national drink and national obsession. We followed the trail down a slope to a large, sandy clearing, sur-rounded by giant banyan trees. About sixty men were gathered here in the late afternoon, squatting around the perimeter, or chatting quietly in small groups. Every man in the village came here at this time each day. A gathering of kava drinkers is known as a *niko*, meaning 'canoe'. In many parts of the Pacific a group of people, or a district of an island, is thought of as a vessel. In Tahiti a leader is called *tira*, or 'mast'.

I sat down on a log beside Sampson Meake. Everywhere around the *nakamal* piles of kava roots stood in neat piles on palm leaves laid out on the ground, along with basins of water. Kava is drunk in almost every island group in the Pacific but in Vanuatu it has an especially exalted status. In Fiji and Tonga I often drank it, although knocking back pints of the stuff had only a mild sed-ative effect. But Vanuatu's kava is far more concentrated. In Tanna the drink is still prepared in the traditional way: the roots are chewed, not pounded.

Sampson fell silent as he stuffed his mouth with the roots and then began to mechanically work his jaws. He was strangely intent for several minutes. Then he squatted on the ground, held up a palm leaf to his mouth and squeezed out a mass of desiccated roots like a fibrous second tongue. The root pulp was mixed with water, strained, poured into a half coconut-shell bowl, and presented to me to drink.

For the beachcombers, the kava ceremony had been a rite of passage. In Fiji, William Cary had not lived on the beach for long before 'I was led into the palace and found the king entertaining a party with a kind of drink called carver . . . He then offered me a cup of carver, which I dared not refuse, although my stomach loathed it, and it was with much difficulty that I kept it down . . . After drinking heartily of it, it leaves them in a kind of stupor, similar to the effect of opium. Disgusting as this beverage was to me at first, my repugnance gradually wore away and after a while I could drink it with as good a relish as I can now swallow a glass of beer, though as I look back it makes my stomach turn to think of it.'

The kava mixture was the colour of dirty dishwater. I drank it back in one go as was required by custom. The brew had an earthy flavour with a sharp aftertaste. The first sensation was a tingling in the lips. Soon, though, I forgot my earlier anxieties about Sampson's saliva, possible TB and hepatitis. Kava is a narcotic, a muscle relaxant containing psychoactive ingredients. Today, in the west, extracts from the pepper plant are used in numerous party pills with brand names like Charge, Euphoria, Rapture, Blast, Exodus and Frenzy. Kava products are illegal in Europe and the United States.

Twilight was thickening and a cool, late afternoon light was filtering through the banyans. Kava heightens the senses so that even shade can seem too bright. Whispers sound deafening. Calm fellowship is more desirable than rowdiness. A few simple words carry great import. The shadowy features of a man's face are loaded with meaning. In earlier times this drink lay at the heart of the islanders' animist beliefs, and the act of consuming it was both a social and a mystical event. It was during the kava trance that men communicated with the spirits of their ancestors whose corpses had once been buried around the perimeter of the *nakamal*. Kava drinking preceded every pagan ceremony. John Frum had first 'appeared' before groups of kava drinkers at Green Point in 1940.

Kava features in most of the beachcomber narratives. In the Marquesas, Robarts describes '. . . a root which is first chewd and then water put in . . . It makes you stupid and inclined to sleep.' In Tahiti, James Morrison comments on how the islanders often drank 'intoxicating peper'. For the missionaries, the kava bowl was Satan's cup and the beachcombers were damned when they took the first earthy draught. But with that first bowl of kava the beachcombers caught a glimpse of the true culture of the Pacific, an animist 'oneness' that was – and still is – scorned by most European and American sailors. In his journals Captain Cook described the islanders' metaphysical beliefs as 'extravagantly absurd'. An exception was Herman Melville; his novel of life aboard a whaler, *Moby Dick*, is set not on an inanimate sea, but a metaphysical ocean infused with the culture of the islands scattered all through it. Melville had been a beachcomber. He deserted from the whaler *Acushnet* in 1842 and lived among the Polynesians in the Marquesas. He described beachcombing as being '. . . much in vogue among sailors in the Pacific'.

The irony of this is that while the vast majority of Pacific Islanders – and even many Tannese – have become God-fearing Christians, we sailors have developed certain animist tendencies. We religiously call our boats by name and refer to them as if they were living creatures – 'she', 'her' – when this is plainly not the case. Sailors have long given names to their boats; those names were painted on the stern but seldom used. Captain Cook rarely – if ever – called his boats by name. They were either 'the ship' or he referred to them by type: 'the barque'. The traders who came in his wake followed the same practice: 'the brig'; 'the schooner'.

At the time of Cook's visit to the New Hebrides, the Tannese believed that the supernatural was a permanently active force in their lives. When fuelled by kava they considered themselves to be constantly surrounded by spirits and mythical figures. Some were benevolent and others malign; they were variously fêted, controlled or ignored. White sailors were assumed to be more of the same. Captain Cook had not been at anchor in the New Hebrides for more than two days before he recorded in his journal that he was being ignored: '. . . not a Canoe had been off to the Ship the whole after noon, so soon was the Curiosity of these people satisfied.' The ships that appeared over the horizon, and the beachcombers and castaways who walked up the sand, were just further players in a world where the natural and the supernatural worlds became blurred.

Heavy swells swept the skyline above the reef passage as I prepared the sloop for sea. The trade wind was remorseless now. The boats anchored in Port Resolution had been rolling hard for days. As the sun set I hoisted a heavily reefed mainsail and began work at the windlass. By the time the anchor clunked into the stemhead the sky to windward was filling with greasy black cloud. Another squall was bearing down on the coast. They had been frequent all day on the disturbed trade. The squalls shifted in from the east, formless but invasive, like a fungal infection eating through the sky. The light was already beginning to fade and I hurried towards the reef passage while it could still be seen.

It was a 50-mile downwind passage back to Erromango. In this fresh trade wind that was an easy distance to complete during the hours of daylight, but I usually sailed between the islands at night. The wind sometimes fell back after dark, and anyway the sea is more interesting at night. In those short, delicious moments as the sky filled with rain, I felt my heart kicking against my ribcage as I turned the sloop towards the darkening sea.

In the approach to the reef passage the boat ducked and climbed through muddy seas. The surface was twitching and disturbed where ocean swells met the waters of the lagoon. Before I reached the 10-metre contour the wind was 40 knots on the beam and rain was drumming on the coachroof. Night had descended with the squall.

I bore off the wind and ran north-west down Tanna's weather coast. A deep, quartering swell heaved out of the night, full of noise and bluster. I crouched beneath the sprayhood, searching the sky to the west for the molten glow in the cone of the Yasur Volcano, but like everything else it was lost in the darkness and driving rain.

Within an hour the squall had gone through and the sky had cleared. The wind was hard and dry. To the west the blunt outline of Cape Enangiang barged stately and calm into the massed seas. In the chequerboard world of moonlight and passing cloud, the sea was white and the land black. I cooked an evening meal and listened to the radio news. Then I dozed in the cockpit as the boat surfed downwind on easing seas, until woken by further showers of rain.

By midnight the brawny southern highlands of Erromango were visible to the north. I brought the sloop under the cliffs at Antioch where the wind and swells fell into order, pressed and regulated as they ran parallel to the coast. In the small hours of the morning I hove to on snowfield seas filled with star and moonlight, then slept till dawn in the calm waters of Erromango's lee. The rising sun was blocked for several hours by Mt Melkum and this side of the island was a monotone cut-out, the waters frozen a lifeless grey in the half-light. I tightened the sheets and beat into the anchorage at Dillon's Bay through a shifty, forest-scented flow of wind.

That morning I sent a message to the gardener, Sempet Naritantop. He should bring his sandalwood plants out to the boat that afternoon as I would sail for Port Vila at sunset.

Sure enough, at 4 o'clock, a canoe was labouring through the swells at the mouth of the Williams River. My cargo of sandal-wood was on its way. Sempet sat at the back of the heavily laden outrigger with a single paddle, manoeuvring over the bar with a lazy nonchalance. Balanced across the gunwales were four wire crates, each containing about forty sandalwood saplings. Even from this distance they stood out as a luminous green fuzz against the dark water. We tied the canoe alongside and he passed up the first crate. It was surprisingly heavy, the rough wire edges drawing blood on my forearms as I struggled to lift it over the rail. The sandalwood plants were 30 cm high, growing in cylindrical seed-raising bags. Each crate weighed about 60 kilograms. We stowed the crates on the spare bunk in the cabin, wedged in behind the lee-cloth and the spare tiller, with a cradle of ropes in support, ready for the overnight passage to Port Vila.

Before he returned to the village Sempet gave me the name of his contact in the capital, and a gift. It was a small piece of sandal-wood, about the size of my little finger, which he had carved himself into a replica ironwood war club. He wanted me to wear the war club and I threaded it onto a piece of whipping twine and tied it round my neck to ensure the scent of sandalwood would never be far away for the rest of the voyage. As Sempet climbed back into the canoe I saw the gift as a personal rapprochement between ship and shore, a hand across the beach as we acted out this tiny footnote to the bloody trade in sandalwood at Dillon's Bay.

It was another wet and blustery night. The trade was a steady 30 knots with occasional stronger squalls. The approaching wind could be heard tumbling down from the mountains, a roar and rush like an oncoming tube train. Leaves and twigs floated past the anchored boat on the ruffled water. There was little point waiting for better conditions. Now that the trade wind season was properly established it could blow like this for days on end. At change of light I put to sea, heavily reefed, for the 80-mile run to the capital.

Short seas and a hot wind pressed the sloop north-west. A line of unbroken cliffs led to Elizabeth Bay where the bush was turning blue in the twilight. Bullet squalls fell down from Mt Santop and the boat was bowled out onto the dark ocean. Strings of sticky spray climbed over the weather rail and beat into the cockpit. Bands of rain clattered against the sails and deck as they were driven through on the trade. Sheet lightning revealed layers of oozing cloud to sea level. A long swell was coming in on the beam sending the sloop into a deep roll.

I climbed down into the cabin, dripping wet, and sealed the companionway. In the halogen-lit world of the cabin, the sandalwood plants made a surreal sight. They moved in perfect unison, dipping and rising with each shift in gravity, like a cartoon chorus. There were 132 plants in total, the tender stems surprisingly stiff and resistant, moving slowly as one dignified mass, even when the sloop buried the leeward rail.

I had never carried cargo before, let alone a living one. The single-hander's life has few responsibilities and I was nervous of the plants at first. These little trees represented a man's annual income. I'd worried that I would somehow contrive to kill the things and arrive in Port Vila with crates of yellowing twigs. But I needn't have fretted. The plants seemed little bothered by this alien world of journey making under sail. Only a couple of leaves had come astray and were lying sodden in the puddle of saltwater that shifted ceaselessly on the cabin sole. I filled the teapot with fresh water from the sloop's tank and dribbled a few drops into each pot to fortify them for the journey ahead. Then I climbed back out into the dripping night.

Plants and boats have rarely been happy companions. The problem of transporting living plants under sail was one of the most taxing issues for Victorian plant collectors. It was a notoriously difficult process and one that few plants survived. Voyages from the Far East or South Pacific could take six months. Because of the need for sunlight and ventilation, it was originally thought necessary to store the plants on deck; yet here they were exposed to the wind and spray that killed them. Plant collectors were never loath to experiment with new means of plant husbandry at sea. The abundant provision of damp moss in the pots was found to be beneficial. So was the use of rainwater in preference to the tainted water found in ships' casks.

Numerous experiments were conducted to find the best method of transporting seeds. They were stored in boxes, bottles, pots and tins. Hermetical sealing was attempted. Seeds were variously bedded in sand and brown sugar, or coated in wax, pitch and resin. Most of these techniques were found to be completely useless. The irrepressible Joseph Banks, after whom the Banks Islands are named, designed a 'plant cabin', a seagoing glasshouse, which could be assembled on the quarterdeck in order to protect vulnerable plants. For many seamen Banks's plant cabin was an abomination. The English explorer George Vancouver (who had been at Tanna with Captain Cook on *Resolution* as a midshipman) strongly objected to having a plant cabin fitted on *Discovery*. When loaded these glasshouses could weigh in excess of three tons and dangerously unbalance the ship. Worse still, they were unsightly. HMS *Guardian* was the first ship to be fitted with one, until heavy Atlantic gales were encountered and the sailors heaved Banks's plant cabin overboard.

More than any other individual, it was Joseph Banks who pioneered the transportation of plants across oceans. As a wealthy amateur, Banks sailed on Captain Cook's first voyage (1768-71) around the world. Banks returned to London with some 3,600 plant specimens, of which 1,400 were new to science, and a hero's welcome which eclipsed that of Cook himself. Within months the Admiralty decided to send Cook on a second voyage, this time in *Resolution*, and it was widely assumed that Banks would be the principal passenger. Banks certainly thought so and arrived at Deptford to announce he would be travelling with four artists, two secretaries, six servants, a private orchestra and a pack of greyhounds. Both Cook and the Admiralty were adamant that this was not to be, and in a fit of pique Banks withdrew from the expedition altogether.

This was probably for the best as Banks's extravagant enthusiasms could more easily be accommodated on shore. As an alternative to voyaging, Banks became engrossed with the management of the Royal Gardens at Kew. This was to become a lifelong passion. He orchestrated the transformation of Kew from a royal pleasure house to a research-oriented botanic garden, the hub of a network for the global transfer of living plants. As his replacement on *Resolution*, Banks ordered that Francis Masson of Kew Gardens should sail with Cook.

When Captain Cook was sent around the world for a third time in 1776 Banks again looked to Kew to find a gardener. David Nelson came highly recommended and was duly dispatched to the Pacific. Nelson returned to Kew with more than 200 packets of seeds, but in the course of the voyage he learned the perils of the beach. While gathering specimens on the foreshore at Tonga Nelson was mobbed, stripped naked and pelted with stones as he ran for his life.

David Nelson worked at Kew Gardens for the next seven years but in 1787 he was again appointed by Joseph Banks to serve at sea. However, the nature of this expedition was unlike any other previously accompanied by a gardener. The man from Kew was sent to Polynesia, not to collect specimens, but to transport living plants aboard a sailing ship on an unprecedented scale.

Such was the horticultural imperative of this voyage that Nelson was appointed even before the captain himself. Given a shortlist of possible ships, Nelson and Banks selected the *Bethia*. An extensive refit was then ordered at the Deptford Naval Yard to transform what had been a coastal trading vessel into a floating greenhouse. The plan was simple but revolutionary: the plants must be stored below deck where they would be sheltered from the elements. The *Bethia*'s Great Cabin was enlarged to include the whole of the lower deck, from a point midway between the main and mizzen masts and the stern. Five rows of shelving were installed in which special holes were cut to take the plant pots. Narrow aisles ran the length of the cabin so that Nelson and his assistant could tend their wards throughout months of passage making. Beneath the false floor the deck was lined with lead so that precious run-off water could be recycled. Two skylights supplemented the light from the stern windows. Gratings mounted in the deck ensured ventilation, while the addition of a stove promised warmth in cold climates.

As this work continued the *Bethia* was renamed *Bounty* and Lieutenant William Bligh was appointed to command. Like David Nelson, Bligh had also served on Cook's final voyage to the Pacific. Both men had been at Kealakekua Bay when Cook was clubbed and stabbed to death on the beach. On this new voyage Bligh and Nelson were instructed to oversee the shipment of live breadfruit seedlings from Tahiti to the West Indies in order to feed plantation slaves.

To assist in the work of tending the plants Nelson chose a 25-year-old Kew trainee named William Brown. When the *Bounty* anchored at Matavai Bay, Tahiti, on 27 October 1788, the two gardeners were ordered to set up camp ashore. Their task now was believed to be crucial to the ultimate success of the voyage. Breadfruit are like bananas; the plant is mainly propagated by shoots from old stock, though the tree can be grown from seed. Banks's instructions were that nothing should be left to chance. Nelson and Brown were to carry both propagating stock and young seedlings. It was the seedlings that were the problem. The *Bounty* had to wait months at Tahiti until the plants were sufficiently strong to survive the return voyage. To help Nelson and Brown in this work, seven sailors were also ordered to live in the camp ashore. This group spent a total of five months on the beach at Tahiti, a longer period of exposure to Polynesian culture that any previous sailors. Even the memory of that shore camp at Point Venus would later cause William Bligh's blood to boil. It was here, Bligh always maintained, as the months passed waiting for the seeds to germinate, that all his problems began. The camp was under the command of the master's mate, Fletcher Christian.

Throughout the month of March 1789 hundreds of living plants were ferried from the beach to the *Bounty* anchored in the lagoon. Bligh records that 1,015 breadfruit plants were brought out to the ship in 774 pots, 39 tubs and 24 boxes, 300 more plants than the original plan intended. The plants were transported in various of the ship's jolly boats and long boats. But they came principally in her 23-foot launch, not an Admiralty-standard design but an uncommonly sturdy little boat with double-diagonal planking, built by John Samuel White of Cowes. It would become the most famous open boat in maritime history. The Europeans at the oars were deeply tanned. Many were now tattooed with Polynesian designs. Those that had lived ashore spoke the Tahitian language, had formed relationships with island women, been accepted into Tahitian society as exalted guests, and generally lived with a degree of comfort and status inconceivable aboard the ship.

When Bligh weighed anchor on 5 April he refused to fire *Bounty*'s guns in salute to his island hosts for fear the flash and report 'would rather hurt the plants'. 'Thus far,' Bligh wrote, 'I have accomplished the Object of my Voyage.'

A week later, running before the trade wind, Bligh wrote that the plants 'continue to thrive finely'. Before the voyage Joseph Banks had written to Nelson with detailed instructions: 'One day, or even one hour's negligence may at any period be the means of destroying all the trees and plants . . . I therefore cannot too strongly recommend it to you to guard against all temptations of idleness or liquor'. Now, as the sun set on each evening of the passage, Nelson and Brown ferried wooden pails down the aisles of the Great Cabin. The breadfruit plants received a half hogshead of water daily, about 26 gallons. Bligh's account is full of praise for the two men from Kew. Whatever other problems were brewing aboard the *Bounty*, the management of the plants was in vigilant hands.

Of all those who sailed on the breadfruit voyage, William Brown is among the least known. The botanist's assistant barely features in the famous first-hand accounts written by Bligh, Fryer and Morrison. In no source is there any suggestion of a falling-out between Brown and his master, David Nelson. Brown's name is simply included at the bottom of Bligh's 'Description of the Pirates': 'Willm Brown. Botanists Assistant. 5Ft. 8In. High. Fair Complexion, Dark Brown Hair, Slender Made, a Remarkable Scar on One of his Cheeks which contracts the Eyelid & runs down to his throat occasioned by the Kings Evil. Is tatowed.' The

'King's Evil' is a reference to scrofula, a tubercular swelling of the lymph glands, once popularly supposed to be curable by the touch of royalty.

When Fletcher Christian, in a fit of frustration provoked by Bligh's name-calling and belittlement, persuaded some of his watch to seize the ship, the division of the crew as a whole was mirrored in the relationship between the two gardeners from Kew. David Nelson climbed into the open boat and was cast away with Captain Bligh and seventeen others. William Brown remained aboard the *Bounty* with the mutineers.

By the time of the mutiny, David Nelson was Bligh's only true friend aboard the ship. Nelson supported the captain throughout the 3,000-mile open-boat passage to Timor. He was loyal even at Sunday Island where, tormented by exposure, exhaustion, hunger and thirst, some crewmen threatened a second mutiny. Being an older man Nelson too suffered appalling deprivations on the voyage. On the Cape York Peninsula, as the battered little launch made its weary approach to Torres Strait, Bligh recorded that the botanist was 'in such a Weak condition that he was obliged to be supported by two Men. His complaint was a burning in his Bowels, a loss of sight, much drought and an incapacity to walk.' Within days of reaching Timor and apparent safety, Nelson was dead. Bligh wrote: 'The loss of this Honest Man bears very heavy on my mind, his duty and integrity went hand in hand, and he had accomplished through great care and diligence the object he was sent for.' It is unlikely Bligh would have used such warm language about any other person aboard *Bounty*.

Nelson's fellow gardener, William Brown, faced an equally perilous future having chosen to stay aboard the ship. In the days following the mutiny Brown assisted the sailors in throwing all 1,015 breadfruit plants into the sea. The gardener undid five months' labour and shed the trappings of his former life at a stroke. According to the minutes of the eventual court martial, Brown played no active role in the mutiny: he was not under arms, nor had he been a sentinel. Nonetheless, William Brown was one of the nine 'hard core' mutineers who chose not to be put ashore at Tahiti. Instead, he followed Fletcher Christian all the way to Pitcairn Island and by doing so he put a death sentence on his head should he ever return to England. Brown was now committed to a life of beachcombing and exile.

It's possible that Brown's skills as a gardener made him of particular value to Fletcher Christian: gardening was also a 'technology' and Brown enjoyed the elevation of status that was sometimes a characteristic of the beach. On tiny Pitcairn, the mutineers' survival would depend on their ability to grow food.

In the decades after the *Bounty* voyage, beachcombers would set up gardens in most of the main island groups where ships called regularly. Like boatbuilding and grog selling, gardening became one of the roles typically fulfilled by beachcombers. On cleared land around the beach settlements at Papeete, Honolulu, Levuka and elsewhere, they cultivated potatoes and reared pigs. Some beachcombers also acted as agents and intermediaries, organising cargoes of produce grown by the islanders for sale to visitng ships: coconuts, yams, taro, citrus, breadfruit. Beachcombers operated what were effectively resupply and reprovisioning depots for European shipping on the shores of many of the principal anchorages in the islands.

According to the most reliable accounts of what happened on Pitcairn, Brown lived quietly on the island for about 3½ years, cultivating a productive garden. It's believed the Kew man was the fourth to die when the Tahitians in their turn mutinied against European command. One of the Tahitians, Menalee, struck the gardener across the back of the head with a rock, then shot him.

3

Tufala Gavman

'The most insane and disastrous experiment in the history of modern colonial enterprise . . . a disgrace to the British Empire.'

Jock Marshall, visiting scientist in Port Vila, 1937

NAILED TO A tree in Dillon's Bay there was a sign in Bislama. '*Mifala I pem sandalwood long price ia antap long dock blong Albert Naupa. Sipos sandalwood blong yu I stap long narafala ples yu mas toktok wetem olman blong boat.*'* It was signed Jonathan Naupa. Naupa was offering 400 Vatu per kilo ($3.50).

Everyone in Dillon's Bay knew Jon Naupa. He was Mr Big of the sandalwood trade in Vanuatu. On the side they also moaned that he didn't settle his bills promptly.

That morning in Port Vila I ferried the sandalwood seedlings ashore in the inflatable dinghy and organized to meet Jon Naupa in a waterfront bar. I knew that Jon was mixed race. His father was from Erromango, his mother from leafy Buckinghamshire. Mostly in jest, I pictured Jon as the successor to James Paddon, fast-forwarded 150 years: a rainbow-nation sandalwooder, dodging and weaving to stay afloat in a precarious island trade. When I met him I found that this wasn't so far removed from the truth.

Jon slid a bunch of keys and pink mobile phone onto the table

---

* 'We buy sandalwood at this price above Albert Naupa's dock. If your sandalwood is somewhere else, please talk to the captain of the boat.'

and pulled up a chair. 'I really wanted to play professional golf,' he sighed. 'That was my dream if you like. But when golf didn't work out I thought, well, I may as well go into the trade.

'They told you I don't pay my bills, right? I know that lot at Dillon's Bay. Well there are two sides to every story. Anyway, it's all sorted out as of two weeks ago. You can check if you like.'

He listed some of the problems faced by the present day sandal-wood trader: cyclones, decrepit shipping, but mostly crooks, rogues and impostors. 'You wouldn't believe this business. I've got EU protocols coming out of my ears. I've got chiefs who'd sell their own mothers. I've got the bloody Tongans with their genet-ically engineered sandalwood . . .'

Jon was in his early thirties, lean and shaven-headed. His scalp was a warm, nutty hue, the colour of *natora*. He had grown up in Port Vila, but spent holidays at Dillon's Bay. His father had been Erromango's first parliamentarian and minister of transport in 1980. 'We were just crazy when we were kids. Racing stolen cars down the runway at Bauerfield, chased by the police. When they saw who we were they never did anything.' With a straight face he said: 'I don't want you to think there's an old boy network or anything in Vila. It's just really important who you know.' Jon had been educated in Melbourne. Now he mostly sold his sandal-wood to Germany where it was used in the cosmetics and phar-maceuticals industries.

'Last year I bought a lot of sandalwood off an old chief in Santo. And like it was really a lot of wood, I gave him more than 10 million Vatu for it ($87,700), all in cash in plastic bags. He was a bushman and buried the lot somewhere in the hills. No one knew where it was. Then he died. His family have been digging up the forest ever since.

'I'm flying down to the southern islands tomorrow. The Erromangans and Tannese aren't any better. You pay them good money for wood and they piss it away. You see them a few days later in the casino with three ugly little girls.'

Jon Naupa stood up and gulped the remains of his espresso.

'I've got to run. I'm playing golf at the South Pacific Games in a few weeks and I'm late for practice.'

More heavy rain had set in as I walked along the foreshore into Port Vila. The road into town was awash. Minibuses plunged into potholes. Women scuttled along faster than the crawling traffic, their soaked Mother Hubbards clinging immodestly.

I cut back to the waterfront across a rubble-strewn lot. On this squally day the waterfront in Vila was a collage of rusting iron roofing, rotting copra sheds, shredded palm fronds, oily puddles and subsiding wharves. I loved everything about Port Vila. I knew that first morning it would be hard to ever prise myself from its clammy human grip. Vila was a true South Sea port. You breathed its history as you walked its streets. As I shuffled along the crumbling sea wall at the back of the Café du Village I smelt fresh baguette and ground coffee overlaid with rotting pawpaw and open drains.

In Port Vila, the veneer of grandeur only ever partly masked the debris littering the beach. In a letter to a friend dated 1913 one Vila resident, Robert Fletcher, wrote, 'You should just see some of the things that haunt the "beach" in Vila. Their only sustenance is absinthe and cigarettes, so fever takes them properly.' These beachcombers were *libérés* from the *bagne*, or penal colony, at Nouméa, who scratched a living illicitly selling grog to the New Hebridians and gambling the proceeds in Chinese opium hovels.

There is something of the beach in all South Sea port towns. The Pacific peoples were village dwellers; there were no towns here in the Western sense. Port towns in the islands are beach towns, bridges between the world of ships and the world ashore, crumbling edifices built on the cusp of two world views.

In Port Vila, the metaphorical beach was even messier than usual because the European world view was represented by two distinct players: England and France.

This elegant harbour had been the stage set for one of the great episodes of theatre in the colonial South Pacific. From 1906 to

1980 the islands were governed by an extraordinary administration known as the Anglo-French Condominium in the New Hebrides. In the 1950s a colonial officer named Reid Cowell penned a musical about the Condominium in the style of Gilbert and Sullivan titled, *Pandemonia, or a Franco-British Fantasy*. The name stuck and the Condominium was vilified as the 'Pandemonium' ever after.

There never was anything else quite like the Condominium. Whereas in the African colony of Cameroon France and Britain administered different regions of one country, here in the New Hebrides they attempted to jointly govern a foreign territory. In the late nineteenth century France had been extremely keen to annex the New Hebrides as a base for settlers and planters – the *colons*. Britain wasn't particularly interested in the islands but was passionate that France shouldn't have them. When the Entente Cordiale was signed in 1904 and the two countries put aside their colonial rivalry, one result was the Condominium: the New Hebrides were to become a 'region of joint influence'. Melanesia was the perfect location for such an ambitious experiment. Tucked away out of sight in the South Pacific, the hope was that no one would find out about the Condominium if things went disastrously wrong.

As the rain cleared I paddled across the anchorage to Iririki Island as the wind dragged tattered clouds from the cliff tops all around. Today, Iririki is an exclusive Japanese-owned resort, but in the colonial era this little island was the seat of British power. I climbed 179 whitewashed steps that twisted between limestone crags to a grassy knoll at the islet's peak. Lawns stretched to the northern escarpment and a vista of sea and islands. The paths were flanked with fan palms, yellow hibiscus, poinsettias, dwarf flaxes, bougainvillea and oleander. The gardens had once been more extensive, but were looted by Australian settlers after independence. The first British Residency was built on this island hilltop in the early 1900s, a ramshackle weatherboard house whose occupants were hard men. Rason slept on rough-cut timber planks with a log for a pillow. King scoffed at the swarms of mosquitoes, claiming any that bit him fell dead. Meanwhile, the French Residency was established on the mainland coast opposite, at exactly the same height above the sea, so that neither flag would fly more proudly than the other. Thus the geography of home was recreated in the tropical Pacific: the French on the mainland, with the English on the small island off the coast, separated by a channel. Even some of those charged with administering the Condominium conceded it was a shambles. Sir Roger du Boulay lived in this hilltop house as British Resident Commissioner from 1973 to 1975. He later described the Condominium as a 'farcical and criminally wasteful system'.

'Portrait of Jean Baptiste Cabri, a Frenchman found on the Island of Nukahiwa, and there become half savage. He carries a slingshot.' Artist unknown, from Georg H. von Langsdorff, *Eine Reise um die Welt*, 1812

The first recorded instance of a Frenchman and an Englishman cohabiting on a Pacific island concerned two beachcombers, Jean Cabri and Edward Robarts. Theirs was a tempestuous relationship. When the Russian navigator Adam von Krusenstern arrived in the Marquesas Islands in 1804, he found the two runaway sailors Cabri and Robarts living on the shores of Taiohae Bay. They were implacable enemies. The nature of beachcombing was such that each felt the other to be a threat to his usefulness and novelty among the islanders. 'Not content to disturb the peace of the whole civilized world,' Krusenstern wrote, 'even the inhabitants of the lately discovered islands of this ocean must feel the influence of [France and England's] odious rivalship without so much as knowing the origin of it.' Krusenstern could have been writing about the Anglo-French Condominium established in the New Hebrides a century later.

The next day I caught a bus out to the airport to pick up Helen. Perspiring, startled passengers emerged from the Auckland flight into the arrivals hall to be garlanded with flowers and fêted by a six-piece ukulele band. Helen looked hot but happy when she finally came through. I'd called her by telephone when I'd first cleared customs in Vila ten days earlier, but hadn't been able to get through from either Erromango or Tanna and she'd been worried. Throughout the whole journey we were plagued by bad luck with the phones. Weeks sometimes passed before I could find one that worked and then, in the most unlikely of places, a villager would lead me to a tin hut beneath the palms where a brand new push-button phone provided an immediate international connection.

My efforts to convince Helen that there was really nothing to worry about were dealt a blow next morning when we woke in the anchorage to find that dawn had produced only the most sickly, yoke-coloured light. Usually it was calm in the anchorage between Iririki and the mainland, but a long swell had set into Vila Bay overnight and now seas were crashing into Iririki's undercut coral cliffs. The lagoon was thick with vegetable flotsam and its surface white with plump, bouncing raindrops. Sheet lightning crackled in the east followed by cannon-roar thunder. More gale-force squalls swept down the Ireriki Channel through the morning and the boats yawed and snubbed at their anchor chains until a ketch finally dragged and grounded on the reef.

It eased in the afternoon and we got ashore, then toiled through the cloying humidity up the hill to the Meteorological Office. Cyclone Gina had formed at 11° south, battering the Santa Cruz and Banks Islands with 90-knot winds. It was two months after the supposed end of the cyclone season so Gina had taken everyone by surprise. The cyclone was weakening now as it travelled south-west towards New Caledonia.

After two days the swell eased and the sky cleared. We motored out past the quarantine anchorage, through the shoals off Malapoa Point, then got up the sails to head north across the open expanse of Melé Bay. The water was gently heaving with residual swell, clogged with mud washed away by the rains. All along the beaches, a mile distant, I could see a trail of flotsam thrown up by the passing storm.

The southern coast of Efaté Island is an exposed weather shore. Over the years it has inevitably been the landing place for ocean debris – including human castaways. The first castaways known to have come ashore here date from the early nineteenth century. As was often the case in these waters, it was a roving missionary, the Reverend George Turner, who recorded the story. A group of about fifty Polynesian seafarers had been washed up on this coast about twenty years before Turner's visit in 1845. They had left Samoa in the aftermath of the Atua civil war, bound south for Tonga in a double-hulled sailing canoe, but the canoe was disabled before making landfall and drifted west for many days before it reached the coast of Efaté. Turner records that they came ashore in two principal groups.

The first was led by Sualo – 'Swallow' to the Europeans – and lived beside the Erakor lagoon, a few miles from present day Port

Vila. As Turner put it: 'They landed, club in hand, fought, conquered . . . Sualo is quite the heathen, has three wives, has been
a great warrior, and is one of the most daring fighters on the
island . . . Chiefs are in the habit of hiring him, for a pig or two,
to join them in their battles.'

The second group of castaways came ashore further west at a
tiny islet called Melé. We could see Melé Island now above the
sloop's bows. It was little more than a coral blip with a tuft of
palms on top, only a couple of hundred metres from shore. The
beachcombers had lived on this islet for more than 130 years,
maintaining aspects of their language and culture. We'd come
here because I hoped to meet a descendant of these castaways, Ati
George Sokomanu, first president of the Republic of Vanuatu.

Unintentional drifts have always been a feature of seafaring in
the South Pacific. In the course of their remarkable voyages, the
Pacific peoples were being cast away long before the first
European ships arrived, and long after. Over the 12 years I've lived
here I've kept newspaper cuttings describing the incidents of drift
voyaging. Most were of relatively short duration. In 2001 a Fijian,
Mateyawa Curubula, suffered engine failure in his open boat and
drifted out from under the lee of Ono-i-Lau Island. He was
located six days later by an RNZAF Orion and picked up by a
local boat.

A more sinister series of drifts occurred the following year
when, over a period of several months, thirteen bamboo rafts
were washed up on atolls in Micronesia, most of them on Yap.
The rafts were all similar in design and many had human skele-
tons on board, on one of which was found an identity card from
Bitung, Sulawesi, Indonesia. It's possible these were accidental
drifts but more likely that the fishing rafts were cut adrift in an act
of foul play. Sulawesi has been the scene of unrest between
Christian and Muslim groups. The distance of the drift from
Sulawesi to Yap is 1,200 miles. There were no survivors on any of
the rafts.

But the longest recorded drift voyage in recent Pacific history began in 1963 when seven men climbed into a 16-foot open boat at Manihiki Atoll in the Cook Islands. Many of the men were descended from beachcomber stock. Teehu Makimare had mixed American and Polynesian ancestry. Kita Marsters was descended from William Marsters, a sailor from Gloucestershire who arrived in the islands in 1862 and never left. Their boat, *Tearoha*, was similarly a European-Pacific hybrid. She carried a Dolly Varden rig, named after the music hall actress and introduced to the islands from Yorkshire in the nineteenth century by a sailor named George Ellis. But *Tearoha* was built on the beach at Rarotonga from local timber by Pastor Takai, continuing a tradition of churchmen building boats on that island initiated by the Reverend John Williams.

The Dolly Varden rig features an enormous elongated boom to catch light breezes and was perfect for fishing in the sheltered waters of atoll lagoons. But when Teehu Makimare and six friends climbed into *Tearoha* on 12 August 1963 they intended to sail to neighbouring Rakahanga for supplies, 25 miles across the open ocean. The boat reached Rakahanga safely where she was loaded with twenty sacks of *taro*, ten of breadfruit, twelve drinking coconuts and a glass Japanese fishing float which contained twelve gallons of drinking water. With these supplies as well as seven adults on board, the 16-foot *Tearoha* was now chronically overloaded. On the return voyage the little boat was blown off by the trade wind and failed to make landfall on Manihiki. The next day the bowsprit and headsail were carried away in a squall and ten sacks of taro were heaved overboard. The men continued to sail down wind, hoping to fetch up at one of the nearby islands, but progress was constantly hampered by the Dolly Varden rig, whose long boom trailed in the water as the *Tearoha* rolled on the deep ocean swells. Worse, the sail was not fitted with reef points so the men had to choose between carrying full sail, or none at all. On the thirty-third day at sea the open boat capsized in a squall and two men were lost, Kita Marsters and Tom Tangimetua. Enoka Dean died of starvation and exposure soon afterwards. By now the rig had been swept away and the compass lost. On 17 October the four survivors were washed up on the weather coast of Erromango. They had been at sea 64 days and drifted 2,000 miles. The Erromangans carried them on stretchers across the island to Dillon's Bay where a fourth man, Taia Tauraki died. The three remaining castaways were brought on to the hospital at Port Vila. All of them recovered and eventually returned home.

It was not only the Polynesians who made unintentional drift voyages. Some European sailors also suffered the same fate. When HMS *Pandora* crossed the Pacific in 1791 searching for Fletcher Christian and the *Bounty* mutineers, the ship's jolly-boat was blown out to sea while investigating Palmerston Atoll. The surgeon, George Hamilton, described how the area downwind of the atoll was thoroughly searched for any sign of the boat until 'All further hopes of seeing her were given up, and we proceeded on our voyage'. The jolly-boat was commanded by 16-year-old midshipman Sival with four seamen aboard. Their only food supply was 'a piece of salt-beef thrown into the boat to them on leaving the ship.' Hamilton records that 'it rained a good deal that night and the following day, which might satiate their thirst,' but the castaways had no vessel in which to contain the water. None of the five men in the boat were ever seen again. Presumably they perished at sea, but it's possible they drifted downwind before the trade to some island where they lived out their days as beach-combers. The loss of the jolly-boat prompted Hamilton to speculate about the frequency of drift voyages in the Pacific. He believed that unintentional drifts were commonplace and the islanders '. . . seldom undertake any hazardous enterprise by water without a woman, and a sow with pig, being in the canoe with them; by which means, if they are cast on any of those uninhabited islands, they fix their abode.'

Later that morning we reached Melé Island where the Polynesian castaways had made landfall in the 1820s. I gybed the sloop off Melé's fringing reef and ran down to an anchorage between the

island and mainland coast. Today, Melé Island is a resort. The castaways had been forced to evacuate the island in 1959 following a
destructive cyclone. They moved onto the mainland and established a new village on the adjacent coast. It was in this latter settlement, also called Melé, that I found George Sokomanu.

In the afternoon we paddled ashore to the beach on the mainland. Helen set off up the coast road to visit the botanical gardens
while I met up with Kali Fatoko, a contact at the Presbyterian
Church who had offered to introduce me to Sokomanu. The sun
was strong now, the ground still sodden. Minibuses churned
through floodwaters bumper deep. Waves of evaporating moisture
and humidity seared the back of the throat. Villagers were pressed
against the walls of coral block houses, seeking shade beneath
narrow eaves. At the back of the village we came to a line of
bushes which offered a degree of privacy to a simple concrete
house, whose blue paint was stained green with moss and accu-
mulated damp. Cracked and overflowing water tanks leaned
against the walls, full of mosquito larvae.

George Sokomanu opened the door and stared at us through
bloodshot eyes. 'I was just reading some papers,' he said in a
croaky voice. We had obviously woken him up. He showed us
into a bare, tiled room. *Pandanus* mats covered the floor. Books
and papers were stacked against the walls. The dominant furniture was a heavy wooden table and upright chairs. This was a
house of meetings and plots, of gambling for power. I sat down
opposite him at the centre of the table and began to take notes.

Castaways became beachcombers when they began the process
of assimilation into the dominant culture of the coast where they
had been washed up. The castaways on Melé had outgrown the tiny
island even before the cyclone forced its evacuation and had started
to come ashore on the mainland. Here, on the outskirts of Port
Vila, the prevailing culture was not Melanesian, but rather that of
the colonial administration, the Anglo-French Condominium.
This was a world where the British played cricket every Saturday
at the British Paddock. The Resident Commissioner batted at

number one, the most senior judge at number two, the Assistant Commissioner at number three, and so on down the order. When Sir Harry Luke cruised through the New Hebrides in 1939 he recorded in his diary that he had never in his life seen anything like the Condominium: 'Port Vila was controlled by a protocol of Continental, polyglot and almost eighteenth century formalism . . . One had hardly expected to find the forms and ceremonies of a minor principality of the Holy Roman Empire projected into the twentieth century in a Pacific Island.'

In Bislama, 'Condominium' translates as *Tufala Gavman**: it was supposedly a joint administration. In reality, Britain and France attempted to govern over the top of each other. Each country maintained its own judicial system, police force, education system and medical service. To keep the peace the Official Gazette was published in parallel columns with both English and French given equal prominence. The Vila Club was equipped with billiard tables from both Britain and France to minimize the chances of unsportsmanlike recriminations. Two currencies were used, two systems of weights and measures employed, and two sets of stamps issued. Carlton Gadusek, an American researcher travelling through the group in the 1960s found Port Vila to be a byword for bureaucratic madness. Cooperating with the British made him the enemy of the French. Working with the French had the opposite result. When he tried to ignore them both they joined forces to oppose him. 'Neutrality is impossible!!!' Gadusek scrawled in exasperation.

This was the world of colonials and missionaries into which George Sokomanu assimilated. In the 1950s the Presbyterian mission had sent a youthful Sokomanu to teacher training college in Fiji. Seven years later he returned home anticipating a life working in mission schools, but instead caught the eye of a British colonial officer named Dick Hutchinson who employed Sokomanu as a clerk. It was the first time a bright New Hebridean

---

*government by two fellows

86

had been given a job with a future in the British administration. Sokomanu worked for the British side of the Condominium for 20 years, including postings as an assistant district agent at Tanna and Malakula.

'The Condominium was a monster,' he told me. 'You had two hospitals, two police forces, two district agents. Everything was divided. The Catholic missions were allied with the French, the Presbyterian missions with the British. Neither side wanted to see the other get ahead. If the British built a school in a village, the French would come along and build a Francophone school right next to it. I saw district agents screaming at each other. Really the British could, and should, have run the administration alone, based on the work of the missions.'

No doubt this was heartfelt, but it was hardly realistic. Indeed, the British were always the junior partners in the Condominium, symbolized by their isolation on Iririki Island. Numerically, Anglophone planters in the group were outnumbered many times by French *colons*. Even among British colonial officials there was tacit acceptance that, in the end, the French would probably have it. One elderly British resident in Port Vila left instructions that under no circumstances were his remains to be buried in the New Hebrides because the islands were certain to become French soil. Instead he wanted to be buried at sea, as the sea would always be English. In the finest traditions of the Pandemonium even this was bungled, and the boat crew allowed his remains to drift back onto the beach. Nonetheless, this man had revived a belief that was more commonplace in the age of sail: the sea was culturally pure, an extension of the culture of the ship.

'The British were always so poor,' George Sokomanu said disapprovingly. 'Their houses were really in a poor condition sometimes. They couldn't afford servants so convicts worked in the gardens. For the French it was never like that. It still goes on today in the French territories, living expenses, tax-free salary paid into a bank account at home, two cars, two boats . . . lavish.

'If you were invited to a British house it was usually in the evening, after office hours. But the French always invited you to lunch. You arrived at noon, there was plenty of wine, lunch wouldn't be finished till 3 or 4 o'clock and by then it was too late to go back to the office. They either went home, or to the club, or the beach.'

By the 1970s, however, it had become obvious – to the British at least – that there had to be change. With independence approaching it was widely assumed that Francophone New Hebrideans would inherit control of the country as a birthright. But as George Sokomanu put it bluntly, 'We British won independence.' The Francophones turned out to be inept opponents. Die-hard French *colons*, some of them Africa retreads from Algeria, were desperate to derail independence and became increasingly erratic in their efforts to do so, at one point even courting the John Frum Cult. At independence in 1980, Father Walter Lini was elected prime minister. George Sokomanu became president, and was re-elected for a second term in 1985.

In the absence of any credible French challenge, Sokomanu's most serious opposition came from a quite unexpected quarter: Moli Jimmy Stephens was the grandson of a Scottish beachcomber who jumped ship and married a Tongan princess. Stephens had assimilated into Melanesian bush culture and had a radically different vision for the group's future.

For a time Stephens had been the skipper of a coastal trading schooner and made evangelical voyages among the northern islands calling himself Captain President Moses. His pagan cult, Nagriamel, won a substantial following on the island of Espiritu Santo. With a bushman's beard and spear in hand, Stephens was an inspirational speaker whose message of kicking out the missionaries and revitalizing traditional animist beliefs drew passionate support. Stephens believed that Sokomanu's Anglicized elite would simply replace the Condominium with more of the same and duly declared Santo's secession. Sokomanu's government had Stephens arrested, charged with seditious mutiny and sentenced to 14½ years in jail.

George Sokomanu was wide awake now. He sat opposite me in a black 'Merry Christmas' T-shirt bearing a picture of a snow-covered tree. His eyes were still bloodshot, but he was focused and alert. If I ever stopped writing he nodded towards my notebook as if I were his clerk – perhaps a satisfying irony considering his first job for the British. His voice had developed a harder edge, he jabbed a finger for emphasis.

In December 1988 George Sokomanu had attempted a coup d'état by dissolving parliament and swearing in his nephew as prime minister. He himself was now arrested, convicted of incitement to mutiny and thrown into the same jail as Jimmy Stephens.

There was little personal antagonism between the two men. Sokomanu remembered that they got on well at the old prison down at the Stade and had many long talks together. They shared a common beachcomber ancestry, but had assimilated in different ways. Sokomanu was Anglophone and Presbyterian. Stephens had gone to live in the 'dark bush' among the pagan tribesmen of Santo.

In the event, their joint occupancy of the prison was short-lived. Sokomanu was rather better connected than the pagan bushman and his conviction was quashed on appeal. Ati George Sokomanu went on to serve as secretary-general of the South Pacific High Commission from 1993 to 1996.

Jimmy Stephens served more than ten years of his sentence for mutiny. On his release from prison he took three more wives to celebrate his seventy-second birthday. When Stephens died in 1994 he had married thirty-one women and left hundreds of children and grandchildren.

Before leaving I asked George Sokomanu one more question about the colonial era. He had worked for the British for 20 years. Did he have anything good to say about the Condominium? 'Well, there were these two countries, Britain and France, and it was perfectly obvious to us that they didn't like each other much. Of course, on a personal level there were good friendships and many good working relationships. But at a government level they had different visions of the Pacific. Sometimes they hated each other, but they never fought each other. It was just talk, talk, talk. That was the worst, but also the best thing about the Condominium – the talk. All the talk fitted in well with our own custom on the *nakamal* of drinking kava and talking things through. When you look at our Melanesian neighbours, New Guinea, the Solomons, Fiji, and the violence in those countries, maybe we didn't do too badly.'

George Sokomanu was hardly the first person I spoke to who mentioned the violence in the neighbouring islands of Melanesia. We heard a similar thing almost everywhere we went in Port Vila. The subject of violence was always strangely accessible in the town, as if conflict were somewhere close to hand. Helen and I stayed in the anchorage at Melé Island for several more days. It was a peaceful spot, beyond the last straggling suburbs and squatter camps, but only a ten-minute bus ride from the town centre.

In a building on the hill above Rue Bougainville I met Godwin Ligo, manager of Radio Vanuatu and a veteran Vila journalist. It wasn't hard to raise the subject of violence. At the time of my visit an Australian-led military force was preparing to intervene in the 'failed state' of the Solomon Islands, Vanuatu's neighbour, and arrest the mutinous warlord Harold Keke. A fracture line of unrest was haemorrhaging through the south-west Pacific. Waves of tribalism, secessionism and banditry were spreading through the islands, from Papua New Guinea in the north, to Bougainville, the Solomons, and south-east as far as Fiji. Geographically, Vanuatu lay in the middle of this group of islands and I asked Godwin Ligo if a similar conflict could happen here. 'It already has,' he said. 'Port Vila had the worst riots in its history a couple of years ago. The government was stealing from the National Provident Fund. It was just here,' he said, pointing behind my head, 'over the road, we had a bird's eye view of the whole thing. Every island was represented in that one. Everyone threw a stone.'

None of this was evident from seaward. After three days anchored behind the reef at Melé we sailed the five miles back into the capital in a sunny breeze, the sloop carrying full sail for the first time in weeks. From seaward, Port Vila was an idyll, one of the most lovely natural harbours in the South Seas, a patchwork of shoals and deepwater channels, a saline palette of blues and greens. Around the amphitheatre of the bay, the hillsides glinted with iron roofs half-hidden in the palms.

The trade was a light but constant pressure through the sky. Strips of washboard cloud appeared spliced into the blue dome overhead. As the boat heeled, the sprigs of frangipani and bougainvillea with which Helen had brightened the cabin now dangled precariously out of the sink where they had been wedged for safe keeping. At the three-metre shoal in the shadow of Malapoa Point we went about, then short-tacked north through the bustling waters of Vila Bay.

Longboats chugged the same way, laden with workers and schoolchildren bound for the town wharf. Minutes later they returned light and empty, planing with their plumb stems thrust high, heading home for the golden strand at Ifira. To the south was the deepwater wharf with its row of stalls, empty today, awaiting the human cargo of the next cruise ship. Further east, rusting hulks were permanently aground in the shallows, their steel hawsers thick with crystalline growth. Young men made their homes in the hold − *damblo** in pidgin. Washing billowed on cables stretched between forepeak and wheelhouse. Distant figures struggled to take it in when squall clouds gathered above the hills of Nambatu.

We anchored again in the sand and coral of the Iririki Channel around which Vila was wrapped like a shawl of warming humanity. Longboats and ferries worked across the anchorage from before sunrise. Nets were laid from boats and beaches. Schools of fish burst and scattered beneath the surface at dusk twilight. At the small town wharf coasters were rafted up three deep. More dried with the ebbing tide up a crumbling gut that led to the old

---

*down below

copra sheds. When the *Dinh I* sailed at sunset one evening, a roar swelled across the lagoon from a mass of well-wishers gathered on the wharf. From the anchorage, Vila bubbled with all the picture book vitality of a port. It was a place of comings and goings, klaxons and gangplanks, ferries and coasters, derricks and cargoes and wharves.

Early morning was the best time to walk the streets of Vila. We were woken before sunup by the ferries and paddled ashore with the first commuters, when the black waters of the lagoon were just touched with pink. In the park beside the waterfront men played pétanque beneath the plane trees as soon as it was light. We climbed up through the Quartier Française while it was still cooled by blue shadows. From the ridge top the sun was glinting on the Erakor Lagoon as we strolled down the undulating ridge into Nambatu. During the war, three radio transmitters had been constructed in the hills above Vila which for convenience were named Number 1, Number 2 and Number 3. Today, Nambatu and Nambatri are prominent Vila suburbs.

In the crowded backstreets trucks jammed the junctions. Dust hung in the air more persistent than fog. Young men leaned against concrete shop fronts, T-shirts pulled up over their shoulders in the rising heat. Gangs of women with bundles larger than their own torsos piled into minibuses. In darkened eateries, men sat hunched over plastic plates, eating earthy tubers in watery stew.

Vila was a thriving, jovial little port town, until you came to the main street. Strangely, it was Port Vila's central thoroughfare that had least life. The Ni-Vanuatu took freely to the water and the hillsides around town, but were still only cautiously reclaiming their capital's heart, more than 20 years after independence. Vila was always a European creation. In Condominium times, Ni-Vanuatu who weren't beyond the town limits before curfew were locked up.

Today, the main street was often quiet and somehow tense. Liquor stores had barred window, like prison cells, except here men stared longingly inwards. There were gloomy steak houses and 70s style fast-food joints. The village-dwelling Ni-Vanuatu seemed uncertain what to do with this urban inheritance.

The Au Péché Mignon café was frequented by the sons and daughters of the new elite. It was the same crowd every day, many of them mixed race, dressed in European clothes printed in bold 'Pasifika' patterns. They were forever rummaging in Gucci hand-bags and lighting each other's cigarettes. While they agonized over the selection of petits fours, bare-chested men shuffled furtively along the terrace.

It was here on the terrace that I arranged to meet Marie-Noëlle Patterson. She was something of a hate figure among the Vila elite. Marie-Noëlle Patterson had been the Ombudswoman during the 1990s. It had been her reports that shattered the dream of independence by first exposing the dodgy shipping register, the insurance scams, the ministers' hands in state coffers. She now worked for the corruption watchdog Transparency International. When I had told George Sokomanu I was trying to contact her, he replied gruffly, 'Why?'

I met Marie-Noëlle Patterson one morning for a rushed cup of coffee. She was the only person I met in Vila who was in a fearful hurry. In a town that was crumbling around her ears Marie-Noëlle Patterson was pin-smart, dressed in a suit, and punctual to the minute. When I asked her first about the poten-tial for violence in Vanuatu she echoed Godwin Ligo. 'Well, it's already here. The South Pacific is a very violent place and it always has been.

'I would say the biggest threat today is the Tannese. Their own island is very overcrowded and there are six or eight thousand of them at Black Sands, just outside Vila. They were put there by the Ifira people who own the land and want to collect rent. They've been shifted around to other places too. A whole lot more were dumped at a place called Freshwind by George Sokomanu's nephew who established a squatter camp that would vote for him. The prime minister doesn't trust either the police or army, so he's created a militia for his own protection – made up of Tannese from Black Sands. When there's more trouble, the Tannese will be involved.'

In Vila, the threat of violence was ever present. People would discuss the prospects for bloodshed as readily as they might else-where debate the chances of rain.

After three more days in the capital Helen flew back home and the boat suddenly seemed vast and empty. I was tempted to sail on straight away and at least fill the emptiness with progress and purpose. But I ended up staying on for several more days in the capital, trying to better understand the legacy of violence that had once been an accepted feature both of sea travel and the beach.

One day I climbed the hill above the anchorage and visited the Cultural Centre where I talked to the archivist Abong Thompson. As I sat with water streaming from my clothes on to the chair, the result of being caught in another Vila downpour, Abong Thompson chatted mildly about his work audio-recording village songs and stories before the last generation to remember the tra-ditional culture died out. Without any change in voice tone he said casually, 'When I was a child growing up on the island of Malakula I would have been killed if I'd accidentally strayed into a neighbouring village. Or, if I'd been very young, one of my family would have been killed in my place because they should have stopped it.' This had been in the 1950s. In pre-contact times villagers had often only encountered their neighbours in order to wage war.

The South Pacific had been a war-torn place long before the first European ship arrived. Competition and conflict on over-crowded islands with a limited supply of food had often charac-terized relations among the Pacific peoples. Melanesian tribes in particular were culturally and linguistically distinct, and almost always hostile to strangers. The early explorers like Bougainville and Cook had rarely stayed long enough in any one place to witness tribal warfare. Rather, it was beachcombers who wrote the most telling accounts as they lived among the islanders for extended periods. Even in the eastern islands of Polynesia, which are generally considered to have been more harmonious, the beachcombers frequently recorded the tribal wars in which they became participants. George Vason had not lived on the beach in Tonga for many months before war broke out and at first he relished the prospect: 'I burned for the fight, and pressed forwards to the first ranks.' But the reality of what he saw soon sobered the lapsed missionary: 'I found their wars were too terrible for the mere gratification of curiosity – that their instruments, wielded with such strength and dexterity, were an overmatch for me, and that such an undisciplined volunteer as I was, would soon be speared.'

Other traders and beachcombers, however, were less impressed by Polynesian warfare. Before he himself was cast away on Penrhyn, E.H. Lamont traded in many of the island groups. Of the Marquesans he wrote: 'Their battles however are not very bloody' being characterized mostly by 'volleys of shouting and hooting. If one or two men are killed in battle, it is considered a bloody one, and is recorded for years in their history.' Later in the voyage he was more scathing still. 'We arrived at Hana-ma-Nu Bay [Hanamenu, Hiva Oa] at an eventful moment, just on the termination, namely, of a three days' battle, in which not a single life had been lost!'

Even in Melanesia, the anthropologists are unconvinced that the body count was significantly higher. One likened pre-contact Melanesian wars to 'Homeric scalding matches'.

It was into this fractious mix that the first European trading ships sailed, armed with cannon and muskets, carrying cargoes of axes and knives. For the most part, the traders are obscure characters. Compared to voyages of exploration, there are few written accounts of trading voyages. But I found one description of a typical trading sailor penned by Thomas Jefferson Jacobs, a crewman on the brig *Margaret Oakley* which traded for sandalwood and bêche-de-mer in Melanesia in the 1830s from her home port of New York. Jacobs describes a fellow seaman on the brig, a man named Benton: 'It was a matter of doubt whether he knew where he was born; he was illiterate and no navigator, but a thoroughly practical and experienced seaman, had been to all parts of the world, and spoke six languages . . . I afterwards saw him bury the glittering blade of his cutlass into the head of a [Melanesian] savage'. For some Pacific tribes, first contact was made with men like Benton, not men like Captain Cook.

'A Chieftain of Tongataboo.' Engraving by H. Wilkins; frontispiece to James Orange, *Narrative of the Late George Vason of Nottingham*, 1840

One of the most detailed accounts of the sandalwood trade is the journal of William Lockerby, first officer on the ship *Jenny* of Boston. Under the command of Captain William Dorr, the *Jenny* made prolonged trading voyages in the early 1800s, mostly in

Melanesian Fiji but also in nearby Polynesian islands. Lockerby's account of these years is short, the violence almost constant. At the conclusion of business at one island in Tonga the sandalwooders 'fired several swivels loaded with grape amongst [the canoes], by the way of wishing them good-bye, and left them to lament over their bad luck'. Shortly afterwards, when the *Jenny* reached Fiji, a seaman and a boy were killed when a longboat was ambushed in shallows off the beach. The second mate 'was severely wounded' in the attack but managed to return to the ship. In revenge, the sandalwooders 'fired our swivel and muskets' into the canoes 'which did considerable execution'. Later, Captain Dorr secured the release of two seamen who had been captured and tortured ashore. When they came aboard the ship the two men were found to be 'so shamefully mangled with spears and clubs'.

William Lockerby was born in 1782 in the town of Lockerby, modern Lockerbie, Dumfries. His family were the traditional masters of Lockerby Castle and prominent local landowners. William moved to Liverpool and married Miss Anna Curran, but shortly afterwards disappeared. Family members explained this by saying he had been press-ganged into service at sea. If he really was the victim of a press gang, Lockerby doesn't mention it in his journal. Indeed, he makes no mention of how, or why, he sailed from Liverpool abandoning his young wife, but begins his account in Boston with the statement that he had taken passage as first officer on the *Jenny* on a voyage to the South Seas and Canton. It may be that William Lockerby, like others who ended up on the beach, was on the run.

What's most striking about Lockerby's account is his utter indifference to the violence on board ship and on the beach. He wrote more passionately about the sandflies that bit him than he did about the men who tried to kill him, or those whom he killed. On one occasion in Fiji, Lockerby was sailing between the islands with a group of sandalwooders in two open boats. The trade was fresh, the men had no charts, and one of the boats went up on a reef. In the heavy seas the boat was soon a total loss, though all of the sailors survived. Not all of them, however, could find space in the second boat. Meanwhile, canoes could be seen being readied at a nearby island. Lockerby realized that 'some must be left to the mercy of the waves and the natives. I therefore concluded to leave the two Lascars.' He doesn't say what happened to these men. The Fijians may have killed them, as they did other castaways, or they may have lived as beachcombers.

Ultimately, Lockerby found himself in the same position as the two Lascars he cast away. Captain Dorr dumped him on a coastline in Fiji after the two men had fallen out. Now a beachcomber himself, Lockerby began the process of assimilation: 'I adopted their manners and customs as much as possible; went naked with only a belt made from the bark of a tree round my waist, that hung down before and behind like a sash . . . I paid particular attention to making myself acquainted with their language, and in a few months I could . . . discourse with them on any subject.' With the benefit of living in close proximity, he came to appreciate some aspects of island life: 'In war they are fearless and savage to the utmost degree, but in peace their disposition is mild and generous towards their friends, and the affection they bear towards their relations is very seldom found among Europeans.' Lockerby was adopted by a chief and afforded chiefly status. This meant he could not feed himself 'it being contrary to the custom of the principal chief'. At meal times he was surrounded by young women who placed the food into his mouth with their fingers.

He had been living ashore for nine months when the brig *Favourite* arrived in the group in October 1808 to procure sandalwood. Being fluent in the language and familiar with the geography of the islands, Lockerby offered his services to Captain Campbell as a pilot, interpreter and guide. But the *Favourite*, like many other sandalwood ships, inevitably got drawn into local wars as the price that had to be paid for timber. Lockerby became a mercenary and turned his gun on the Fijians he had lived among for the previous nine months. In one attack on a Fijian village the sailors 'fired about a hundred canister and grape shot' into the grass houses. When they subsequently stormed the village he 'saw upwards of two hundred corpses of men, women and children whom the grape shot had dreadfully mangled'.

This was the nature of beach violence. Trading vessels arrived among islands that were often already at war, bringing guns and greed. The result was a spinning storm of bloodshed that was devoid of any simple rationale as the participants constantly changed sides. The beachcombers both lived among and fought the islanders; they fought each other; they fought on behalf of any ship that would have them; and they incited the islanders to attack ships. The missionaries despised the beachcombers in their own time and, still today, some anthropologists see them as little more than brazen sociopaths who brought only destruction to the islands. As I read Lockerby's journal I shifted several times between seeing him as victim and perpetrator of violence. In the end I realized he was both: brutal and brutalized. By the time he quit Fiji for Canton on the *Favourite* it is unclear if he even understood for whom or what he was fighting. Once a sailor trod the sand his sense of loyalty and identity became muddied in the shifting theatre of ships, ocean, islands and cultural confrontation.

One of the (few) leaders in Port Vila whom Marie-Noëlle Patterson hadn't discredited was Kalcott Matas Kele-Kele. He had been part of George Sokomanu's 'British elite' and was, by all accounts, the brains behind independence. I was told his office was at the northern end of town. When I got to the right area the only possible office building was a cabin above a wrecker's yard where men were breaking up trucks with sledgehammers. A ramp led up to the cabin, beneath a cliff daubed with graffiti supporting the Vanu'aku Pati. A soggy piece of paper was pinned to the door with 'LAWYER' scrawled in biro. The door was locked but when I came back that afternoon I met Sara, his secretary. Mr. Kele-Kele would be in court all day but if I returned next morning at 10 o'clock I should find him in the office. I asked if I could telephone to confirm the appointment. Sara rolled her eyes.

The phones had been disconnected as the result of an outstanding account.

Many of the political leaders in Vila had considerable reputations, usually for embezzlement, fraud, kickbacks, gerrymandering and multiple adultery. Stories about these people were rife, and if even half of them were true the islands were being fleeced. But the story I heard about Kalcott Matas Kele-Kele was different.

In the 1970s Kele-Kele had been studying law in Papua New Guinea and would become only the third Ni-Vanuatu to be awarded a university degree. One evening while at home he went out on the town in Vila with a Francophone friend. Later on the two students ended up at the British Ex-Servicemen's Club, hallowed ground for white expatriates and colonial administrators. At the bar the two visitors asked for a drink. They were refused and told to leave, which they declined to do. The police were called and in the ensuing scuffle a framed portrait of Queen Elizabeth was broken over the shoulder of Superintendent John Liddle of the British police. Both students received a two-week jail term, suspended for a year. The law student Kalcott Matas Kele-Kele went on to become a Supreme Court judge.

The next day, at 2 p.m., I was shown into his office. A dusty black court gown was hanging on the back of the door. There were few shelves on the walls: books and papers were stacked on the floor. Three large Melanesian slit drums, known locally as *tamtams*, stood in a corner, turned to face the wall. From the window I could see a plume of sparks flying from the wrecker's yard below.

Kalcott Matas Kele-Kele was sitting behind a desk piled high with papers. We talked about the Condominium, particularly its legal system and the notorious 'Joint Court', once described as a 'comic opera' and lampooned as the 'Joy Court'. But inevitably the subject of violence was raised. 'Don't feel too confident it won't come here,' he said. 'And don't underestimate how terrible it would be. I saw it myself in Papua New Guinea – tribal warfare with axes in the street. I thought I was going to die. Two men ran up to me with long-handled axes but recognized I wasn't from a local tribe so they left me alone.' He had a slight, boyish body. His arms and legs were tensely entwined, but his eyes were calm and he selected his words with an advocate's poise. 'If there is violence here it will be about land. Perhaps a dispute between settlers from other islands and local people here on Efaté.' He paused a moment and chose his next words with particular care. 'But you know, it may be that our great luck is our small population. Our whole population is smaller than that of Malaita Island alone in the Solomons.'

The subject of Vanuatu's 'small population' was never going to be an easy one. Estimated at more than a million pre-contact, the population fell below 41,000 in the 1930s, the result of pathogens to which the islanders had no immunity escaping from ships and crossing the beach. This was the other legacy of violence left by trading ships and beachcombers, an unintentional but devastating pall of death. Writing in the early 1900s one Vila resident, Edward Jacomb, believed that 'the population will inevitably disappear if the present regime is allowed to continue'.

A decade later the extent of mortality in the islands was captured by the anthropologist Bernard Deacon in a series of moving letters to his lover, Margaret 'Margou' Gardiner sent from Deacon's camp on Malakula in the late 1920s. 'There seems nothing here but Death . . . My notes read like the last confessions of a dying man. They die so simply, unassumingly, uncomprehendingly: and all with this tragic swiftness. In one village of twenty, nine died in one week. Men have become carelessly ironic about death. It's not like death in war or crisis – it is the final death, the death of a people, a race, and they know it more clearly than we do.' Deacon himself died of blackwater fever near South West Bay in 1927. Among colonial administrators throughout much of the twentieth century there was a kind of 'overlord' mentality of the sort expressed by Arthur C. Clarke. For a time it seemed the Condominium's ultimate role among the New Hebrideans would be to ease their passing as a people.

The islanders had long associated white sailors with disease and danger. When Captain Pease of the *Planter* reached the Ellis Islands (Tuvalu) in 1853 he was obliged to undergo a ceremony of cleansing: 'Their manner of receiving strangers is most tedious and ceremonious . . . The stranger is required to stop at the water's edge five or six hours when the King and all head chiefs are engaged in religious ceremonies . . . that the stranger may prove good friends.' As part of the ceremony the islanders gave Pease a thorough scrubbing. But the *Planter*, like most trading ships, carried a mixed-race crew and the Pacific Island seamen could step straight ashore.

In the same year, 1853, the brig *Chatham* was wrecked on Penrhyn Island 1,300 miles to the east. The brig's owner, E.H. Lamont, described how he was similarly cleansed in a 'little pool of fresh water' on coming ashore. The surprise here is that the Penrhyn Islanders had never seen a white man before; they knew nothing of European ships until the *Chatham* crashed onto the reef a few hours before dawn. Yet still the sailors were associated with danger and were scrubbed before they could begin the process of assimilation.

In the New Hebrides, the dire predictions of men like Jacomb proved to be unfounded. The population of the group stabilized at around 40,000. Today it is 200,000. 'We have the same tribal tensions as elsewhere,' Kalcott Matas Kele-Kele said. 'Our luck is that we are small and manageable.' 'Luck' seemed an unlikely word to use, but perhaps he was right. He stared at me mordantly across his desk, as if willing me to understand the pathos of his words. Kele-kele was suggesting that Vanuatu's 'small population' might possibly be its salvation.

In the end I did find an expression of beach violence on the streets of Port Vila. It was more obvious than I had ever imagined. Just before I left the capital I walked up to the campus of the University of the South Pacific to meet John Lynch, professor of linguistics. I was hoping to talk to Professor Lynch about Bislama, the local contact language. I knocked on his door (*killem doa* in Bislama). I knocked repeatedly (*killkillem doa*). In the event, I found his door was locked and the admin office said he had just phoned with his apologies but was sick today and we would have to reschedule. I was putting to sea that evening, but John Lynch later sent me some notes which provided the information I needed.

Bislama is the creole or pidgin English used throughout Vanuatu. All Melanesian societies were highly localized. John Lynch has identified 106 languages in the islands of Vanuatu of which 81 are still actively spoken today, one of the highest language densities in the world. Bislama is the common tongue that binds the country together.

I never tired of reading or listening to Bislama. It is a kaleidoscopic mix of logic, brutality, innocence, inventiveness and most of all, wide-eyed wonder towards the world of ships. The trade goods which the sandalwooder James Paddon brought in the hold of the *Brigand* mesmerized the islanders. A 'saw' was explained in Bislama as: *wan tingting i gat tith blong kaekae wud; i kam i go i kambak; brata blong tamiok.**

One of the first missionaries to arrive at Tanna was Reverend John Paton in 1858. Among the many trappings of European culture that Paton helped unload from the *Hirondelle* onto the beach at Port Resolution was his wife's grand piano. The Tannese had never seen a piano before and it was translated as: *bigfala bokis blong waetman; tith blong im sam i black sam i waet; sipos yu killem, im singaot.*†

During the time I was in Vila there was a group of hard-drinking sailors who spent their nights in the Waterfront Bar and Grill. When I saw these guys next morning they would refer to their hangovers by saying: *'Hed blong mi hemi bagarap gud.'*‡

---

*Something with teeth for eating wood; it goes backwards and forwards; brother of the tomahawk.
†A big European box; with black and white teeth; if you strike it, it sings out.
‡'I've got a frightful headache.'

Bislama originated as a simple form of pidgin English used between Europeans and Aboriginals in the Sydney area from about 1790. But Bislama developed as a ship-based contact language through its use by mixed-race crews and in trade negotiations between ship and shore.

The number of Pacific Islanders working as crew on European ships is one of the little-told stories of the sea. This is likely to remain the case as there is scant documentary evidence. As European and American crewmen were killed or deserted to live on the beach, they were inevitably replaced by Pacific Islanders, there being no other source of labour. One sandalwood trader named Burns who ran four schooners, *Cheetah*, *Vulture*, *Coquette* and *Adolphus Yates*, wrote that three-quarters of his crews were black Melanesians – 'Kanakas'. The skipper of the American trading schooner *Antarctic*, Benjamin Morrell, commented of the Maori: 'They make excellent sailors too, after a short course in training; as I can vouch for from experience, having had several of them at sea with me'. The Australian gold rush in the mid 1800s only increased the problem of finding crew. When the *Chatham* sailed from San Francisco in 1852 her owner made no secret of the difficulties of finding good seamen. The captain was a drunk, as was the second mate, who had never been to sea before. The *Chatham* was a brig of 300 tons burden; some similar-sized ships carried a crew of up to twenty men. Before the mast on the *Chatham*, however, there was only a British deserter from a man o'war, a Portuguese, and two Kanakas. Her owner explained this in the following way: 'Wages being very high [in California], 60$ per month for seamen, we sailed as light-handed as possible, as least as far as the islands, to which there is generally a fair run, and where men may be had for 10$ or 12$ per month.'

The name 'Bislama' itself is derived from 'bêche-de-mer', also known as sea cucumber. The 'fish', as it was always called by the traders, was considered a delicacy in China and, like sandalwood, was one of the few commodities the Chinese would trade for tea.

As the bêche-de-mer fishery was dependent on local labour, a contact language was essential.

The same was true of the whale fishery. One estimate suggests that between 20 and 50 per cent of crews on whalers were Kanakas. Some of the best glimpses we have of these men are in literature, such as Queequeg, the Maori harpooner in Herman Melville's *Moby Dick*. Another Yankee seaman in the 1800s, John D. Jones, described spending a night watch listening to a Polynesian seaman teaching Bislama to a Portuguese-speaking hand from the Cape Verde Islands. On board ships, where instructions were sometimes urgent and comprehension essential, there was an obvious need for a lingua franca among mixed-race crews. Bislama is the language of unlettered sailors mixing with pre-literate islanders as they climbed aloft in squalls. It is the voice of the beach, of the ship as melting pot, where culture and syntax were boiled down along with the whale blubber.

Almost everything connected with the beach and the idea of cultures merging has long been derided. Bislama is still often called 'broken English', 'mongrel English' or 'bastard English' – a *langwis blong rod*.*

It is also a language that is riddled with references to the violence of the beach. The Bislama for 'to strike' something – *killem*; 'to play the drums' – *killem tamtams*; 'to be unconscious' – *ded*; 'to be dead' – *ded finis*; 'to hit someone' – *killem*; 'to kill someone' – *killem ded finis*.

This is a language conceived in terror as sandalwooders negotiated for timber, watching for an ambush. I had come to the islands hoping that my own voyage might help me recreate these historical encounters on the beach. But on the streets of Port Vila this violence wasn't consigned to history; it was a living legacy, part of the vocabulary in use every day.

---

*Literally, a 'language of the road'; in Bislama, an 'illegitimate child' translates as *pikinini blong rod*.

4

Trading in the Backwaters

'I lived only upon the gills, and fins, and bones of fish, after
they had passed the table of Henneen, the chief whose slave
I was.'

Leonard Shaw, beachcomber, 1830

T HE NIGHT WAS humid. A slack and sticky trade wind was
easing over the ocean. There was no moon, no horizon, and
the open sea felt cramped, airless, as if it had suddenly shrunk.
Nguna Island lay out in the blackness to the east. No lights were
visible from ten miles offshore. I lay dozing on the cockpit bench,
the night becoming muggier still as the wind fell further. The
sloop settled into an ever more docile onwards nod.

The humidity and lethargy aided my sense of fatalism at sea. It
was an 85-mile passage from Port Vila to Malakula, a simple trip
with the trade wind on the beam. Before leaving the capital I'd
anticipated reaching Port Sandwich early the next morning. But
now, as the night wore on, the languid pool of sea and sky around
the boat became the whole world and it seemed large enough to
hold me indefinitely.

Through the small hours a coaster crawled past, heading north.
Its grinding engine could be heard drifting over the water long
after the navigation lights had faded from view, the sound laden
with heat and vibration. Far ahead the volcano on Ambrym
appeared as two glowing piles of embers suspended in the sky, the
colour of a dying coal fire.

I sailed under the lee of Cook's Reef but felt no change in the seascape. The reef is a coral formation that has long been a hazard to shipping heading to and from the capital. The *Alize II* came to grief here in the 1970s. Steaming north overnight from Port Vila the ship struck the rocks near Safuti Point and screeched up onto the coral shelf. Next day chaotic scenes developed as a column of villagers trudged across the reef to inspect the castaways. Peering aboard the ship they saw that the passengers, mostly French planters, were sitting down to a four-course luncheon in the main cabin, after which they spent the afternoon drinking wine.

Ships provided the only transport between the islands in Condominium times, and for much of the era it was feast or famine — but mostly famine. The original British Residency steam yacht, *Euphrosyne*, burnt to the waterline in the 1920s and was not replaced until 1961 for reasons of economy. In the intervening years the Condominium chartered whatever was available. *Bonite* was infested with cockroaches, stank of copra, and was thought unfit to carry human beings. *Honey* sank at anchor. *Astralabe* was a total loss on the reef at Maewo. And the original *Alize* was destroyed in appalling conditions by a cyclone in the Banks Islands.

As dawn approached the breeze died back to a trickle of wind and the sails hung limp in the rig. I made coffee as twilight struggled over the black ocean. The sloop was becalmed in a windless hollow surrounded by the high islands of Epi, Malakula and Ambrym. The sea was so still this could have been an inland lake. In the gathering light both land and water were the same pallid grey. Now a column of smoke and steam could be seen rising vertically from the volcano on Ambrym. Even before the lower limb of the sun had cleared the horizon, it was intensely hot.

When the tide turned an hour later, the breeze picked up with the flood. To the south-east, tidal eddies and white caps spread like an insect plague over the glassy waters until the sloop was overtaken by a wave of momentum and set on its way towards the coast of Malakula. Late in the morning I reached Lamap Point, the entrance to Port Sandwich. Cattle roamed heavily along the beach. The reef was wide here, the silvery expanse of its surface studded with green pools and black boulders. Along the escarpment, half-hidden among the palm fronds, were the iron roofs and curved eaves of time-worn planters' houses. Many copra planters in the outer islands had lived on the margins of European society. I had come here to trace the life and death of the man who built the first European house on this cliff top, a trading sailor, would-be planter, and beachcomber named Vernon Lee Walker.

Port Sandwich cut far inland, parting the bush like a gorge. I eased the mainsheet and ran dead down wind under Ashuk Bluff. Palms crowded to the water's edge on both shores. In the stifling heat of the morning sun, Port Sandwich was cool and green.

I gybed close under the palms at Middle Bay and ran clear of a milky shoal that butted across much of the fairway. On mudflats off the west shore the rusting remains of the copra steamer *Pervanche* were the colour of blood. Mangroves burst profusely from the wheelhouse giving the hulk a schizophrenic appearance of both decay and rude health. I ran the sloop behind the spit at Planters' Point, anchoring off the wharf in a pool of still water.

'NO SWIMMING' read a sign nailed to the wharf. There have been many shark attacks in the shoal waters of Port Sandwich. An American woman was killed before independence, and a girl had her calf bitten off while swimming from a yacht in the 1980s. Local people have long been wary of the water here. When men were forced to swim the harbour for want of a canoe, they rounded up as many dogs as possible and swam across Port Sandwich surrounded by a pack of hounds, hoping any sharks would attack the dogs first.

A faint rumble could be heard spreading over the water. Moments later the grey steel bows of a warship slipped from behind the palms. The ship steamed cautiously around the spit at Planters' Point and tied to the rotting jetty outside the old Ballande store. Within ten minutes the beach was thronged with villagers. About fifty more had formed a line on the jetty, waiting to tour the ship.

La Glorieuse had come north from its base in New Caledonia. The French tricolour flapped sporadically in the disturbed trade. Lamap had once been a prominent French settlement, the third town of the colonial New Hebrides. But today it was no more than a village with a line of gutted concrete shells where the administrative buildings had been. When George Sokomanu had boasted to me that 'We British won independence', then it was French settlements like Lamap that had 'lost'. *La Glorieuse* steamed up from Nouméa every few years to keep the flag flying in this abandoned outpost.

I took the tour of the ship along with the villagers. The sailors were a mix of French and Kanaks, and conducted us round the ship in high spirits. Signalman Bertrand pointed out the two cannon (40mm and 20mm) while the villagers stared open-mouthed. On the flybridge he showed us the half-shredded wind-surfer board they had found drifting at sea and now used for target practice. The villagers stared spellbound.

It had been in this harbour, 229 years before the visit of *La Glorieuse*, that the islanders first saw cannon and made their first tours of a European ship of war. On 22 July 1774 Captain Cook had anchored HMS *Resolution* near the entrance to the harbour he named after his patron, the Earl of Sandwich. I paddled the kayak round the spit at Planters' Point and down the harbour to find Cook's anchorage, which he described as lying 'some thing more than a Cables length from the South Shore and a Mile within the entrance.' On the second day Cook had gone ashore on the nearby beach, his first landing in what was then a group of islands barely known to Europeans. The sand all along that southern shore at Port Sandwich is the colour of turmeric, overhung by the trailing boughs of *navele* trees. At night the *naveles* produce spectacular flowers with long white spines tipped in pink. The flowers are released at dawn so that the beach and lagoon are littered with fallen blooms. Cook's longboat grounded on the fringing reef, and as the sailors waded ashore they must have pushed the flowers aside with their knees.

Gathered on the beach to meet him there were, by Cook's esti-
mation, four to five hundred armed men. The beach is very
narrow here and these forces would have stretched for hundreds
of metres on either side. For the sailors wading ashore, both fight
and flight would have been difficult. When I read Cook's account
of first contact in the New Hebrides, and then came ashore in the
same place, the real wonder of the man wasn't only his genius for
navigation, but that the death he ultimately met on the beach at
Kealakekua Bay hadn't occurred years earlier.

Cook made peace on the beach at Port Sandwich, but his short
stay here was not altogether successful. The disappointment that
many on board *Resolution* felt towards the New Hebrides was syn-
thesized in the account of the ship's scientist, Johann Reinhold
Forster. Of first contact at Port Sandwich Forster wrote: 'The
natives of Malicollo [Malakula] are a small, nimble, slender, black
and ill-favoured set of beings; that of all men I ever saw, border
the nearest upon a tribe of monkies . . . their women are ugly and
deformed . . . their complexion is sooty, their features harsh, the
cheek bone and face broad, and the whole countenance highly
disagreeable'. From their physical appearance Forster concluded
that the New Hebrideans were unpredictable, untrustworthy,
vengeful and cruel.

He was certainly not the only European to disparage the islanders. I found similar remarks dating from the first European voyages
through to the mid-twentieth century. But Forster's theorems
gave the gloss of scientific respectability to what becomes, in the
literature, a litany of racist denigrations: 'very ugly . . . wild
savages . . . black devils' (Prado 1606); 'brute barbarians' (Fray
Munilla 1606); 'They are short, ugly, ill-proportioned . . .'
(Bougainville 1768); 'An Apish Nation . . . the most ugly and ill-
proportioned people I ever saw . . .' (Cook 1774); 'very low in the
scale of human beings . . . filthy, ill-looking, insolent, monkey
like' (Belcher 1842); 'degraded creatures' (Paton 1858); 'deeply
sunk and debased' (Murray 1862); 'inhuman . . . unclean, despi-
cable and repulsive individuals' (Thurston 1871); 'I had been

expecting to see a fine, stalwart race . . . [but] the people are as *black,* and *ugly,* and as *dirty* as they can be . . . [his italics]' (Robertson 1902); 'loathsome . . . simply hideous, mis-shapen, lice-stricken savages . . . The average kanaka of these parts is a phthisic wreck . . .' (Fletcher 1925); 'considered as among the lowest people in the world' (Harrison 1937); 'wizened, pygmy-like, ugly little creatures' (Luke 1945).

I noted down these remarks while reading the accounts of previous sailors and visitors to the islands. The quotations reproduced here are a small portion of the whole. At the same time, I recorded observations I found describing beachcombers in the islands. Similar vocabulary was used to account for both groups. As the beachcombers crossed the cultural divide, wore native dress, were tattooed and learned the local language, their supposed degeneracy and barbarity was emphasized, as was their 'darkness'. Reverend John Williams had railed against the beachcombers: 'the vilest of the vile, the scum of the crew'. Most other missionaries concurred: Turner described beachcombers as 'vile . . . degraded . . . monsters'; for Murray, they were 'evil . . . vagabonds'. Two bêche-de-mer traders came across many beachcombers in the course of their voyages and recorded their impressions. John Eagleston described beachcombers as 'devils of the blackest stamp'. Captain Freemantle thought them to be 'degraded characters . . . they mostly hail as shipwrecked mariners'.

I left the kayak on the powdery sand at Port Sandwich where Cook had come ashore waving a palm frond as a sign of peace. It was late afternoon and the air was filled with glancing sunlight and birdsong. Kingfishers and green parrots perched in the *navele* trees, chessboard swallows fluttered overhead. Smoke from cooking fires was bleeding through thatched roofs, giving each house I passed an air of impending disaster. Children peered from the doorways, then chorused '*Bonjour Monsieur*–hello–*bonsoir*–goodbye–goodnight–good morning–*au revoir*,' continuously, until I was out of sight.

But the dominant feature here were the coconut plantations that stretched almost unbroken up this weather coast of Malakula. Scores of copra-drying sheds lined the track, each one surrounded by piles of husks. Villagers shovelled split logs into the fireboxes while others tipped fresh sack loads of coconut meat onto the grills. The men were jet black, their bodies dusted with ash. I climbed up into one shed where women were stuffing cooked flesh into sacks. The smell was only just pleasant, an overwhelming wave of baked coconut-compress.

Beyond the drying sheds the coconut palms covered the hillside, reaching further than the eye could see. The fronds heaved and crashed in the trade wind, making a roar like breaking surf. Occasionally the sun penetrated chinks in the canopy and stroboscopic beams of light scattered among the trunks. The trees here were very old. The steps cut in the trunks were worn and weathered black. Names had been carved into the bark to identify the original European owners. Most were unreadable; the letters had swollen out of shape as the tree had grown, so that they now resembled undecipherable hieroglyphics from a forgotten tongue.

Three days earlier I had met the last surviving member of one of the most prominent copra dynasties in the group. Isobel Ohlen was 75 years old. She came through the bedroom door of her villa in Nambatu, Port Vila's most exclusive address, supported by three young Ni-Vanuatu women. Her blue-rinsed hair formed glossy ringlets. She wore a white nightdress, a quilted satin dressing gown, rouge, and carried a Pekinese dog in the crook of her arm.

We sat on the terrace and she told me about the tranquil afternoons of her childhood when she would take the pony and trap to bathe at the beaches on the Pango Peninsula or go further afield, through the settlement at Melé to her father's plantations at Devil's Point. Occasionally she joined him on the steamer for a longer tour, cruising 100 miles north to the plantations here on Malakula and neighbouring Ambrym Island. 'This was a wonderful place then,' she told me. 'It was a paradise. The people were so kind and simple.' I asked if there had ever been conflict between the French and English. 'No. No. This is not true. There was never any problem between the French and English. All of it is untrue. The Condominium was the best time here. Look at the country now. Look at Port Vila. It was the war that changed everything. There was a sudden evolution and development, new ideas, American culture.' The Ohlens had been among those planters who had done well out of copra. When I asked another French resident in Vila about Isobel Ohlen she rubbed the fingers of one hand against her thumb and said, 'She's very rich. She's done nothing her whole life.'

I asked Madame Ohlen about her nationality. 'I am French,' she replied tartly, as if the question had been absurd. Her family had lived in Melanesia for four generations. She had been born in Port Vila in 1928. In many ways the more successful planters like the Ohlens represented the complete opposite of the beachcombers. The *colons* brought their own culture with them to the islands and, even after four generations, were still defiantly European.

But for every family like the Ohlens, there were many other planters who struggled. It was the missionaries who had first collected coconut oil for commercial purposes. In Tahiti, the price of a copy of the Gospel according to St Luke had been ten gallons of coconut oil in the early 1800s. By the 1870s the Godeffroy company perfected the technique of making copra from the dried white flesh on mature coconuts. Over the following decades the New Hebrides became the third largest producer of copra in the world, after the Philippines and New Guinea, and some planters made considerable fortunes. But copra was never a reliable commodity. When the price was high the shelves of the trade stores were stocked with champagne, but when it plunged the planters went native, eating a local diet of *taro* and fruit. Stuck on outer islands, afflicted by fever, boredom, financial insecurity and unbearable solitude, the planters faced a constant battle to maintain their European identity. One observer of plantation life in the colonial era was the American film-maker Martin Johnson, who first sailed to the South Pacific with Jack and Charmian London on the *Snark*. 'The traders and planters lead lonely lives,' Johnson wrote in the 1920s. 'They have just three things to look forward to – the monthly visit of the *Pacifique*, a trip once a year to Sydney or New Caledonia, and dinner.' Johnson was amused at the way the more upright planters still dressed for dinner each evening, believing that if they did not, 'the islands will get them'.

I followed the track along the shore of Port Sandwich and reached the abandoned French colonial town of Lamap – now little more than a village. On the escarpment overlooking the ocean with fine views east to Ambrym and Epi was a derelict villa. The louvered shutters were smashed or hanging by a solitary hinge. Scores of wasp nests were tucked under the eaves of the veranda. I wandered through the deserted, echoing rooms followed by a group of children. In an alcove I stopped to make a few notes and they crowded round. As I wrote one of them touched my watch. I could feel frizzy hair against my bare arms. They touched my pen and muttered '*stylo*' and rubbed their fingers over the page of my notebook and whispered '*cahier*'. They smelt of copra and wood smoke; everything here did.

I walked out onto the lawn and from the lip of the escarpment looked down over the reefs at the entrance to Port Sandwich. A little more than 100 years after Cook had sailed through this reef passage, another Englishman arrived here under sail. His name was Vernon Lee Walker. He berthed his schooner in Cook's anchorage and bought a parcel of land on this escarpment overlooking the harbour entrance where he built his house. In every respect bar one, Walker's Pacific voyages could not have been more different from those of Cook. His schooner carried no scientists, painters or astronomers. He was a trader and his crew were mostly black Melanesians. But ultimately, both Cook and Walker shared the same fate on the beach.

When he quit the Black Country town of Wolverhampton for the South Seas in 1878, Lee Walker never imagined he would end up living in a backwater like Port Sandwich. It was to Sydney that

Lee went first on the heels of his domineering brother Howard, who appears from Lee's letters to have been the driving force behind their scheme to establish a South Seas dynasty.

Sydney in the 1870s was a town eager to make good, a place of merchants and prospectors. Port Jackson bustled with trade and commerce as the gateway between the young colony and the South Pacific Ocean. Some settlers planted their gaze in the east towards those islands that lay beyond the Coral Sea; hopes were high that the Melanesian islands might be for New South Wales what the West Indies had been for England: plantation gold. In Sydney the Walker brothers enjoyed carriages, parks, picnics and dinners while they developed contacts and scouted for business opportunities.

It's probably not unreasonable to assume that one of the Sydney merchants whom the Walker brothers aspired to emulate was my great-great-great-great-grandfather, Anthony Hordern. I came across one reference to my ancestor by chance. It was a small article in the *Sydney Morning Herald*, the same edition that reported the attack on James Paddon's *Brigand* at Ile Maré, dated 14 December 1843. A newspaper man, George Cavanagh, had suggested that Hordern came from convict stock having been 'transported to the colony for an offence of frightful atrocity', namely, a bank heist to the tune of £25,000. Hordern maintained he'd arrived in Sydney as a free migrant 19 years earlier, sued the hack for 'malignant libel', and won his case.

Anthony and Anne Hordern reached Sydney in 1825 from their home in Retford, Nottingham, after a 25-week voyage in the *Phoenix*. Family portraits reveal them to be two of the most po-faced people I have ever seen. The following year Anthony set up a corset and bonnet shop in Sydney's King Street. The family business evolved into 'Anthony Hordern and Sons, Universal Providers, Palace Emporium'. The Horderns became the merchant princes of retail in Sydney, a rags-to-riches saga once dubbed 'Draper to Squire'. Their trading empire spanned the Pacific, India and England. The principal Hordern store in George Street became an institution in Sydney with the stated aim of supplying 'all the daily demands of the domestic economy of the people in every rank of life'. The Hordern family homes were at Darling Point and Bellevue Hill. The latter had so many bedrooms that one was given over to the exclusive use of a dairy cow. By 1904 one of Anthony's grandsons, sadly not in my line of the family, employed 4,000 people and had 500 horses in his delivery service.

Today, the Horderns are best remembered not only for their ability to make money, but for their even greater facility for losing it. In the first decades of the twentieth century the decline of the Hordern trading empire was as spectacular as its earlier expansion. The store in George Street was promoted with the slogan, 'While I live, I grow,' beneath which some unkind soul added the words, 'slower and slower'. The store closed in 1969.

My own branch of the family was never among the high flyers and managed to lose their money even more readily than the rest of them. 'Fast women and slow horses,' my father once told me by way of explanation. My great-grandfather returned to England, but couldn't settle and escaped to the island of Jersey in the English Channel. My grandparents lived in a small semi-detached cottage beside the slipway at Le Bourg and ran an unsuccessful chicken farm.

Nonetheless, in the late 1870s, when the Walkers arrived in Sydney, the Horderns would have perfectly represented all the New World promise of opportunity and social mobility to which the two brothers aspired.

For the Walkers, however, there was to be no boom before the bust. After five years' struggle it was becoming clear that the Walkers' dreams of founding a Sydney-based trading empire were unlikely to be realized. Howard's business projects repeatedly failed and, pursued by creditors, Lee fled into the Pacific.

He went first to Nouméa but increasingly spurned the society of white colonists, preferring to live on board ship and keep the company of Kanaka seamen with whom he spoke Bislama. He ran a modest trading store and made long coastal voyages to collect copra. Lee described his life aboard ship at this time in a letter to his mother: 'I slept on the boards with just a blanket around me and went about without boots all the time as one has to walk through the water so much . . . Dangerous as it is, travelling around the coast, I would far sooner be doing it, than having to live in Nouméa.'

The sea was the great discovery of Lee's short life. His letters home amount to a gloomy correspondence, but in those written at sea there is a spark of life and hope. Only on the deck of a roving ship did Lee manage to slip beyond the reach of his over-bearing brother Howard and escape the yoke of his own unattainable ambitions. In 1886 he made his first voyage to the New Hebrides. The supercargo on one of Howard's schooners had been speared to death on the beach and Lee took this man's position. He wrote, 'I can get along with the natives better than most people and have no fear of them. You would hardly know me now, I am more than brown almost black from the sun. Clothes do not trouble one much in the Islands.' Life aboard the small schooner was undoubtedly hard. His bed was now a sack of rice, the heat and stink of copra unbearable, and malaria inescapable. 'However in fine weather it is not so very bad, and there is a kind of fascination in the risks you run.' Becalmed off Nouméa Lee wrote in pensive mood, 'Now I come to think of it, in four more days it will be my birthday, but I cannot for the life of me, think how old I am. It must be somewhere about thirty.'

Lee's last letter home was written aboard his 50-ton schooner as it again drifted becalmed. 'We are now about thirty miles from an island called Erromango, with hardly a breath of wind and a smooth sea.' Lee's crew were Kanakas – 'They are Maré boys' – from the same island where James Paddon's *Brigand* had been attacked 43 years earlier. It was Christmas Day 1886 and the sailors ate a breakfast of cold fowl, roast leg of goat and jam roll. While the sailors sang carols, Lee wrote his letter and thought of home: '. . . what is the use of my going home, after being down here so long, I would be fit for nothing at home.'

The following year Lee bought 1,000 acres of land at the

entrance to Port Sandwich for £75 worth of trade goods. On this bluff at Lamap Point, with fine views east across the ocean, he built a homestead he christened Bellevue Station. Along the escarpment he planted coffee, maize, tobacco and vegetables. In a paddock he raised pigs and turkeys.

A column of children was still following me about as I wandered through the gardens of what had been Lee Walker's home. When their Sydney businesses had collapsed, my own family had beaten an impecunious retreat to an island in the English Channel, like Lee Walker, not wanting to go home. Lee had retreated to this steamy hilltop in the New Hebrides. Looking back across the weeds and tall grasses at the collapsing villa I got a sense that with a slightly different roll of the historical dice, some greying, weatherboard homestead like this one beneath the palms might have been part of my own ancestry.

The sun was setting by the time I got back to the anchorage at Planters' Point. In the last of the light I followed the coastal track as far as the French cemetery. It was a peaceful place, a small clearing surrounded by bush. A detachment of sailors from *La Glorieuse* had been here earlier in the day to maintain their forebears' graves. The coral blocks marking each of the twenty graves had been whitewashed and flecks of paint were visible on the mown grass. None of the graves bore an inscription, but the sailors had designated each stone with a neat French flag. In one case, though, the flag was an error. This was the grave of the Englishman, Vernon Lee Walker.

I sailed from Port Sandwich at dawn next morning, following the course Lee had steered on his final voyage. From between the fringing reefs at the harbour entrance I could see the site of Lee's Bellevue Station on the southern headland. The sky was lightening, filled with white cloud, as the sun rose above the channel between Paama and Ambrym Islands. A steady trade wind was flowing up the coast giving an easy beam reach to Pentecost Island, 50 miles distant. Lee Walker's schooner had made this same passage to Pentecost on 16 December 1887. The voyage had no grand design. The garden at Bellevue Station was not yet fully established and he sailed to Pentecost to trade for yams.

By this time Lee Walker had sailed many thousands of miles in the islands and suffered his fair share of scrapes. In New Caledonia the schooner had once fetched up on a reef '. . . and I never expected to see land again, as it was nasty weather at the time, however we were lucky enough to get off, with not much damage to the ship, but it took us two or three days to recover our spirits again.'

But whatever the perils of navigation, they were eclipsed by the dangers of the beach. Going ashore to trade required a small-scale military manoeuvre which Lee had refined to a well-practised routine. The schooner would be anchored offshore and, dressed in pyjama trousers and a singlet, armed with a revolver or a Winchester rifle, Lee Walker climbed into the longboat. He would be rowed into shallow water by four of his 'boys' – 'all black fellows are called "boys" down here' – each armed with a rifle. The long-boat was backed in towards the beach, ready for a quick getaway in case of trouble. Lee jumped ashore alone, then the longboat pulled out into deep water where the 'boys' stood by with their rifles, ready to put up covering fire. 'The first thing on landing I am surrounded with from 100 to 300 (according to the place) natives all armed with muskets, rifles, or bows and poisoned arrows . . . The one that speaks to you the fairest is the one that will be the first to lift [h]is hand to kill you . . . I never trust one of them.'

I had a fast passage to Pentecost that day, the sloop dipping its rail as the trade freshened mid morning, driving over the swells at more than six knots with a rush of wind and spray. I pictured Lee's schooner sailing this same course on a powerful beam reach, the main boom thrown wide to leeward, its tip kissing the brilliant seas.

Late in the afternoon I reached the small bay at Batnavni on Pentecost's eastern shore. A mushroom-shaped pinnacle of rock stood on the fringing reef, glowing as a radiant orange beacon in the afternoon sun. I anchored in sand off the mouth of a small stream. A stony beach stretched away to the north. South of the anchorage craggy limestone cliffs fell straight into the sea. The houses of a small village were scattered along the foreshore and among the trees.

In the 1880s this anchorage was known as Steep Cliff Bay. Lee Walker's schooner anchored a mile offshore and, as usual, he was rowed to the beach by his 'boys'. But this time, as soon as the long-boat grounded in the shallows, the traders were attacked by about a hundred islanders. Lee got off two rounds with a Winchester rifle before being shot in the arm and tomahawked in the back of the head. His Melanesian boat crew were all killed. The attack was over within two minutes; those left aboard the schooner could only watch. The next day, with the help of a Fijian schooner, Lee's body was recovered. According to a letter written by his brother Howard, '. . . it had not a stitch of clothing on & was simply hacked to pieces, two fingers gone (evidently to get his ring), the body was brought on here [to Port Sandwich] & buried in the French Soldier's quarters, all hands turning out . . .

'I am sending a report to H.B.M. Consul at Nouméa, & also to the English men of war, but the English will do nothing . . .

'I have got two vessels placed at my disposal one American flag & the other Danish & we intend to go to Pentecost & get our revenge, I have got 20 volunteers here, all white men, splendid shots & accustomed to the Islands, & I expect [an]other 20 from Nouméa & being under foreign flags no-one can interfere with us, & we will make it hot for the natives.'

No doubt they did. But no record is known to exist of this attack, nor is it likely that one would. Unlike the voyages of Captain Cook, few journals, theorems or oil paintings resulted from trading voyages. If Howard's promised revenge amounted to more than bravado, the attack on Steep Cliff Bay was just one more unrecorded chapter in the cycle of violence on the beach.

Lee's brother Howard also died a typical island death, though his was non-violent. The cause was malaria, as it was for count-less others.

*

The trade was fresh in the pre-dawn darkness next morning. Its bullish rush could be heard stampeding through the forest to windward. There was no chink of light in the night sky and I ran out onto a black seascape filled only with noise and motion. The sloop surged west through the last of the night in rising but still regimented seas. Soon the sound of white caps hissing down the quarter replaced the fading crash of bush ashore. In the deep swells beyond the island's lee the boat surfed down into the empty pits between each crest with a heart-quickening lunge. I sucked black, sweet coffee though chattering teeth as the frigid tropical twilight climbed over the back of Pentecost and flooded across the ocean ahead.

By mid-morning the coast of Ambae was visible away to the north, a wet green frill between the sea and cloud. To the south a wobbling blob was shifting on the swells. Ten minutes later the blob had stiffened sufficiently to be recognizable as a ship. As our courses converged I saw a small island trader bound northwards. The waist was stacked with 44-gallon drums, sheets of iron and an upturned lighter. About a dozen passengers were crowded round the rail, Mother Hubbard dresses flapping uncontrollably round the women's knees. It looked a wild, wind-tossed little world, rolling heavily on the beam swells. As the sloop sailed under the ship's stern I read the name, MV *Keidi*, and passed through a corridor of smells which trailed in its wake, an unmistakable cocktail of copra and cement. The whole 120 feet of the rusty little ship was infused with it after a lifetime of shifting the same cargo.

The sky had partially cleared when I approached the coast of Espiritu Santo early that afternoon. The town of Luganville was in shadow at first, but as I ran down the Segond Channel in a brisk easterly a smattering of iron roofs stood out from the verdure, glinting in the sunshine like a vein of quartz after rain.

The MV *Keidi* was tied to the wharf at Luganville, grinding against the concrete piles as it shifted on the short seas running up the Segond Channel. A truck was pulled up beside the ship and boxes of supplies were being unloaded for the ship's store. The storeman was Chinese, overseeing with folded arms and proud chin as the provisions came aboard, barking orders. 'We go to Ambrym,' he told me, 'buy copra.' I asked if it was a straight exchange, copra for trade goods. 'No, pay cash for copra.' His lips spread into a smile. 'Then they spend cash in ship's shop.' I looked through the goods being unloaded from the truck. Some of it hadn't changed much since James Paddon's days trading for sandalwood. The tomahawks were still here, and bush knives, spades and axes, along with instant noodles, rice and shampoo. I climbed up onto the ship where an effusive woman named Constantine dressed in a brilliant Mother Hubbard squeezed my hands and kissed both my cheeks. Chickens roosted in the fo'c'sle, a deckhand was cleaning three *mahimahi* fish caught earlier in the day, while the derrick hoisted yet more drums of diesel and sheets of iron into the waist. I climbed up to the bridge hoping to meet Captain Roy. The equipment here was spartan to say the least: a wooden wheel, a rev. counter, dials for engine temperature and oil pressure, two throttles, a compass and GPS. There was no depth sounder. From behind the closed door to Captain Roy's cabin I hear the faint strains of 'Onward Christian Soldiers' being rendered in Bislama.

The waterfront at Luganville was a wasteland of broken hardstanding, head-high weeds, rubble and abandoned warehouses. The main street was a windswept, dusty highway down which logging trucks occasionally thundered. In its colonial prime Luganville had been the Wild West of the Pacific basin. Jeeps full of planters concluded drinking binges by racing down this street firing rifles into the night sky. Hookers were shipped in from Hong Kong or the Philippines and Monsieur Laborde's nine-foot wide bed became the celebrated venue for multi-racial orgies. It was hard to picture any of this in today's town. As another logging truck crawled past in a cacophony of crashing and screaming metal, it was hard to imagine anyone had ever had a good time in this blighted little town. A shopkeeper told me that the independence celebrations, normally the highlight of the social calendar, had been cancelled this year because of repeated violence. Only the Chinese traders had stayed on after independence, though the shop fronts were so thick with dust the names were hard to read: Valient Leung, Ah Pow, Tak Ying & Co., General Stores and Electrical Repairs – Bake a Better Biscuit.

The Hotel Santo stood at the western end of town, a legacy of Luganville's last days of pitiful grandeur – the 1970s. The barman was dressed in white, like a ship's steward. It was so dark in the bar that his black hands and face were all but invisible and he appeared as a disembodied drill suit. The Hotel Santo was a white man's haunt, in denial of the tropical sunshine outside. The décor featured black vinyl upholstery, dark formica tables and velvet curtains the colour of kelp. An English father and son were the only other patrons. The son was teaching on a program for young offenders in the Australian outback and they had met here in Santo for a diving holiday. 'Luganville is upside-down,' the father told me, 'the sights are all underwater.' But the seas in the Segond Channel were too rough today for diving, so instead they were swilling beer in the sub-aqua gloom of the Hotel Santo.

Luganville is a poor anchorage for small boats. The trade wind howls up the Segond Channel putting a boxy chop on the water. When the tide turned that night, spray broke so hard over the quarter I needed to close the companionway at anchor. I had spent many more comfortable nights in mid-ocean and left the next morning as soon as the tide turned.

Distant to the south the islands of Aore, Abokissa and Tutuba just broke the skyline in the charcoal skies of dawn twilight. The islands rose from the sea no more prominent than saucers, painted with palms, a yellow fringe of sand and coral around the lip. Cream-coloured cloud poured overhead on the trade as I beat back out to the east through clotted seas, warm and rich with sediment.

Today the Segond Channel was a benign and empty place. There was no other boat in sight. But in the single month of April 1944 a fleet of more than seventy cargo ships had steamed into these narrows. In the Pacific War this had been a great, muscular waterway, churned by steel. Two thousand five hundred tons of cargo could be unloaded from the docks at Luganville in one day. Along the shores of the Segond Channel the US military built its largest establishment west of Pearl Harbor, known as Base Buttons.

The US war plan for this theatre was simple. In 1942 Admiral King devized a three-point initiative to halt the Japanese advance: 'Hold Hawaii; support Australasia; drive north-westward from the New Hebrides'. Santo became the supply depot for the war in the Pacific. After decades of hand-wringing missionaries, broken-down traders, sybaritic planters and effete colonials, the GIs had arrived.

From my position at the eastern entrance to the Segond Channel I could see the sites where three bomber airfields were built in a matter of months to cater for the B17s. Fighter One was constructed from Marsden steel matting in the bush behind Turtle Bay, close to where I planned to anchor that night. Twelve hundred planes had lined the new airstrips. On the Segond Channel there was a seaplane base, several hospitals, an aviation fuelling and repair shop, docking and port operations, a ship communication control centre and 165 magazines. Beside the Sarakata River a jungle-fighting school was established. Fifty thousand troops were stationed at Santo in 3,174 Quonset huts and 1,236 tents. The largest floating dock in the world, ABSD-1, was built in Palikulo Bay. Two hundred miles of new roads were laid down and 12,000 loaves of bread baked each day. The US commanders thought the Condominium authorities were a joke and ignored them. French and British copra plantations were bulldozed to make way for it all. There were farms, a radio station, a Masonic temple, the *Santonian* newspaper, twenty-three cinemas and a golf course.

Artie Shaw, Isaac Stern and Bing Crosby all flew to Base Buttons to keep up morale. Bob Hope pulled a crowd of 18,000. *Withering Tights* was playing at the cinema. Soldiers staged theatrical reviews including *Khaki Wacky* and *Sex Takes A Holiday*. Base personnel formed bands like Jojo Politi and the Santo Swingtet.

But there was never enough bootleg booze to go around, and soldiers took to drinking torpedo fuel to dull the fear.

James Michener was just one of half a million GIs who passed through Santo. But despite his romantic tales of lagoon-side love, there was in reality remarkably little contact between the GIs and the New Hebrideans. The anthropologist Lamont Lindstrom has estimated that no more than fifty mixed-race children were born to US wartime fathers, a staggeringly small number given the scale and duration of the US deployment. Base Buttons was an insular, self-contained community and the GIs never lived on the beach.

After two hours beating into a patchy trade I finally cleared Million Dollar Point. The seas were calmer today, and I could see one group of divers already in the water and another on shore struggling into wetsuits. The culture of excess in wartime Santo had been notorious. At the war's end the US forces simply had more equipment than they could possibly repatriate and in August 1945 Santo staged the mother of all garage sales. A ten-ton truck cost $25. You could pick up a patrol boat for $300. But Base Buttons was too big to ever be flogged off in this way and most of the equipment was dumped into the sea here at Million Dollar Point. Trucks stuffed with the contents of naval dockyards, aircraft hangars, magazines, hospitals and canteens were hoisted out into the Segond Channel with their engines still running, along with tanks, jeeps, ambulances, bulldozers and tankers. Diving on this bounty today attracted scuba enthusiasts from around the world. Vivid pink fins and fluorescent masks bobbed and ducked on the grey wastes of the channel's surface.

The flow of wind was no stronger when I reached the entrance to the Channel and the sloop wandered noiselessly north on a long, indifferent swell. Late in the morning I ran through Diamond Passage and crossed the lagoon to the north-west. The water was a deep blue, as rich and lush as the groaning plantations along the coastal strip. Seed pods of the *navele* tree lay on the surface, little woody pyramids that were flushed gently aside by the bow wave. A metre down the water was thick with jellyfish,

opaque patches that struck the self-steering rudder with a yield-
ing clunk.

Behind islets on the west shore there was an inner lagoon. I ran
through a second pass in the reef and entered a complex system of
coral gardens, palmed islets, limestone pinnacles and cays over
which shoal water cracked and popped at high tide. The anchorage
in the lee of the reef was slightly exposed and groundswell refract-
ing within the confines of the lagoon left the water trembling.

When darkness fell I paddled the kayak west through the shoals
towards Oyster Island. As I followed the coastline, the mangroves
gave way to hibiscus and palms. There was supposed to be a resort
here but 'resort' can mean almost anything in the islands. In the
fading light I could just see half a dozen whitewashed bungalows
on the beach. They were in darkness and looked deserted. Perhaps
the resort had closed down.

I paddled silently, just off the beach, listening for any sounds
ashore. Behind the sand there was the faint glow of an oil lamp.
A woman was working in the light of its smoky flame. I called
out a greeting and saw her jump with surprise. Immediately a
large dog started barking and ran down onto the beach. I
shouted that I was from a yacht anchored round the corner. She
said she would call the manager. I heard her feet crunching along
a coral path.

The dog stood barking at the tree line as I pulled the kayak up
the sand. Finally I saw the lamp coming back, held high by a small,
worried-looking man trying to find me in the darkness. 'Yes?
Yes?' he called, 'Can I help you?' I asked if there was still a resort
here and explained again that I had come from a yacht. He
lowered the lamp, came forward and patted me on the shoulder.
'Bien sûr, of course, this way, please, come, come.'

I followed him up the path, then heard heavy switches being
thrown. Strip lights flickered into life all around us. Music was piped
from somewhere inside. Slowly the familiar trappings of a resort
came into view. It was a low-key place, modest bungalows, paths of
crushed coral between banana palms and flaxes, a woven bamboo

bar and outdoor kitchen with wood fires. I walked inside where Jean-Pierre introduced himself and got us beer from the fridge.

His last restaurant had been in Alice Springs. 'I was there 15 years. Half a million tourists go to Alice each year, half a million, you know, they don't all want to eat burgers and pizzas. I cooked kangaroo, buffalo, crocodile, emu. After 15 years in Alice I wanted to live on the beach.'

I asked if the resort had closed. When did they last have guests? 'This year is terrible, you know. Maybe last month some Germans were here. Now we have no tourists. We have terrorism and SARS – and in the Solomon Island, you know, this is a bad place now, so now no one comes to Vanuatu. Once we had twenty yachts anchored out there, eating in the restaurant at night.' I didn't know if this was true, or just an old man's dream of cargo.

Jean-Pierre also owned the Café du Village in Port Vila. 'My son is the manager there, but next month we are going to swap. My son will come here for one month and I will go to Vila to run the Café.' He obviously couldn't wait. 'In Vila I am up till two or three in the morning. Here I am in bed at 8 o'clock at night. My wife is already in bed now, she went as soon as it got dark. She won't come to Vila with me any more. No, she doesn't like it. Too many people. Too much noise.' He told me the Café du Village was also struggling. 'It's the mentality, you know, the mentality of these people here. They are the kindest people in the world, but to work with? No, you cannot do it. At the Café we have twelve chefs working in two shifts – but you never know how many will come to work. You can never get a regular supply of anything. We put carpaccio of tuna on the menu. Suddenly the fishing boat disappears – we have no more tuna. And people get up and walk out. I've seen it, a table of twelve, if they cannot have carpaccio they walk out. I'm going broke. I want to leave Vanuatu. It's not a place for an old man. But how can I sell? Who will buy this? Anyway, my wife will not even go to Port Vila anymore so what does it matter. What are you going to eat?' Jean-Pierre cooked me a blue steak of Santo beef and green pawpaw soucroute.

'Come ashore in the morning. I bake the bread early, it will be ready by 9 o'clock. We can settle up then.' He left the girl to clear up and walked down the path into the darkness, saying his wife would be worried.

The bread was still warm when I beat out through the reef passage next morning. The breeze was very light from the east and the sloop made only an ambling way across the lagoon towards Mavéa. Soon the wind died altogether, and for an hour the boat drifted over a shoal which cleft the dark water with a slash of colour. Twelve metres down the seabed was visible as a series of serrated shelves and terraces across which fish occasionally darted and flashed. It wasn't until noon that the wind freshened and I could set a course to the north under three sails as the sky slowly filled with rain cloud. On each inshore tack the coastline of Santo would suddenly bulge from the cloud, a bold and ominous green strip.

Contact with European shipping had long made this weather coast of Santo cult-prone. The Ronovuro Cult briefly thrived here in the early 1920s. Ronovuro claimed divine powers as his lungs had supposedly been filled with the final breaths of a dying seaman. Ronovuro was hanged by the Condominium for murdering a deaf planter, John Clapcott. Later, at the end of the Pacific War, a man named Tieka recruited villagers to a cult whose central tenet was nakedness. Under Tieka's leadership, the Naked Cult strived for a pristine new beginning. Tieka demonstrated his personal rejection of the old ways by getting married to his own brother and sister. Cult members took off all of their clothes, killed their animals, burnt down their houses, abandoned their villages and went to live communally in the bush, determined to remain in this state until a great cargo arrived from the land of the white men. The Naked Cult held out until 1951 when the Australian government took pity on the malnourished, miserable villagers and sent aid. Tieka decreed that the prophecy had thus been fulfilled, whereupon his followers returned to their villages and got dressed.

Late that afternoon I reached Port Olry in the aftermath of a heavy shower of rain. On every side of the anchorage there were sweeping beaches glistening in the emerging sun, spits awash in turquoise water, precipitous islets, freestanding coral columns, and milky green shallows. But the village itself was in disarray. Port Olry had recently been hit by Cyclone Zuma and parts of the settlement were still strewn through the adjacent plantations, torn iron sheeting and broken beams scattered among the palms.

On the beach I met Father Fred. He had been rebuilding part of the mission and now pulled off his sweat-stained felt hat to shake my hand. As we talked a group of boys on ponies galloped by in the surf, kicking up clods of heavy sand and spray. Father Fred led me through the village as the sun set. He came from Lau, an isolated group of islands on the eastern side of the Fijian archipelago. It is a chiefly group and had been off-limits to yachts for many years. 'Then they made a change,' Father Fred told me frowning, 'and allowed the sailors to come into the islands. You know what we found? Six propane cylinders on an uninhabited island, all full of heroin. They think the drugs were left there to be picked up by another yacht. So now we say, no more sailors in Lau!' The men of God were still wary of the men who came under sail.

For the last three days I'd been working my way north to reach the great bay which cleaves the north coast of Santo. This was a remote shore, seldom visited by boats today, but the traders and beachcombers had been here in the 1800s. You could tell the haunts of the traders by looking at the place names that adorn the chart. Great explorers like James Cook left their ship's or patron's names behind them: Port Resolution, Port Sandwich. In the decades following Cook's voyages this habit became so profligate among explorers that some within the Admiralty grew irritated by it. Captain Francis Beaufort, Hydrographer of the Navy in the early 1800s and also the man who invented the famous wind scale, believed that '. . . it would be really more beneficial to make the name convey some idea of the sense of the place, or some allusion to the inhabitants, or still better to adopt the native appellation, than to exhaust the catalogue of public characters and private friends'. Beaufort would have approved of the traders who, having no patrons to toady up to, preferred the brute obvious when it came to nomenclature: Steep Cliff Bay, Reef Bay, Black Sands, White Sands, White Grass. Likewise, the vast gulch that divides the north coast of Santo goes by the plainest of names: Big Bay.

It was early afternoon by the time I beat around the cape and out into the wind-whipped entrance to Big Bay. The wind had climbed to 25 knots and the water was streaked with white caps. In the west the Cumberland Peninsula formed the skyline for more than 30 miles. Patches of rain cloud were tugging at its ridges and forests as the trade ripped down its length. The alluvial plain 12 miles to the south was still out of sight and the bay had the appearance of a yawning terrestrial mouth, its lips partially lost in cloud, only a great tongue of breaking water pouring out of the island's throat.

I put in four long tacks that afternoon and evening, beating across the ten-mile breadth of Big Bay. Land lay on three sides but for long periods nothing of it could be seen, the sloop lost in a cocoon of rain cloud as it pitched and bucked on the steep seas. Navigation in these waters, though, was simple enough. Big Bay was clear of reefs or shoals; cliffs of dripping black rock tumbled into deep water when I finally reached either coast.

The first trading vessel to beat south through the white caps of Big Bay was the *Margaret Oakley* in 1834. She was 'a rakish brig' according to one crewman, and took full advantage of the wide, unobstructed bay: 'So deep is the water close inshore, that we almost grazed the land in sailing along . . .'. Captain Benjamin Morrell anchored off the black sand beach that flanks the alluvial plain and 'next day carried on a brisk trade with the savages, who surrounded us in numerous canoes'. When the islanders showed him some 'gold' he 'politely pocketed it' and sailed on, convinced his fortune was at last made. But Morrell was a man who believed he had found 'gold', 'onyx', 'precious gems' or other 'rich

Right: Dillon's Bay, Erromango. The sandalwood trader Sempet Naritantop and my cargo of seedlings. The once-bloody trade in sandalwood continues on a small scale today, 178 years after the first European ships arrived. The cliffs in the background are those on which the schooner *Elizabeth* was wrecked in 1848

Below: The sandalwood seedlings being secured in the cabin ready for the overnight passage to Port Vila

Left: A dancer at the John Frum village, Tanna

Below: The burnt-out village at Yanekahi, Tanna, where the deckhand Fred Nasse – aka 'Prophet Fred' – attempted to form a breakaway cargo cult in 2003. More than 170 years after their inception, 'sailor cults' and 'sailor religions' are an ongoing saga in the islands

The beach at Melé where the Samoan and Tongan drift voyagers came ashore in 1825

Port Vila. The Court House of the Anglo-French Condominium in the New Hebrides. Properly known as the Joint Court, it was lampooned as the 'Joy Court', described by one visitor as 'pure musical comedy'

Planters' Point, Port Sandwich, Malakula. The English trader, sailor and beachcomber Vernon Lee Walker is buried behind the beach

Matantas Village, Big Bay, Espiritu Santo. The Spanish expedition of Pedro Fernandez de Quiros celebrated Corpus Christi on the beach here in 1606. Today, the stream in the foreground divides Matantas into two parts: one Christian, the other pagan

Right: The anchorage at Sola, Banks Islands. The group was sighted by William Bligh in 1789, seventeen days after the mutiny on the *Bounty*. Too afraid to land, Bligh named the group after his patron, Joseph Banks, and continued west to Torres Strait in the *Bounty*'s 23-foot launch

Below: Pacific Island seamen, the descendants of the 'Kanakas' who once worked on many European trading ships. Sola, Banks Islands

Above left: Village on the sandbank at Tikopia

Above: A Tikopia woman smoking a pipe

Left: Nau Vairiki preparing a meal on the inland – 'profane' – side of the house, Tikopia

Below: Tikopia from the summit of Reani – *Te Uru o te Fenua* – the Head of the Land

False killer whales (*Pseudorca crassidens*) in the Labyrinth, Great Barrier Reef

Approaching Albany Passage, Cape York Peninsula. The *Pandora* castaways found a spring of fresh water on the coastline to the left

Thursday Island in Torres Strait. The settlement was conceived as a coral gateway between Asia and the Pacific, an 'Austral Constantinople'

Approaching Croker Island, northern Australia

cargoes' at almost every island he visited. Little of it turned out to be of any value.

The purpose of his 1834 voyage in the *Margaret Oakley* was to return home two Melanesians kidnapped in the islands four years earlier. Morrell had taken the two to New York with the inten-

Benjamin Morrell, captain of the schooner *Antarctic* and the brig *Margaret Oakley* in the South Pacific. Morrell aspired to being an explorer, the American equivalent of Captain Cook, but in reality was little more than a trading skipper who scavenged cargoes of sandalwood, bêche-de-mer, turtle and pearls. Frontispiece to his *Narrative of the Four Voyages to the South Sea*, 1832

tion of training them to be beachcombers. He had become convinced of the potential value of beachcombers in Melanesia as a result of his crew's experiences at a group he called the Massacre Islands (the Kilinailau Islands, New Guinea). In that group Morrell found plentiful stocks of bêche-de-mer but a party of sailors sent ashore to construct a drying shed were attacked and killed. Only one man survived the massacre, Leonard Shaw, who was kept as a slave and exotic pet by the chief for 108 days. Shaw suffered a broken skull and near starvation, only staying alive by eating rats and the gills of fish. In addition, he was tortured by children who pulled out his facial hair: 'I wore, at the time I was taken, a very large pair of whiskers, – long, full, and bushy; and my beard had grown to a great length'. Both were plucked out 'in large bunches' until he prayed that God would 'take me from such monsters to himself'. Shaw finally managed to escape while the village was being bombarded with cannon fire. When he came on board the ship Morrell wrote, '. . . his wasted emaciated form was lacerated with wounds . . . In short, he was the spectre of wretchedness.'

Nonetheless, Morrell was convinced that trade in these islands was still feasible if only there were beachcombers who might act as interpreters and intermediaries to explain one world to the other. Clearly, no white man was going to volunteer for this work so later in the voyage Morrell seized two Melanesians, whom he named Sunday and Monday. On board ship they learned to speak Bislama, and after a period of time in New York Morrell pronounced them to be 'civilized, intelligent men, well fitted to becoming proper agents, or interpreters . . . to open an intercourse with their native isles, which cannot fail of resulting in immense commercial advantages.' As a sideline, both men were 'advertised as cannibals' and publicly exhibited in New York and other American cities.

It took Morrell three years to raise the finance for a new voyage but in 1834 he was given command of the trader *Margaret Oakley* for a return voyage to the Massacre Islands. One of the brig's midshipmen, Thomas Jefferson Jacobs, wrote that Sunday was '. . . gentle, affectionate, inquiring and intelligent'. Monday, however, was '. . . suspicious, moody and difficult of restraint'. Three bitter New York winters had 'chilled his temper as well as his frame; he hated the confinement of dress and the restraints of orderly and civilized life, and often wept in bitter agony . . . he rapidly declined, and soon died in New York.'

The *Margaret Oakley* sailed from the Hudson River on 9 March. Jacobs befriended Sunday and in the tradition of shipboard language exchange, learned to speak the islander's tongue. He transcribed Sunday's native name as 'Prince Telum-by-by Darco' and learned he was the son of a notable chief. Prince Darco was 25 years old and a great favourite on board the brig, particularly on account of his 'praiseworthy habit of minding his own business'. Darco had the keenest eyes of all the sailors and 'was our principal "look-out" at the masthead'. For entertainment on the voyage the seamen often challenged Darco to wrestling contests 'but with one tender hug, he lay them sprawling and discomforted on the deck'.

Morrell was always cagey about exactly which island he had kidnapped Sunday and Monday from, but it's clear from his account it lay somewhere in the Bismarck Sea, immediately off the north coast of New Guinea at approximately 144° 55′ east.

Sunday, or Prince Darco, met a rapturous welcome from his own people when the *Margaret Oakley* dropped anchor. Morrell kitted him out with those trappings that made some beachcombers so powerful in other parts of the ocean, particularly in Polynesia: a musket, pair of pistols, cutlass, lance, harpoon, powder, shot, grindstone, cleaver, axes and carpenter's tools. Darco told his people New York 'was situated in the moon, and peopled by spirits and hobgoblins'. The islanders called his musket the 'magic war club from the moon'.

Morrell's original design of training an indigenous beachcomber proved a masterstroke. The crew of the *Margaret Oakley* '. . . had as much as they could well attend to in exchanging gratulations with the young women'. Better still, Darco set the islanders to work, diving for bêche-de-mer and pearl shell and hunting turtle, until 'a large quantity of these articles awaited [Morrell's] command'.

The *Margaret Oakley* sailed north to Canton where the South Seas' products were exchanged for tea and fancy goods. Then she headed south to Singapore, followed by a six-week passage across the Indian Ocean to Fort Dauphin, Madagascar. This was as close as Morrell would get to sailing in triumph back up the Hudson River.

After three days at anchor at Madagascar Morrell and part of the crew went ashore to trade for cattle when the wind changed suddenly and blew onshore with some force. 'The vessel plunged and staggered, and the waves completely buried the bow, sweeping the deck.' Morrell arrived back at the beach just in time to see the brig 'drive on shore' where her back was broken in the surf. The hatches were thrown open and all hands endeavoured to save the cargo. At the same time, however, about 200 islanders arrived and the contents of the hold came ashore amid scenes of considerable confusion. According to the midshipman: 'Boxes of costly silks and lackered ware were broken open and pillaged by the savages, many of whom were seen scampering into the forest with flowered shawls, and remnants of silks, satins, crapes, and handkerchiefs ornamenting different parts of their persons, while underneath their arms were boxes of tea, bundles of sewing silk and other valuables . . . Captain Morrell paced the beach to and fro like a maniac, with a brace of pistols in his hands, threatening to blow out the brains of the first man who broke open a box . . . [but] the moment he turned his back, open went a box, and away ran the savages with the contents.'

The *Margaret Oakley* was a total loss, as was the vast majority of her cargo. The crew lived on the beach in Madagascar for several months after the wreck. Some determined to stay here for good and 'took unto themselves Malagashe wives'. As for the captain, 'after the wreck of the vessel he became partially insane'. Morrell was eventually taken off by a British ship and after a period of obscure wanderings returned to the east coast of Africa, where, at Mozambique in 1839, he 'took the prevailing fever and suddenly died'.

'Thus perished the *Margaret Oakley*,' the midshipman observed, 'and her enterprising but unfortunate captain, the ribs of the former being buried on the eastern, and the bones of the latter upon the western side of the Mozambique Passage.'

Shortly before midnight, in heavy rain, I reached the anchorage in the south-east corner of Big Bay used by the *Margaret
Oakley* 169 years earlier. Through the sodden night I could see
nothing of the land up ahead but the wind could be heard in the
bush on two sides, scratching and tearing as if the sky were filled
with thousands of angry birds.

At dawn next morning the anchorage was still, save for a clang-
ing resonance hanging over the water as a bell was struck ashore.
A few grass huts of the small village of Matantas, black with moisture, were visible in the bush. The village was split in two by a
small stream. The western part of Matantas is today Christian,
under the leadership of Chief Moses. But on the eastern bank of
the river I met a man named Tavue who told me that none of the
families here went to church. It was hardly a defiant stand, but still
Tavue was the only Ni-Vanuatu I met who openly embraced
paganism. '*Velej ia, olgeta blong kalja.*'*

It was the anniversary of Vanuatu's independence and Tavue
invited me to join the village that evening for the celebrations.
About fifteen people were gathered inside one of the larger grass
houses in the semi-darkness. We ate *laplap*, a gummy meal of
manioc, coconut and *taro* cooked in the earth oven. The band
consisted of four guitars, a ukulele and a 'bush base' – an old tea
chest. The villagers sang for several hours, celebrating the
memory of Jimmy Stephens, the grandson of a Scottish beachcomber who at independence had tried to lead Vanuatu back into
the pagan past. This village had been one of the strongholds for
Stephens' Nagriamel Cult; in 1980 it had been strafed with
machine-gun fire from a Papua New Guinean patrol boat which
came in support of George Sokomanu's government in Vila in
order to bring Matantas into line.

'Was anyone killed?' I asked.

'Only a cow,' came the reply.

---

* 'In this village, everyone is culture.' In this context, 'culture' refers to the pre-
contact animist system of beliefs, also known as '*kastom*'.

Early the next morning I paddled the kayak along the beach that trails for seven miles around the head of Big Bay. The seabed was steely grey sand, the water perfectly clear. Two men on piebald ponies were galloping this way. When they saw me they heaved the ponies to a halt, then urged them through the small surf until they were standing beside the kayak, knee deep in the waters of the bay. The men's names were Nixon and Walter. Walter was holding an oilcan in one hand and plaited vine reins in the other. A rusty chainsaw was lashed across his back. They were headed for the far side of the river to clear bush for new gardens. I asked if the river was safe for my kayak. Were there any crocodiles? 'Safe,' Nixon said, 'no problem.' I wanted to be certain. The anthropologist John Baker had seen the tracks of a large saltwater crocodile on this beach in the 1920s. One of Baker's carriers had described the animal as '. . . big fella all same bullock, but e long fella; backside blong im e all same pine-apple; e no drown, e swim all same dog'.

'Straight?' I said, 'no crocodiles?'

'*Stret. Hemi ded finis.*'

All along the beach a mix of fine black sand and pebbles had been thrown into a pattern of arches by the action of the waves. I paddled for two miles, then dragged the kayak up beside a greying tree trunk that had been washed up below a wall of yellow and rust hibiscus.

Vanuatu's tempestuous relationship with European sailors, and their religion, had first begun on these flotsam-strewn sands almost 400 years earlier. In 1606 the Spanish ships of Pedro Fernandez de Quiros had anchored off this beach, the culmination of the most enigmatic of all European voyages to the South Pacific. The beach was the only clear land in the whole bay so it was on the sand that Quiros indulged his passion for ecclesiastic pageantry and celebrated Corpus Christi. According to his account a column of men marched through three palm-enlaced arches and entered a cloister specially built for the purpose. The procession was headed by one sailor and one friar, the twin representatives of Quiros' seaborne mission to establish Christianity in the South Seas. Acolytes sporting red cassocks stood on either side as three companies of soldiers marched past flanked by twirling drummer boys. Eleven sailor lads dressed in green and red silk taffeta with bells on their feet performed a sword dance; garlanded youths dressed as Indians sang canticles to an accompaniment of tambourines and flutes. The Father Commissary wore a cloak of yellow silk six yards long borne by six royal officers. In his hands he held a coffer of crimson velvet, fastened with gilded nails, which contained the most blessed sacrament. As Quiros saw it, 'When the smoke cleared away, there were seen amongst the green branches so many plumes of feathers and sashes, so many pikes, halberds, javelins, bright sword-blades, spears, lances, and on the breasts so many crosses, so much gold, and so many colours and silken dresses, that many eyes could not contain what sprung from the heart, and they shed tears of joy.' Quiros named this land Espiritu Santo, believing it to be part of a great continent.

As the sailors conducted their fancy dress parade, body parts were hanging in the trees behind the beach. A Moorish drummer boy belonging to the Spaniards severed the head and foot of one islander shot by the arquebusiers and strung them from the branches behind the beach as a warning. 'With such wild savages,' the nobleman Prado wrote in his *Relación*, 'it is impossible to use politeness.' Prado described the 'Chinese confection' used to treat those struck by poisoned arrows: one and a half ounces of human excrement mixed with water. Once this potion was drunk, the victim vomited up the poison and recovery was rapid. Only one crewman, a Portuguese, refused to drink the remedy and he died, though his wound had been relatively minor.

The weather was deteriorating by the time I got back to the sloop. To the west the Cumberland Peninsula stretched 30 miles into the distance, its layered crests and ridges alternately picked out by shafts of moist sunshine and lost in squalls of rain. As I got up the mainsail the prospects for the overnight passage to the Banks Islands were uncertain. The trade wind burst down from the Tabwemasana range sending the sloop yawing around its anchor chain. Running north down the cauldron of Big Bay, white water was breaking down the boat's quarters within a mile of the beach. Night had fallen by the time I had cleared Cape Quiros and came out into the fray. A long, deep ocean swell was rising from the east. The sloop climbed and plunged over the seas for two hours, shuddering through the blinding gloom.

It was here, on the seas just north of the bay, that Quiros's expedition had collapsed. The sailors had endured 35 days of processions, devotions, silk accessories, investitures, choirs, galas, feasts and, as Prado put it, '. . . other absurdities I omit to avoid tiresomeness'. Prado doubted that this bay was part of a great continent; more likely it was just one more small island in this sea. In a letter to King Philip III of Spain he described Quiros as an 'impostor' who should be 'confined as a lunatic'.

The two Spanish ships had tried to beat south down the coast of the island but been driven back by the strong trade wind. The second ship made it back to the anchorage but Quiros's *Capitana* did not. Somewhere in the entrance to Big Bay, on the night of 11 June 1606, there was a breakdown in command. Prado believed that the crew mutinied. He describes how Quiros was made a prisoner in his cabin while the crew got drunk on Portuguese wine. The mutineers had planned to kill Quiros and his aides but didn't bother 'seeing how submissive they were'.

Perhaps there was a mutiny; perhaps Quiros's voyage simply collapsed under the weight of its own folly. The result was the same either way: Quiros sailed back to Mexico and the second ship, *San Pedrico*, was abandoned at Big Bay. The captain of the *San Pedrico* was a highly regarded Basque pilot named Luis Váez de Torres. Quiros had gone to some lengths to secure Torres's services '. . . because my will asks none other, nor is there anyone else who satisfies me, and the crew ask for him'.

Torres was determined that something could still be salvaged from this so far disastrous expedition. He ordered that the remaining ship would not return to Mexico, but continue west on a voyage of exploration. 'This plan was against the inclination of many [of the crew], I might say the majority, but my condition is different from that of Captain Pedro Fernandez de Quiros . . . I was right to act in this manner for these are not voyages made every day.'

Torres sailed north-west and navigated the shallow, dangerous strait that separates New Guinea and Australia. It was a voyage through the tidal margins that separate brilliance and recklessness. No European ship would repeat the passage for 164 years. Some navigators believed it to be impossible.

In the strait the *San Pedrico* met the most difficult conditions of the voyage. The water was shallow, littered with reefs and sand cays, and the currents were strong. The *San Pedrico* was blown out of one anchorage: '. . . at dawn there came a storm of wind which broke our cable and we lost an anchor. We ran without sails until it ceased . . .'. Another night '. . . there came such a great wind and tempest while we were anchored that it seemed as if all the elements had conspired against us; so that at midnight we all made confession and prepared to die'.

In the midst of the strait the Spaniards found that among the twenty or more Melanesians they had kidnapped was a pregnant woman: '. . . when her pains began, which was at nightfall, she sat on the open deck on a cannon and a negress fetched sea-water in a bucket and poured it over her neck . . . for with the dashings of water they do not feel the pains so much'. Later, the woman was taken below deck and lay on a gun carriage until her child was born.

For more than a week the *San Pedrico* ran west between the reefs within the strait. The currents were so strong '. . . it was necessary to have two men at the helm to keep the ship's head against the stream, and this lasted for eight days and nights'.

Torres and Prado returned to Spain with limited charts or other information about the strait. Of the Melanesians they kidnapped, most were baptized in Manilla and left there, but one young boy was sent to King Philip III as a trophy where he joined a troupe

of pages at court and is thought to have been included in paintings by Velasquez.

But Torres's voyage was never lauded in his own lifetime. What
little official interest remained was still focussed on Quiros, who
spent seven years selling his bedding and pawning his possessions
to petition the Spanish crown for a ship to take him back to
Espiritu Santo. Torres's voyage was considered to be a sideshow
and details of his route slipped from Europe's collective memory.

I would be sailing in the wake of Torres for much of the
remainder of the voyage.

Late in the evening the sky had partially cleared. Lightning silently
flickered along the leeward horizon as the squall moved through.
After midnight I sailed five miles downwind of Gaua Island – still
given Quiros's name of Santa Maria on Admiralty charts. Gaua
was high and mountainous, only visible as that wholly black part
of the sky where there were no stars. The wind was very light
under the island's lee and the seas were hardly formed. I dozed in
the cockpit, relishing this interlude of peace and stillness, as the
boat ghosted north-east at little more than a knot.

At dawn, Vanua Lava rose bold and beautiful to the north,
climbing to 1,000 metres close behind the reefs. But there were
no sharp edges here. The jumble of peaks and ridges were smooth
and domed, like a pile of green velvet eggs.

In the Dudley Channel the roar of breaking water filled the air
with tension. Close beside the sloop the blue meat of fully formed
ocean swells crashed onto the fringing reefs. The hiss of sea spray
hung over the water with the menace of a reptile about to strike.
To the south a bay was squeezed into a slot between the mountains, and I followed the reefs round to an anchorage at Sola, the
main settlement in the Banks Islands. A white stone cross was
planted on a grassy knoll overlooking the bay. The imposing lines
of the mission were visible in the bush behind.

I spent my last night in Vanuatu drinking kava in the *nakamal*.
It was dark inside the small iron bar. Kava drinkers will seldom

allow any light in the *nakamal* as it dazzles their heightened senses. I knew the barman was just in front of me because I could hear him breathing. Once my eyes had adjusted I saw a bench against one wall. Two men sitting there moved apart and I took my coconut shell of kava and sat between them. 'You've got your shell then,' one of them said, 'good, good.' The two men were Father John Sovan and Father Baldwin Lonsdale. In the *nakamal*, the islanders' hospitality could be insistent. 'That's a good full shell, you should drink that down now,' Father John said. There was always unease if my shell was full, and once I'd drunk it they twitched and fussed until I had another. 'That's your shell there, you should drink that down. That's it, well done, well done. Spit over there by the door. That's your first shell, you'll be ready for another now.'

The Fathers asked me if I had ever had 'two-day kava' – a brew reputedly so strong the effects last for two days. 'It was shortly after I was ordained,' Father Baldwin told me. 'We went down to Tanna for a bible group and they took us straight onto the *nakamal*. It really is something, this two-day kava. You should try it if you get the chance. I had my shell, a good shell too and – Hooo! – my legs just went out from under me!' They both hooted with laughter. 'We were lying on the *nakamal* all night, ten priests, we just couldn't move!'

The missionaries had struggled for decades to kill off the habit of drinking the narcotic kava. Sometimes as I sailed through Vanuatu it seemed that the islanders had learned to be ashamed of almost everything about their past: nakedness, headhunting, their treatment of women. But guilt about drug taking had never caught on here. Anthropologists are fond of the subversive speculation that so long as kava is being drunk in the islands, pagan beliefs haven't entirely died.

'You'll be coming to the service in the morning?' Father John asked as I lurched towards the door.

I heard the bell at 7:30 a.m. The Anglican church had walls of bamboo and an iron roof. The congregation had spilled out at the back of the building, sitting on mats, logs, bricks and lumps of coral. I perched here, squinting into the strong sunshine, rather dazed. Beside me the church 'bell' hung from a bamboo frame: an old yellow scuba bottle struck with a piece of iron. Father Baldwin was standing before the altar draped in a white chasuble, a lappet embroidered with gold around his neck.

At the end of the service the small choir broke the silence. Father Baldwin led the procession down the central aisle holding a crosier of ebony inlaid with mother of pearl. Behind him came the precentor and choristers singing 'Hark Hark My Soul'.

5

An Island Apart

'It is hard for anyone who has not actually lived on the island
to realize its isolation from the rest of the world . . . They find
it almost impossible to conceive of any really large landmass
. . . I was once asked seriously by a group of them, "Friend,
is there any land where the sound of the sea is not heard?"'

Raymond Firth, 1936

THE CUSTOMS OFFICER at Sola was named Harold. I collared
him as he was leaving church in his Sunday best and asked if
he would mind giving me a clearance now. Harold led the way
sullenly to his small office beside the beach.

They are much the same, these government outposts in the
islands: geckos scaling the whitewashed walls, torn linoleum,
scratched wooden desks, empty drawers, the louvres thrown
wide, the world beyond cut into slices of fronds and foaming seas.

I told Harold I was bound for the Australian coast. He nodded
in resignation and began to fill in the clearance form. I'd assumed
he was understandably annoyed at being asked to work on a
Sunday, when his office was closed. But I realized now it was
something else. I'd played a couple of games of pétanque with
Harold and the previous day eaten a meal at his home. On this
small island where little changed from one week to the next, he
was reluctant to see the stranger leave.

A watery rainbow was spreading above the hills as I paddled out
across the bay. Cloud was shifting in from the east to obscure Tow

Lav, the mountain that towered over the anchorage like a head-stone, and drizzle had already greased the sloop's deck. The wind was light and uncertain. The Great Barrier Reef is 1,500 miles due west from the Banks Islands, but the first course I set was in the opposite direction, north-east, across a loose and lethargic swell.

To windward, Mota Island was shaped like a coolie's hat, coloured the darkest green. Above the peak the sky was lighter, with streaks of blue swelling through the cloud. Distant to the south, the outline of Gaua faded and re-formed among rain cloud. The trade wind was patchy; wheezing puffs came through on the crest of each swell, but the sails slatted as the sloop rolled down into the airless troughs. Imperceptibly, the outline of Mota changed shape, the hat developed a second peak, until the island better resembled an Asian camel, its head outstretched, drinking from the trackless deep.

The first European to see Mota Island was Lieutenant William Bligh, who described it as '. . . most remarkable having a Sugar Loaf Hill'. As the sun rose on 15 May 1789 Bligh found islands on the horizon all around. On this seventeenth day after the mutiny on the *Bounty* the men crammed in the boat had already sailed more than 1,000 miles.

I had with me on the sloop a transcript of the notebook that Bligh carried in his jacket pocket throughout the open-boat voyage, 'kept in my bosom as a common memorandum of our time'. At the point where I crossed his track Bligh records that the launch was 'Constantly Shipping Water and very Wet', his crew were 'suffering much Cold and Shivering in the Night'. With these lush islands all along the horizon, the men were 'Starving with plenty in View'. Bligh drew a sketch chart of the islands, named them after his patron Joseph Banks, then embarked on the 1,500-mile passage west towards the Australian coast and Torres Strait.

The prognosis for the boat crew was anything but rosy. The quartermaster, John Norton, had already been killed in Tonga, where the boat had landed to search for food and water. Crucially, though, Bligh did have one thing in his favour. In the course of the mutiny his clerk, John Samuel, had managed to get a number of essential documents into the open boat. 'To Mr Samuel I am indebted for Securing to me my Journals and Commission with some Material Ships Papers. Without these I had nothing to Certify what I had done, and my honour and Character would have been in the power of Calumny without a proper document to have defended it.'

The question of paperwork and documents is a recurrent theme in the narratives of beachcombers and castaways. One boatload of starving castaways who arrived at the East Indies in 1791 without papers were imprisoned by the Dutch for a month under suspicion of being Fletcher Christian and his fellow mutineers. Bligh was more terrified of the beach than he was of the sea: of losing his status as a ship's captain and becoming indistinguishable from the riffraff on the sands. Without some sort of paperwork, castaways might be condemned to roam the sea as outlaws. Not all those who sailed in open boats had the security of Bligh's commission to hand.

Thirty-seven years after Bligh's voyage, another boatload of castaways crossed these waters east of the Banks Islands. In 1826, under cover of darkness, Charles Stewart waded into the chill waters of the Derwent River in Van Diemen's Land (Tasmania) and swam out into the stream. Ten other men followed him. In mid-river they climbed aboard a ship's longboat belonging to Captain Walker and cut the moorings. All eleven men were prisoners in the penal colony and had to choose – quite literally – between hell and high water. They chose high water. Before dawn the longboat was offshore, heading north-east into the Tasman Sea.

It was an open boat, about 20 feet long, equipped with oars and a single mast. In his former life Charles Stewart had been a ship's mate, but was transported to Van Diemen's Land for falsely billing his owners with a forged account. Stewart now adopted the role of both leader and navigator. Unsurprisingly, the longboat was poorly provisioned for an extended ocean voyage and Stewart's most pressing need was to find some shore where they could better make their preparations for sea. After a passage of 1,000 miles he made landfall on Lord Howe Island where the sloop was dragged up the beach. In a large pot scavenged from Van Diemen's Land they boiled seawater to make salt. The convicts then set about curing scores of fish and birds for a proposed voyage of 4,000 miles across the equator to Hawaii.

The sloop made the New Hebrides before the shortage of food and water again made landing an imperative. Charles Stewart sighted Futuna and brought the longboat in towards the surf. One of the crew slipped over the side in deep water and swam ashore carrying pieces of hoop iron the convicts hoped to trade for provisions. The man walked cautiously up the sand until the islanders burst from where they had been hiding in the bush. In the longboat Stewart could do nothing. The single musket they had with them could not be made to fire. Stewart ordered that the sloop put to sea, leaving the tenth man to his fate.

Too frightened to try a second landing Stewart beat back south, still desperate for provisions. After several days they sighted Ile Walpole. I had used Walpole as a waypoint on my own passage north from Auckland to Port Vila at the start of the voyage, and had passed it at night: a grim, castellated formation that is little more than a rock in mid-ocean where landing is difficult in anything other than a calm. Most of the coastline consists of cliffs rising to 100 metres; at their summit lies a narrow tableland covered in scrub. The convicts landed the sloop in a small cove on the west side and dragged the boat above the swells. They scaled the cliffs and on the tableland found coconuts, killed birds and collected birds' eggs. From the rocks they were able to catch many good fish. After a period of rest Stewart decided to sail back to Lord Howe Island. The plan was to provision the sloop more thoroughly this time before making a second attempt for Hawaii. Four of the men, however, had been broken by the sea and refused to leave Ile Walpole. None of the four men was heard from again.

The six remaining crew attempted to sail south-west to Lord

Howe but were blown off by the trade and instead reached the Ile des Pines. Stewart believed the island to be uninhabited, but as soon as they pulled in towards the beach the Melanesians came streaming out of the woods and down into the water. The convicts this time managed to fire off the musket using a firebrand, which brought sufficient time to gain the safety of the sea. When Lord Howe Island was finally reached the sloop was again loaded with cured fish and Stewart again set a course for Hawaii. Now they met nothing but northerlies or calms and the convicts made their next landfall 1,500 miles to the east in Tonga. On the beach they met no opposition and found plentiful coconuts, fish and turtle.

Stewart now sailed north-north-west and made landfall in Fiji's Lau group. The convicts brought the sloop in to a bay, set one man down on the beach to look for yams, then quickly pulled back into deep water. The crewman walked slowly up the sand, armed with their only axe. There was no other person in sight. After spending some time on the beach he walked into the woods and disappeared from sight. Stewart and the four others waited all that day in the sloop, but the man never returned. Before nightfall Stewart ordered the boat to sea.

In political terms, Charles Stewart's original decision to sail to Hawaii was inspired. In the early 1800s, Hawaii came as close to a beachcomber haven as the Pacific could provide. Kamehameha, who had received Captain Cook's hair after his death on the beach at Kealakekua Bay, was known throughout the ocean as the chief most likely to give beachcombers a favourable reception. By using customary warfare and social networks coupled with beachcombers serving as guides, advisors and mercenaries, Kamehameha united the Hawaiian Islands and created a power base akin to a European monarchy. Isaac Davis and John Young, two seamen captured from the *Fair American*, were rewarded for their service with extensive grants of land and high-born wives. From 1802 to 1812, Young even served as governor of Hawaii Island. Kamehameha surrounded himself with beachcombers who played any number of roles: carpenters, masons, blacksmiths, oracles, priests, gardeners, doctors, jesters. He ran a fleet of thirty trading schooners so seamen, pilots, sail makers, coopers and shipwrights were always in demand. One advisor in Hawaii, Archibald Campbell, recognized it was the beachcombers' knowledge of ships and western technologies that made them valuable: '. . . the natives should be taught nothing that would render them independent of strangers . . . [or] they will soon know more than ourselves'. By the time of Charles Stewart's voyage in 1826 Kamehameha had been succeeded by his son, but otherwise little had changed in Hawaii. One 1825 visitor to Honolulu described the beachcombers as dividing each day into three parts: 'Drinking, gambling and sleeping'. Honolulu was by now one of the largest ports in the Pacific with a population of 9,000 Hawaiians and 1,000 beachcombers. There were hotels, boarding houses, billiards rooms, bowling alleys, lotteries, amateur theatricals, trade stores and countless opportunities for beachcombers as cultural go-betweens. After the horrors of the penal colony, even the thought of making landfall at such a place must have filled Stewart and the other escaped convicts with a passionate resolve.

Too passionate perhaps, because from the point of view of navigation, sailing to Hawaii had always been a difficult proposition in such a small boat. The first part of the route, as far as the equator, was the easiest and after months at sea the little sloop had yet to complete the distance. They then faced the equatorial doldrums, followed by a passage of 1,200 miles beating directly into the north-east trade winds. With the loss of this last man in Fiji, Stewart now abandoned the plan to reach Hawaii altogether.

Instead, he determined to follow the route William Bligh had taken in the open launch after the mutiny on the *Bounty*. Bligh, too, had come through Fiji, then headed north-west via the Banks Islands to Torres Strait and on to the Dutch settlement at Timor. Stewart sailed north-west for 800 miles until a high, craggy island was sighted some time in May 1827. Cautiously, the open boat closed the shore. Suddenly, as the convicts dragged the longboat over the fringing reef and up onto the beach the islanders came flooding down the sand. But something was different here: they were waving palm fronds and entreating the men to land.

More than six months had passed since Stewart had fled Van Diemen's Land. The stolen sloop had covered 5,400 miles of open ocean, nearly twice the distance of Bligh's post-*Bounty* voyage. By now the little longboat had started to fall apart, while the men themselves were malnourished and exhausted after an uninterrupted series of hardships. Even if they could navigate Torres Strait and reach Timor, they faced the real possibility of being sent back to England and re-transported to Van Diemen's Land. Unlike Bligh, Charles Stewart had no ship's papers or commission with which to defend his honour and character.

John Young, beachcomber adviser to Kamehameha I and later governor of Hawaii. From a drawing by Jacques Arago in Louis de Freycinet, *Voyage autour du Monde*, 1827

The five men all agreed that this island was markedly different from any they had yet encountered. Better still, it was very small and offered only a temporary anchorage: European ships were unlikely to call here and it might remain beyond the reach of the law indefinitely. The escaped convicts decided they would sail no further. If a ship ever did arrive here Stewart would have to rely on his powers of persuasion: he would tell a story that the group were survivors of a ship which had sunk with the loss of all other hands and so quickly that no identification had been secured. Charles Stewart and his men had arrived at the tiny Polynesian island of Tikopia.

I hadn't mentioned Tikopia to Harold, the customs officer in the Banks Islands, saying only that I was bound for Australia. Charles Stewart's prediction that Tikopia would remain beyond the reach of the law has proved partly accurate: it is the only island I know of in the South Pacific where western conventions of clearing customs and immigration do not apply. Tikopia is still governed by its chiefs and it is to them that any visiting sailor must apply for permission to land.

Tikopia is an island apart in other ways. When the peoples of Oceania migrated into the Pacific basin they did so from west to east, populating the westernmost islands of Melanesia first, and later inhabiting the eastern islands of Polynesia. Geographically, Tikopia is part of Melanesia but culturally the population is Polynesian. For reasons that aren't entirely clear the Tikopia 'back-migrated' from the Polynesian heartlands, sailing west against the general flow of migration about 1,000 years ago. Today the island is technically part of the Solomons, but it is largely autonomous, its Polynesian inhabitants surrounded by a Melanesian archipelago. The island's culture has evolved far removed from the main currents of Polynesian society that lie more than 1,000 miles to the south-east in Samoa and Tonga. Today the island has no airstrip, no wharf, no white residents, no electricity and no telephones. The Tikopia have been called 'museum pieces' and 'human anachronisms'. Ethnographers see the island as a crucible for the study of an untouched Polynesian culture.

It is also an island where beachcombers and castaways have long been washed up. Beachcombers had the knack, born of desperation, of winkling out a friendly shore.

By midday the trade had climbed above ten knots. I hoisted the light number one genoa and set a more purposeful course to the north-east. A few white caps were fizzing on the lazy swells and the sun was now strong among broken cloud. Just behind the sloop the last foaming remnants of its wake spanned the entire Banks group, from Mere Lava in the south to Ureparapara in the north. Ahead, the skyline was empty.

By twilight the trade was at 15 knots. As the sloop drove over the deepening swells, heavy bursts of spray were thrown into the big genoa, threatening to split the foot of the sail. I released the sheet and climbed to the foredeck, pulling the cracking canvas to the deck as the boat lost way and pitched benignly on the seas. Drizzle had set in again; the stars were obscured by cloud. I let out a portion of the furling headsail and spent a few minutes tinkering with the steering vane until the sloop was again balanced on its course.

Close reaching is my favourite tack – the wind just forward of the beam, the sails drawing hard, the boat surging over the swells. On no other point of sail is the power created by wind in canvas so apparent. On a small boat in the deep ocean there is pleasure in this wilful rampage into the opposing forces of wind and water. But on the passage to Tikopia the pleasure lay deeper than this. I knew that this was probably a once-in-a-lifetime voyage. Tikopia was so remote it was unlikely I would ever come back this way. And there was a sense that this was a passage through time as well as space. I suspected that making landfall on Tikopia was as close as I could get in the present day to experiencing Pacific voyaging as it might have been for the first Europeans in this ocean; of seeing and feeling what the beachcombers saw and felt as they stepped from the surf.

I slept little that night. For a moment between showers in the early evening the incoherent outline of a ship was smeared onto the horizon. After that the darkness was complete. Through the night I searched to find a skyline, but saw nothing more distant than soapy seas pouring round the stanchions as the sloop heeled to the trade.

In the months before my voyage Tikopia had made an unlikely appearance in the news. In late December 2002 the island was hit by tropical Cyclone Zoe. It was a category 5 storm, the highest rank in the scale, producing sustained winds of 180 knots and 10-metre swells. In New Zealand I read a newspaper report about a local anthropologist, Judy MacDonald, who had worked on Tikopia and was now trying to organize a relief ship. This was more difficult than it might sound. The Solomon Islands had no fuel and for many days it was uncertain if a ship would sail at all.

I wrote to Dr MacDonald at the University of Waikato offering the services of my own sloop. This offer was hardly the answer to all her prayers and I said as much in my letter: I wasn't leaving for several months and anyway the five-ton yacht could carry little in the way of supplies; but perhaps she might have something for me to take to Tikopia? She phoned two days later and asked me to take two sacks filled with clothes and tools to give to the family she had 'belonged to' while living on the island. It wasn't possible, she explained, to live on Tikopia without 'belonging' to a family. The sacks were sent up to my home on Waiheke Island and I stowed them in the sloop's forepeak, the airless V at the very front of the boat. Once at sea, they had soon been buried beneath sails, the dinghy, warps and other stores for the four-month voyage. Now, in the early hours of the morning, with Tikopia just below the horizon, I wriggled up into the forepeak to find the sacks. It was often damp in the forepeak. Wet sails were stuffed in here in squalls; moisture came in with the anchor chain. With no through-draught it rarely dried out. When I dug them out from beneath the crush of gear, the two plastic sacks were dappled with mould and the heavy tape with which they were bound was beginning to perish. The simple address, though, was still clear to read: 'Vairiki. Tikopia. South Pacific Ocean.'

A mob was waiting on the beach. About fifty naked children came wading hungrily into the lagoon as I paddled the kayak over the fringing reef. After months in Melanesia the contrast in these

Polynesian children was obvious. Their skin was the colour of copper. The hair of some was bleached blond. Most had flowers in their ears, or a tightly rolled leaf to stretch open the hole bored in the lobe. They swarmed around the kayak, rubbing its smooth deck until there was almost no part of it not covered by competing fingers. When I climbed out they hoisted the boat onto their shoulders and carried it from the water in accordance with Polynesian custom. I thought of Charles Stewart and his fellow escaped convicts coming ashore here 176 years earlier after an open-boat voyage of more than 5,000 miles. As I waded through the lagoon towards the beach the children slipped their sandy hands into mine. Others took hold of my clothes, wrists and elbows; like a chain gang bound together, we shuffled up onto dry land.

Dugouts had surrounded the sloop as soon as I'd dropped anchor. These boats came ashore now bringing the sacks I was delivering for the New Zealand anthropologist, and other gifts of my own. Boys threw the sacks onto their shoulders and we walked up the dazzling sand towards the shade of palm and casuarina trees.

It was here behind the beach at Faea that Tikopia's most famous foreign resident, the New Zealand-born anthropologist Sir Raymond Firth, had made his home in the 1920s. Apart from the beachcombers, Firth is the only white man to have lived here for an extended period. He returned many times and wrote a total of ten books about the island. His classic work, *We the Tikopia* (1936), is today thought to be the most comprehensive study of a pre-literate people to have been compiled. When Firth died in 2002 his official obituary described him as the father of modern British anthropology.

Tikopia is governed by its four hereditary chiefs, or *arikis*, each of whom presides over a separate district. In the 1920s Firth had come under the jurisdiction of Ariki Tafua, the number two chief and headman of this district of Faea, and as my anchor was sunk in Ariki Tafua's lagoon, the same was true of me. I owed the chief tribute. Firth described the incumbent in his own time as a '. . . strong willed old man with an eye for the main chance'. His grandson had clearly inherited the same characteristics. Ariki Tafua showed little enthusiasm for the gift I had brought. Instead, he told me he had a severe headache, a boil and a sore knee. Did I have any Aspirin on the boat? I brought him half-a-dozen Codeine and a brace of Valium. After that Ariki Tafua was always pleased to see me.

When I crawled back into the sunshine the boys were waiting. They heaved the sacks I had brought from the New Zealand anthropologist onto their shoulders and we set off to find the Vairiki family on the far side of the island. The path led through rich volcanic gardens divided by coral block walls. Villagers were everywhere at work, stripped to the waist, replanting beds of yams, *taro* and bananas washed away by mudslides caused by Cyclone Zoe. As we walked down the twisting path, dozens of people could be seen at any one time. I hadn't seen this sort of population density anywhere in Vanuatu outside the capital. On Tikopia the struggle had always been to balance the population with the food supply. In *We the Tikopia* Firth captures the sometimes suffocating intensity of 1,200 people living crammed together on an ocean-girt island from which the only means of escape was death. He records several incidents of suicide, particularly among those disappointed in love, usually achieved by swimming alone out to sea.

Tikopia's geography is simple and stunning. The island is a volcanic cone, the crater filled with fresh water to form a lake, locally named Te Roto. On the windward side, one section of the crater wall was blown away by a later eruption and the lake is only separated from the sea by a broad sandbank a few metres above the waves. Before the cyclone this sandbank had been the site of the largest village, shaded by breadfruit and coconut trees. But when we came out onto the beach I saw this whole area had been devastated by ten-metre ocean swells. Piles of fallen, greying timber stretched far into the distance.

The Vairiki family had lived here before the storm, but their house had been destroyed along with most of the others. The site where they had chosen to rebuild was on the far side of the crater lake, near the sacred *marae* at Uta. My guides returned with an outrigger canoe and we pushed off across the cold, deep waters of the lake. The crater walls rose almost vertically on three sides, the raw blue disk of the sky like a lid overhead. White, long-tailed *tekiake* birds circled on the thermals. The boys barely used their paddles: the trade wind coming off the ocean swept over the water and pressed the little boat inland.

There is no part of Tikopia from where the breakers on the reef cannot be either seen or heard. The ocean is ever present in the islanders' lives. The terms 'inland' and 'seaward' are used for all sorts of spatial reference on Tikopia. Firth described being in the gardens one day when he heard a man say to another: 'There is a spot of mud on your seaward cheek.' The houses are divided into two parts: inland/profane and seaward/sacred. By tradition, the dead are wrapped in bark cloth and interred beneath the sand floor of the family home on the seaward side. In the cyclone some houses had been so badly damaged that bones had been brought to the surface.

Outside the Vairiki's house at Uta I called a greeting, then crawled on hands and knees through the tiny doorway. Inside, the air was still, heavy with smoke. Even beneath the dense thatch, the rumble of distant surf was still audible. It is rare to use personal names for married couples on Tikopia and I called my hosts Pa (Mr) and Nau (Mrs) Vairiki. I watched them open the sacks I had brought and carefully pick through the buckets, knives, fishing tackle, torches, towels and clothes. Two elderly women were sitting against the wall on the inland/profane side of the house, smoking pipes. Their jawbones were etched with tattoos; further bird and fish motives adorned the skin around the corners of their eyes. A single tattooed line extended down their throats, between their breasts, and under the wraps around their waists. When Pa Vairiki had finished going through the gifts he put them aside with a nod, but said nothing. Reciprocity and gift-giving are taken for granted on the island. There is no word in the Tikopian language for 'thank you'.

It was hot and hushed under the thick sago thatch. The floor was springy with many layers of woven matting. Having sat up on watch much of the night I felt myself starting to doze off to sleep on the floor. The Vairikis seemed quite at ease with this and sent a small boy to sit over me and fan away the flies. When I woke an hour later, nothing had changed.

Nau Vairiki served us a meal. In an earth oven she had baked *taro* and yam tubers to form a starch, which she then pounded in a carved pudding bowl to make a sticky paste known as *kai tao*. She mixed this with coconut cream made by grating and then wringing out the hard white flesh of mature coconuts. In ordinary times such a meal would be commonplace, but today it represented a considerable honour as almost all the island's coconut trees had been destroyed in Cyclone Zoe. The pudding was served with *nukunuku*, a fish found in the cool waters of the crater lake. The boy continued to fan me throughout the meal while the Vairikis asked for news of Judy MacDonald. It was more than 20 years since the anthropologist had lived in their home, but every time her name was mentioned Nau Vairiki's beetlenut-stained lips spread into a smile.

At the time of my visit to Tikopia I had not met Judy MacDonald. But when I returned home to Waiheke Island after the voyage I phoned her to say I had safely delivered her gifts to the island. It turned out that Judy had worked with Raymond Firth at the London School of Economics. 'I think I pissed Raymond off,' she told me on the telephone. 'You couldn't get onto the island in those days without his say-so. God knows what'll happen now he's dead.' A few days later I drove down to Hamilton to meet her.

Perhaps the most valuable legacy left by the Pacific beachcombers was their written descriptions of everyday life in the islands. Beachcombers lived as family members, took wives and fathered children, learned the local language, observed the ceremonies and participated in almost every aspect of daily life. They arrived in the islands with the first ships, stayed longer than any other sailors, and left an unmatched written record of Pacific cultures at the time of first contact. The narratives of Edward Robarts, James Morrison, George Vason, William Mariner, Samuel Patterson and several others amount to works of amateur anthropology. Perhaps the finest of these accounts is that narrating the experiences of William Mariner in Tonga. As a 14-year-old clerk on the *Port au Prince*, Mariner was one of the few crew members who survived when the Tongans seized the ship in November 1806. He subsequently lived as a beachcomber in Tonga for more than four years. When he finally stepped ashore at Gravesend in June 1811 Mariner was immediately seized by a press gang and held captive for some time before he could secure his release. In London, he then met Dr John Martin, a man who '. . . thought it a great desideratum to obtain, if possible, an intimate and domestic history of an uncivilized people. I mean such a history as would introduce the reader . . . with the genius of their language, their intellectual and moral character, their ordinary discourses, sentiments and habits.' Martin was a friend of the London publisher John Murray and, based on extensive interviews with William Mariner, Murray published his *Account of the Natives of the Tonga Islands* in 1817. The second volume narrating Mariner's four-year residence in Tonga is comprised solely of ethnographic notes and a 2,000-word vocabulary of 'genuine Tonga words'.

Beachcombers were often the first to transcribe Pacific languages. Boultbee drew up a crude phonetic Maori vocabulary and Campbell did the same in Hawaii. A much more comprehensive vocabulary of the Tahitian language was compiled by the beachcomber Peter Heywood which was, according to the Second Secretary to the Admiralty, Sir John Barrow, 'a very extraordinary performance; it consists of one hundred full-written folio pages, the words alphabetically arranged, and all the syllables accented'. A copy of Heywood's vocabulary was carried by the missionaries on the *Duff*, one of whom thought it 'more useful than every aid besides'; the missionaries preached the gospel with words first transcribed by the same beachcombers they so greatly despised.

In the twentieth century, scientific anthropology arrived in the Pacific Islands with the coming of the Polish-born ethnographer Bronislaw Malinowski, and his student Raymond Firth. Both men adopted some of the beachcombers' unwitting methodology. At the outbreak of the First World War Malinowski was conducting fieldwork in the Trobriand Islands. Since he was Polish born the Australian authorities wanted to intern him as an enemy alien, but Malinowski persuaded them to leave him where he was; he could do little harm in the remote Trobriands. As a result he spent several years living on the beach and wrote about the importance for anthropologists of immersion in the culture they were studying: living as a family member, eating local food and, most important of all, speaking the local language. By the time Judy MacDonald arrived at Tikopia in 1979, this was mainstream practice for anthropologists.

When I reached Hamilton I found that Judy's house was in a leafy avenue close to the university. We sat at a polished mahogany table and she served smoked salmon roulade, leftovers from the dinner party the night before. And for a moment I couldn't quite place this. I remembered the heat and sweat beneath the domed thatch roof of the Vairikis' house, the total lack of privacy, the swarms of flies by day and mosquitoes after dark. I wondered how Judy MacDonald had swapped this comfortable suburban home for a grass hut; smoked salmon roulade for bony *nukunuku*. Had it been hard, I asked her, to adjust to the Tikopia's way of life. But she dismissed the question with a wave of her hand. 'Oh you get used to it,' she said. 'You can't sanitize the environment out in the field.'

I asked her about the character of the islanders. I'd taken many photographs and noticed that they seemed to love posing. Even when I was putting the camera away they continued to gaze heroically at the horizon. 'I might have read this wrong,' I said, 'but are they rather vain?'

'Oh, they have a terrifically high opinion of themselves,' she laughed. 'Although they are Polynesians they share some Melanesian characteristics, particularly their insularity. I remember once I was trying to describe an elephant to a group of women on the island and I heard one whisper to another, "What nonsense! She always tells lies." Remember that much of their contact with the outside world has been with anthropologists like Raymond Firth who have found everything they do absolutely fascinating. *Of course* you want to take our photographs, that would be their view, we are the Tikopia. You know where the title of Raymond's book comes from? They would always be telling him, "We the Tikopia think this, We the Tikopia think that, We the Tikopia believe something else." They have always considered themselves pretty special and since Raymond made them famous it's only got worse. There is plenty of justification for it – they're highly intelligent and confident. Seven little boys were taken from the island to Honiara in the 1950s. By the 1980s they were a bishop, the comptroller of customs, the chief of police, and the rest were headmasters. Today in Honiara, the Tikopia are all over the prime minister's office, they're in the church, and they're doctors. If they get off the island and get an education they do extremely well. But their sense of superiority hasn't always made them popular in the rest of the Solomons.'

The telephone rang several times during our conversation. It was the car mechanic trying to source spare parts for her Jaguar. Judy MacDonald put her hand over the mouthpiece and said to me, 'A few years ago I was waiting for a hip replacement operation, blasted out of my mind on opiates, so bought the Jag to cheer myself up. Getting the thing fixed has turned out to be nothing but a curse.'

I remembered her telling me on the telephone that she had pissed off Raymond Firth and I asked why. 'Well, Raymond wanted to say that women had real status on Tikopia. They were *tapu* or sacred, so you mustn't hit a woman for example – it was all very Victorian, preserving the vessel in which you breed. He argued that there was genuine sexual equality on the island but my research didn't support this. The women on Tikopia are infantilized. They use a very simple vocabulary, "the cat sat on the mat", that sort of thing.'

When I mentioned the division of the houses into 'inland' and 'seaward' parts she said, 'It's actually more complex than that. The houses are divided into an inland/profane/female side and a seaward/sacred/male side. Tikopia is not like other Polynesian islands in this respect, where women have a much higher status. You know the *mahu* of Tahiti or the *fa'afafine* of Samoa – boys are raised as girls. You don't get that on Tikopia – who'd want to be a girl? They're much more Melanesian in that respect. They have the Melanesian hang-up about menstruation. By the time you get up to Papua New Guinea they're hysterical about it.'

I knew the effect of the arrival of Christianity in Vanuatu and asked Judy MacDonald if the missionaries had been similarly influential in Tikopia. 'They wear their religion fairly lightly. The first missionary didn't arrive until about 1911 – very late – and he was from the Reef Islands – they wouldn't have a white missionary. They didn't finally convert until 1956 and took a cavalier approach to the whole thing. They thought the Catholics were a bit funny because the priests didn't get married. They weren't sure about the Seventh Day Adventists because there were too many dietary restrictions – they didn't like the sound of that at all! Anglicans seemed the least bothersome, so in the end they went with them.

'Tikopia was really a lovely, easy place to work. After I came back from the London School of Economics I couldn't get a university position straight away so in the end I took a job working on a luxury cruise ship. It was quite a small ship, very exclusive, caviar and champagne for breakfast, all of that stuff. All the passengers were extremely rich Germans. We cruised around the Pacific Islands and every evening I gave a talk, a few anthropological aspects of the places we were visiting, but mostly fluff stuff – "Tribes I Have Known: a Woman Anthropologist's Adventures in the Savage South Seas" – you know, that kind of thing. But honestly, living on Tikopia for a year was a delight. Wealthy German tourists are much the most difficult tribe I have ever worked with.'

Tikopia has always been a backwater. The island is removed from the main currents of its own Polynesian culture, and was also largely bypassed by the process of European exploration. Quiros sighted the island in 1606 but otherwise none of the great voyages of discovery came this way. Tikopia's exposure to the west came with a later and altogether different breed of sailor. Most of the island's early contact was with the Irish trader and beachcomber, Peter Dillon.

Dillon is usually remembered as the man who discovered the fate of the expedition of the celebrated French explorer Jean François de la Pérouse at Vanikoro Island in 1788, 120 miles northwest of Tikopia. But the pages of his two-volume *Narrative and Successful Result of a Voyage to the South Seas* (1829) record numerous other brushes with castaways and illustrate the extent of the role played by castaways and beachcombers in Pacific voyaging.

Peter Dillon was born in Martinique in 1788, the son of an Irish immigrant from County Meath. He joined the Royal Navy as a midshipman and served at the Battle of Trafalgar, but brawling sometimes marred his career and he left the navy and sailed to India. In 1808 he voyaged on the *General Wellesley* to the Pacific and reached the south-west corner of Vanua Levu, the largest island in Fiji. Just four years earlier this area had been virtually unknown to Europeans. It was a drab stretch of scrubby hillsides, mangrove-lined bays and tidal river deltas. Then castaways from the wrecked ship *Argo* struggled ashore through the surf and found green gold growing on the arid hillsides: forests of sandalwood trees. Almost overnight the 'Sandalwood Coast' at Bua Bay attracted ships – and beachcombers – from around the Pacific basin.

At Bua Bay Dillon himself went to live on the beach, obtaining cargoes of sandalwood for visiting ships. This was beachcombing in its classic sense, an agency for the tortuous process of negotiating for timber. Peter Dillon haunted a metaphorical beach: he was an intermediary between two worlds. Chameleon-like, the beach-combers slid back and forth along a continuum between two cultures: the indigenous life of the island, and the copper-sheathed universe of the ship anchored in the lagoon. In anthropologists' jargon these beachcombers were 'transculturists'. They lived among the Fijians, spoke their language ('Beetee' as Dillon called it), abided by their taboos, and were dressed and tattooed like islanders. As such, beachcombers were of incalculable value to trading skippers because they understood the violent and complex world of Fijian tribal politics. Beachcombers knew best how to play one chief off against his rivals and orchestrate the delicate balance of persuasions and threats necessary to initiate trade. Peter Dillon was a master of the art. In one three-week period he obtained 150 tons of sandalwood for about £30 worth of trade goods. At this time sandalwood fetched £80 a ton on the coast of China so Dillon's haul was worth £12,000 – a considerable sum in the 1800s. The beachcombers, however, were paid only scraps. In reality, the beach was often a trap and the men who haunted it were caught between two worlds, trusted by neither. Life on the beach was brutal, often short. Having learnt the ropes for four months, Peter Dillon got out and again took passage on a ship.

Only a matter of weeks later more castaways landed in Fiji after the brig *Eliza* was wrecked on Mocea Reef. On board the *Eliza* at the time of the wreck were more than 30,000 Spanish dollars, numerous muskets, and a man later dubbed 'the most notorious beachcomber in the Pacific', Charlie Savage. The only account of the wreck was left by another of the crew, Samuel Patterson, who described how, on the night of 20 June 1808, the *Eliza* was sailing among the Fiji Islands when 'the man who had the lookout on the forecastle, seeing breakers just ahead, cried out with the greatest vehemence, and gave us the alarm . . . But before we could get on deck the vessel struck the rocks.' The seamen cut away the masts, one of which broke the whaleboat in two as it fell, 'but we got the long boat out and put the money in it to the amount of

34,000 dollars, the navigating implements, muskets, a cask of powder and balls . . .' Next day, the long boat came ashore at Nairai Island, nine miles distant from the site of the wreck. As the castaways walked up the beach they were surrounded by Fijians who stripped them naked. But most alarming for Patterson was the loss of his identity papers. One Fijian 'took off my hat, in which was my pocket book, which contained my protection and other papers . . . they took the papers and rolled them up and put them thro' the holes in the rims of their ears and wore them off'. For Patterson, life on the beach only truly began with the loss of his papers.

In the aftermath of the wreck the castaways broke up into different groups. Some, such as Patterson, were held captive at Nairai. The captain and most of the officers were taken off by another ship. But according to Peter Dillon's account, some others, including Charlie Savage, managed to escape and fled into the islands with as many dollars and muskets as they could carry. Over the following months other sandalwooders deserted and went hunting for the dollars now scattered throughout the Fiji Islands. All brought guns and powder and '. . . were on that account thought highly of by the Islanders, from among whom they procured wives and lived very comfortably'.

At Bau, Charlie Savage became a personal favourite of Naulivou, the *Vunivalu*, or high chief, primarily by offering his services as a gun for hire. With Savage and other beachcombers now among their number, Ratu Naulivou ordered an attack on the enemy strongholds at Nakelo and other towns. For the beach-combers armed with muskets, these engagements against men equipped with spears and clubs presented few risks. Fijian oral trad-ition remembers piles of corpses and riverbanks stained with blood while the beachcombers fired with impunity from behind barricades. For the beachcombers the rewards were many. The exact number of Charlie Savage's wives is unclear, but he certainly had several, one of whom, Kapua, was a woman of rank, being the daughter of the chiefly line of Roko Tui Bau.

One description of Charlie Savage's power was written by the castaway whaleman William Cary, who lived in Fiji in the years after the beachcomber's death: 'The king then made him head chief, giving him command of the whole tribe, and he conquered the entire group, but he was very severe with the natives and would shoot them for the most trivial offences.'

This was the situation that Peter Dillon found in Fiji when he returned in 1813 as third mate on the *Hunter*. What is apparent from Dillon is that Savage was just one of many beachcombers at Bau. Among that group was the Prussian seaman Martin Buchert, a Chinese cook named Luis, a Lascar deserter whom the sailors called Joe, Thomas Dafny a castaway, McCabe and Atkin, both deserters from the *City of Edinburgh*, a Tahitian, a Tongan, and at least one escaped convict from New South Wales.

Dillon found that the presence of this armed gang had changed the nature of the sandalwood trade beyond recognition. Now the chiefs spurned trade goods; the price of sandalwood was war. The chiefs expected sandalwood crews to work as mercenaries on their behalf and Captain Robson of the *Hunter* had little option but to agree. Peter Dillon was among the twenty sailors armed with muskets who manned three of the *Hunter*'s boats, one of which was mounted with a cannon. They were accompanied by a fleet of forty-six canoes which carried a thousand armed men for a proposed attack on the fortified island of Bekavu while a still larger Fijian force travelled overland. Bekavu was razed and the corpses of the dead were 'despatched in a fast-sailing canoe' to provide a feast for the chiefs on the Sandalwood Coast.

However, in return for this attack the *Hunter* secured only 150 tons of timber, one-third of the full cargo Robson believed he'd been promised. His attempt to assert his authority over the recalcitrant chiefs only provoked an attack on a shore party – made up of his own sailors together with Charlie Savage's beachcomber gang – in which fourteen of the men were killed.

Among the survivors were Peter Dillon and the core of the beachcomber gang. This group were now cut off from the ship and, according to Dillon, surrounded by Fijians who 'stood in thousands on each side of the path'. Norman was speared and killed. Dafny's shoulder was pierced by a spear and four arrows stuck in his back. Luis was killed with a heavy war club. Charlie Savage was 'seized by the legs, and held in that state by six men, with his head placed in a well of fresh water until he suffocated'.

As night was falling Dillon made the safety of the sandalwood cutter *Elizabeth* together with the remains of the now decimated gang: the Prussian Martin Buchert and Joe the Lascar. Dillon assumed command of the *Elizabeth* and put to sea, but for six days the ship was thwarted by calms while still within sight of land. Dillon described how both of the beachcombers were miserable to find themselves back aboard ship and 'begged to be landed on the first coast we met with'. When the trade finally built the *Elizabeth* sailed north-west. A week later, on 20 September 1813, Dillon sighted a small and unusual looking island. It was a volcano with one section of the crater missing that appeared on no charts. The island was Tikopia.

Dillon brought the *Elizabeth* to anchor in a bight in the fringing reef. Soon the Tikopia were climbing all over the ship. Dillon wrote that they were unarmed ' but very wild' and he assumed they had never seen white men before, which was virtually the case. 'They came on deck without reserve, seized upon bars of iron from the forge, and jumped overboard . . .' One man was carrying off the ship's compass when a Fijian woman aboard the ship seized 'him by the throat with one hand and by the privates with another [and] in this way got him under her, where she certainly would have strangled him, had I not interfered'.

However, after an exchange of gifts good relations were established and the two beachcombers, Martin Buchert and Joe the Lascar, insisted on being put ashore. Dillon protested that the island was quite unknown and their reception uncertain, but in the end he reluctantly consented. Dillon sailed west that evening and eventually reached Sydney.

Peter Dillon did not return to Tikopia for 13 years. He reached the island in May 1826 as captain of the *St Patrick* and was curious to know the fate of the two beachcombers he had abandoned here. Even while the *St Patrick* was still out of soundings, canoes put out from the beach at Faea. Joe the Lascar was standing in the bows of the lead boat but had no recollection of the captain. Dillon wrote that communication was very hard as Joe's 'conversation was composed of a mixture of Bengalee, English, Beetee [Fijian] and the Tucopia [Tikopia] dialects'. Martin Buchert was in the following canoe. He too failed to recognize Dillon until reminded of their flight after the massacre at Fiji 13 years earlier. Buchert said that no ship had called at Tikopia for the first 11 years, since when three whalers had visited. Neither of the beachcombers had considered being taken off.

Dillon returned to Tikopia in September the following year for the third and final time. He came in command of the *Research* on a voyage sponsored by the East India Company to make one last search for La Pérouse. When he came ashore Dillon found a group of five new beachcombers were now living on the island. These men had arrived a few months earlier, half-starved, in a battered open boat. Their leader, a man named Charles Stewart, claimed to be mate of the ship *Mary* of Liverpool commanded by Captain Williams. According to Stewart, the *Mary* had foundered at sea with the loss of the captain and all other hands. The ship had sunk so quickly that no papers or other means of identification had been secured. Stewart and four other survivors had reached Tikopia after a desperate voyage in one of the open boats.

The Prussian beachcomber Martin Buchert didn't trust these castaways and asked Dillon to take them off the island. Dillon didn't believe the men's story either, suspecting they were escaped convicts from Botany Bay or Van Diemen's Land. But he liked Charles Stewart, describing him as a 'shrewd young man, about twenty-five years of age, with a good understanding, improved by tolerable plain education'. Like many other ship's captains in the Pacific, Dillon was short of crew. Whether Stewart was a genuine wreck survivor or an escapee, he had certainly once been a ship's officer and Dillon recruited him to join the crew of the *Research*.

When the *Research* quit Melanesian waters some weeks later Charles Stewart sought leave to stay in the islands. He had made friends ashore and intended to embark with them in an indigenous canoe. For Stewart, this option was preferable to staying on board the ship and risking being re-transported to Van Diemen's Land. Dillon agreed. Charles Stewart was never heard from again.

The last reference I found to Dillon dates from 1834, seven years after his final voyage to Tikopia. He was seen in Sydney by Thomas Jefferson Jacobs, midshipman on the trading brig *Margaret Oakley*, still keeping the company of beachcombers and Kanaka seamen. Jacobs wrote in his journal: 'A handsome and trim little clipper sloop lay anchored in Neutral Roads; she was owned and commanded by Captain Dillon . . . a large, fat, jolly man, and had with him a tattooed savage'. Dillon still sailed the ocean's backwaters: 'He traded to nameless islands, and still finds his business very profitable . . .'

Peter Dillon's anchorage at Tikopia is the only one the island boasts. Under the lee of a prominent bluff on the crater wall there is a bight in the fringing reef. The water is deep, as clear as the open ocean. The bight is surprisingly free from ground swell although a dirty wind falls down from the peaks overhead. If the wind shifts out of the east, this is a weather shore and you must put to sea.

Nestled at the base of the cliffs, thatched roofs were visible among the palms. For several hours after dawn the beach was still in shadow. Through the first smoky light of day, black figures could be seen bathing in the grey waters of the lagoon.

Every morning at Tikopia I was greeted with the same overwhelming raptures. As soon as I slid the kayak from the sloop's deck there was a roar from the beach and a group of about fifty children ran splashing down into the lagoon. As I came ashore they held the canoe aloft and, chanting, carried it above the tide.

Then it disappeared into the village. When I came back later in the day it was only necessary to stand for a moment on the sand before a platoon of naked tots trotted from the grass houses with the kayak held on their heads.

Late one morning I was sitting with Pa Vairiki on the summit of the peak which towers over the island, called Reani, or *Te Uru o te Fenua* – the Head of the Land. As Raymond Firth put it, 'Many an ocean rover has expressed in song his feelings of the instant when Reani, the Head of the Land, is buried beneath the waves, or conversely when on his return it breaks once more into view, assuring him of his course and of an end to his wanderings.'

From the summit of Reani it was clear how monstrously impractical Tikopia was as a place to live. The total land area is less than three square miles and much of that is precipitous. The lives of the islanders have always been utterly dominated by the daily imperative of finding enough food to stay alive. A wealthy man is *taŋata kai kai lasi* – a 'man who eats greatly'. A long life was the only measure of prosperity.

After ten centuries living on this vertiginous rock the Tikopia learned it could sustain a population of 1,200 people and no more. In pre-Christian times only eldest sons were allowed to marry and have children. There was no taboo on sex: others were free to take as many lovers as they liked, but any progeny were killed. Even so, starvation in the aftermath of cyclones was commonplace. Firth recalled how in one famine a chief took his young sons out to sea in a canoe so as not to be a burden on precious food supplies. An ancient song of Tikopia refers to drowning at sea as 'sweet burial'.

Now the islanders' days are filled with gardening and fishing. The Tikopia swarmed all over their blue-bordered rock, digging gardens on any ledge where soil had formed. From the summit of Reani I occasionally caught sight of them, stick figures glued to the emerald outer flanks with breakers foaming on the reef beneath their heels. When Pa Vairiki saw I was impressed by this he pointed out more. 'Look friend, there, look,' and after a moment's fruitless stare I would see a man tilling the soil on a giddy-making slope, the black waters of the crater lake 300 metres below. 'Over here, brother, look here.' In *We the Tikopia* the islanders' dialogue is usually prefixed with the word 'friend', especially when they are addressing Firth himself. 'Friend, is there any land where the sound of the sea is not heard?' In the five days I spent at Tikopia I was never once called by name, only 'friend' or 'brother'.

That morning a young man named Michael had greeted me on the beach. I'd met him the previous night when we'd paddled outriggers far into the island's lee and scooped up flying fish attracted by the hissing light from hurricane lamps. Michael gave me a *taonga* – a treasure – a carved pearl-shell pendant, and asked me to become his 'friend'. When I told Pa Vairiki about this as we sat together he looked slightly disapproving and explained in broken English that if I were to form a 'friendship' on the island, it should be with a man of rank, not a commoner.

This question of 'friends' and 'friendship' crops up constantly in the Pacific Islands. Indeed, in today's tourism industry it is so constant as to have become almost meaningless. However, at the time the first European ships ventured into the islands it meant a very great deal. Captain Cook, Joseph Banks and Johann Reinhold Forster all recognized its importance. It was so prevalent that Cook named the group centred around Tongatapu 'The Friendly Islands'. The Polynesian institution of 'bond friendship' has no direct equivalent in western culture. It was the product of those island societies that revolved around the needs of sailors and castaways.

The Polynesian world had never been a closed one. The Tikopia had regularly voyaged 120 miles to the neighbouring island of Vanikoro, returning with turtle-shell ornaments, arrow-heads and the *Canarium* almond. The practice of attaching feather lures to bonito hooks was introduced from Tuvalu, 600 miles to the north-east. The Tikopia's experiences at sea are remembered in many of their songs and laments: the loss of a famous Tikopian, Pa Veterei, and a great fleet of canoes near the Banks Islands; one of Ariki Tafua's ancestors drifting disabled for many days on a passage from Vanikoro. Some families on the island trace their ancestry back to the arrival of drift voyagers and castaways.

In this fluid world of sea travel and landfalls the arrival of strangers in boats had once been an accepted part of life in the islands, and Polynesian cultures developed social mechanisms for the rapid assimilation of visiting sailors and castaways, notably through adoption and marriage. The crews of Louis Antoine de Bougainville and Captain Cook all reported that Polynesian women, especially at Tahiti, were unreserved about entering into sexual relations with few preliminaries. Some of these women were little more than girls. The response from European sailors was unequivocal; competition was fierce to sail on ships bound for the South Seas. William Bligh had little difficulty recruiting crew for the *Bounty*. One of his seamen, James Morrison, had previously been a midshipman but was prepared to suffer a reduction in rank simply to be included on the crew list; on the *Bounty* Morrison sailed as boatswain's mate.

James Morrison ended up living on the beach at Tahiti where the institution of 'bond friendship' was known as *taio*, a connection between men so strong that they swapped names and social identities. As Morrison put it, 'We were treated like the rest of the Family, but with more attention and respect.' It was perfectly acceptable to sleep with the wife of your *taio*; indeed, it was considered rude not to. So close was the bond of friendship, however, that it was usually taboo to sleep with your *taio*'s children; it would have amounted to incest.

Inevitably, as ships called more frequently at the main centres like Tahiti the institution of *taio* could not keep pace with the numbers of arrivals. Today, it is only in the most remote islands like Tikopia that sailors find residual traces of the same thing, although the sexual element has disappeared; the missionaries saw to that. But in the early 1800s *taio* affected the lives of European sailors in the Pacific every bit as much as the conditions prevailing at sea. Most of all, it determined the nature of the beach. The status and security of beachcombers and castaways was dependent on the Polynesian concept of 'friendship'.

Taio wasn't unconditional, nor was it universal. Some sailors were adopted and assimilated into tribal culture; others were killed, especially when they arrived in such numbers as to threaten the indigenous group. Here on Tikopia *taio* was known as *tau soa*. As I walked around the island I often tried to picture the lives the beachcombers might have led here. The only option was conjecture, as few facts were known. I had asked the anthropologist Judy MacDonald if she knew what had become of the beachcombers. 'There was a rumour that they killed Martin Buchert,' she said, 'but I don't know that I'd believe it. There are no records at all. Dillon is the only source.'

When Peter Dillon sailed from Tikopia for the final time he tried to persuade both the Prussian Martin Buchert and Joe the Lascar to come with him: it might be their last chance. Buchert insisted that he wanted to stay on Tikopia, 'there to end his days in retirement from worldly affairs'. Joe was equally determined to stay on the island, telling Dillon that 'he had lost his caste, and would therefore be disowned by his friends and relations' if he returned to India. Both men would have been adopted by the islanders and given wives of high rank to hasten their assimilation.

Even when Judy MacDonald arrived in 1980 it was impossible to live on Tikopia independently; she *had to* 'belong' to a family. In the nineteenth century, beachcombers were often damned for having crossed the cultural divide, but in some cases they really had little choice in the matter. This was certainly the experience of E.H. Lamont in 1853 when the *Chatham* was wrecked on Penrhyn, a Polynesian island with a similar culture to that of Tikopia. The *Chatham* castaways went through a series of religious ceremonies and hours of bathing after which the women tore at their bodies with small clam-shells until 'their legs, arms and faces were streaming with blood'. At the end of the formalities, Lamont realized he had been adopted by a chief: 'The worst of it was, I soon found that I had so many relatives, even

fathers and mothers, that I was always forgetting my nearest con-
nexions [sic], and falling into ridiculous mistakes. The laws of
the island forbid marriage with any relative as near as a second
cousin; and I occasionally horrified some young lady, who
proved to be a near relation, by the tender advances which in
amorous moments I made to her.' Robarts, Morrison, Vason,
Mariner, Cary and Lockerby were all similarly adopted by chiefs.

Tattooing was often an integral part of the adoption process. In
Tonga, Vason found it was unavoidable and received a full body
tattoo: 'It was performed only every third day, the pain being so
exhausting . . . When it was completed I was very much admired
by the natives . . . I looked indeed very gay in this new fancy covering'. It's unlikely many Europeans would have thought so. Tattoos
became the insignia of the beach. A man who would permanently
change the colour of his skin aroused understandable resentment
among those whose culture he had abandoned. Tattooing was
sometimes thought to make rejoining the European world impossible. A seaman named Bruce sailing through the Marquesas in 1838
described one beachcomber he met: 'He is tattooed across the face,
and will therefore probably never return to England.' Ships' captains
and missionaries used the number of a beachcomber's tattoos as a
yardstick to gauge the extent of his depravity.

But in Polynesian culture tattooing physically identified adults
as being members of a family or tribe. It was part of the adoption
process and not something the beachcombers could necessarily
have refused. In the Caroline Islands, James O'Connell observed
that he could not take a wife until he had been tattooed. Similarly,
an English sailor named Peter Heywood who lived on the beach
in Tahiti for 18 months explained the rationale for tattooing in a
letter to his mother. 'I was tattooed, not at my own desire, but at
theirs'; an adult with no tattoos was regarded as '. . . a mere outcast
of society'. On Tikopia almost all adult men and women had
once been tattooed, regarding it as an important physical attrib-
ute and a statement of identity.

One legacy of the beachcombers was their numerous mixed-race children. On Penrhyn, Lamont had three wives. A visitor to Fiji recorded that the beachcombers lived in a state of unblushing polygamy: 'the number of their wives and women is unlimited, and it is not uncommon for two or three of them to be confined at the same time'. One Fiji beachcomber, William Diapea, could not keep count of his progeny: 'I am the reputed father of thirty-eight children and ninety-nine grandchildren.' On Tikopia the beachcombers would also have left children. When I was talking to Judy MacDonald about Martin Buchert and Joe the Lascar she said: 'Who knows, maybe all the children today have a few drops of Prussian and Indian blood.'

Most beachcombers met an unknown fate. Charles Stewart's remarkable boat voyage from Van Diemen's Land is only documented because at Tikopia he met Peter Dillon who recorded the details. I've never seen Stewart's story repeated elsewhere. Beachcombers are often no more than snippets in the accounts of other men's lives, shadows on the sand. Exactly how many there were and where they all lived and died is impossible to tell.

On my final day I saw Ariki Tafua as I was walking through the village. The chief was wearing a wrap around his waist, standing beneath a stream of water, enjoying a shower in the sunshine. He smiled enthusiastically and waved me over. The Tikopia have rigged up an ingenious system of pipes so that rainwater flowing down the crater walls is channelled to the principal villages where it emerges at communal standpipes. The chief's mane of grey hair was plastered against his scalp, neck and shoulders. Two small motifs of seabirds and fish were tattooed beneath his cheekbones. I could see more tattoos on his biceps and further marks on his back as he spun about beneath the silver stream of water. The pigment used for tattooing is made from the soot given off by burning tree gum; the chisel is crafted from the wing bone of a seabird.

The loss of interest in tattooing on Tikopia can be precisely dated. Since the island converted to Christianity in 1956 enthusiasm has waned. Ariki Tafua was in his fifties, so his skin was a living record of these changing values. A generation earlier the chief would have been heavily tattooed across the back and chest. The present Ariki Tafua had only a handful of marks. The missionaries have never liked tattooing. A common explanation heard on the island today is: 'We must not spoil God's body.'

'The ship is coming soon,' Ariki Tafua told me. 'Maybe tomorrow it will come. We hoped last week, but in the end nothing.' Where had I heard this before? The ocean was full of islanders waiting for a ship. 'Some of our people will be leaving for Honiara,' he said. 'We will have dancing in the village tonight to farewell them.' Ariki Tafua invited me to return that evening to join his family for the dancing and I promised I would come.

But as the sun set that day the wind picked up markedly from the east. Bullet squalls fell down from the crater rim so hard the sloop dipped its rail at anchor. In the gathering darkness the wind was lifting spray off the water. The anchor chain was like a solid bar.

I had anchored *Gordian* in 22 metres of water, marginally too deep for the ground tackle I carried. Worse, I could hear the chain rubbing against coral on the seabed: the holding was poor. The dancing would be starting soon. I should have been launching the kayak now to go ashore. But I couldn't leave the boat. There was little margin for error in open anchorages like the one at Tikopia. If the anchor dragged while I was ashore the sloop would drift out to sea.

An hour later the conditions had deteriorated. I decided to put to sea anyway, in good order, rather than wait to be blown out of the anchorage. As I started working at the windlass I could hear a gong being sounded from the village above the howl of the squall and the rattle of rain. I had only taken in five metres of chain when the anchor broke out and the sloop was blown off into deep water. Within a few seconds the glow of the hurricane lamps behind the beach at Faea had faded and Tikopia disappeared into the night.

I got up a double-reefed mainsail and set a course due west for the Great Barrier Reef and Torres Strait.

6

Pandora's Box

'You dam'd infernal Scoundrels'
Lieutenant William Bligh, 1789

INDISPENSABLE REEF IS a series of three large coral formations 480 miles west of Tikopia. Each of the reefs is circular, enclosing a lagoon. The channels between them are so narrow that the reefs in effect create a chain of coral stretching 60 miles from tip to tip. It is these isolated formations in an otherwise open ocean that give the Coral Sea its name and proved such a hazard to shipping before these waters were fully charted.

A strong wind and rushing swells pushed the sloop west through that first unexpected night at sea. I sat at the chart table and plotted a course from Tikopia to clear the southern tip of Indispensable Reef, my first waypoint in the eastern approaches to Torres Strait. Then I climbed out into the cockpit. The oceanscape was a warm, powerful, tight presence in the darkness. A ceiling of cloud filled the sky; there was no moon to light the way ahead. The wind was a hard, barrelling force; big seas loomed up behind the quarter, their crests slapping into the topsides. Tepid strings of spray spun into the cockpit as if coughed up from the belly of a waking beast. These were perfect, strong trade wind conditions. In the small hours of the morning I again sat at the chart table and walked the dividers across the chart. If this wind kept up, I'd reach Indispensable Reef in three days.

By dawn though, the wind had fallen lighter. Soon the rising sun was swallowed by squall cloud. For a moment it appeared as a drained disk behind the cloud, the same colour as the moon, before it disappeared altogether. The squall systems were toothless, full of rain but little wind, they shuffled without conviction across collapsing seas. The raindrops fell vertically, the empty sails shaking off plumes of water.

In the afternoon a five-knot trade pushed the last rain over the western horizon; the sloop plodded the same way in ever-easing seas. To windward the sky was now deep blue without a cloud in sight. Heat and stifling calm spread over the ocean. At twilight the blinds were pulled down on the passage: the wind failed completely and I dropped the sails to the deck.

I woke next morning to a flat calm. It was hot even before the sun had cleared the horizon and I lashed the small awning over the boom to provide shade in the cockpit. I read here for several hours but by mid-morning was becoming manic so buried myself in housework. I had to scrub the galley, food lockers and bilges before I restored any inner calm.

In the afternoon I read Peter Dillon's account of his discoveries at Vanikoro Island, 80 miles to the north-west. His ship *Research* must have crossed this same patch of ocean on the short passage from Tikopia to Vanikoro in September 1827. From discussions with the islanders at Vanikoro, and evidence he could see from himself ashore, Dillon pieced together what had happened to the ships of the celebrated French explorer Jean François de la Pérouse that had been wrecked here 39 years earlier. In a violent storm one of the ships had struck the fringing reef on the north-west side and broken up in deep water. Most of the crew drowned in the wreck and the Melanesians killed those that had struggled ashore in the surf. The second ship was driven onto the southern barrier reef, then beat over the coral into the sheltered waters of the lagoon. According to islanders' account, most of the men from this ship got ashore in good condition, still under the command of officers. A palisade was built from which the castaways undertook expeditions to fish and gather fruit. Dillon was shown a clearing of axe-hewn stumps in the forest where scores of trees had been felled. He estimated the clearing to be seven acres in extent. After many months' work the French castaways launched a two-masted boat they had been building in the forest. Dillon saw the imprint of a shallow trench down which the boat had been dragged to reach a creek leading to the sea. Several of the sailors had developed friendships and chose to remain on Vanikoro. One had subsequently become a chief, but had died some years before Dillon's visit. Another, a commoner, had left with Melanesian friends in a canoe and the old man was possibly still alive somewhere in the group. The remainder of the white men put to sea, intent on reaching some European settlement.

The course steered by the French crew is unlikely ever to be known with certainty. But the most obvious destination was Timor, following the route Bligh took from the Banks Islands. Timor was the closest European outpost; better still, it was a downwind passage the whole way. The French boat was never seen again. It was probably wrecked somewhere in Torres Strait.

On the third day a stuffy breeze was gasping over the horizon with the first rays of light. I got up the sails and made coffee as the buzz of wind and progress began to percolate through the boat. But within an hour the wind had stalled; the cloud patterns overhead were fractious and at odds. An hour later still I was sipping cold coffee, expecting another day of calm, when the trade came in hard from the south and didn't let up.

For four days the trade remained stubbornly in the south while the sloop pushed west-south-west into the Coral Sea. The wind was a mechanical force at 25 knots, dragging rain and cloud across the ocean without respite. Swells came in just forward of the beam, their crests obscuring the weather horizon in the moment before they rolled beneath the keel. Aerated spray peppered the topsides and landed with a wet clatter against the cabin windows. For hours at a time, foaming crests were the brightest things in sight on a seascape suppressed beneath frowning cloud.

That night the wind fell back slightly, and I arrived on deck in the dawn twilight to find the boat was underpowered. As I worked at the mast, shaking out the reef in the mainsail, the first sepia rays of sunlight rose along the eastern horizon. The sky was filled with a veil of dry cloud in which the light found kinks and splits, until the heavens appeared to be paved in cracked glass. The sun came up like a colourless kaleidoscope, twisting and reforming in the film of cloud. Part of what makes sea travel a distinct world is simply that time afloat is differently structured. I rarely see the dawn on land, but on board the boat sunrise is part of the seascape every day. Dawn is a peculiarly maritime experience. Occasionally, I could sit quietly in the cockpit with breakfast and watch the coming of the light slowly unfold across the seas of Melanesia. But more often dawn was a busy time. The last few hours have passed lazily, and if the wind has changed I'm restless to make amends. Sunrise equates with putting things right, shaking out a reef, rebalancing the steering vane, snatching drinks and pieces of fruit. Dawn was something I caught glimpses of over my right shoulder as I worked at the mast. The first feeble rays of light played on the steel ring of the reef point as I slipped it from the horns on the boom and hauled it up into the sky.

At noon that day I sailed north of the Torres Islands. From 20 miles distant, the land appeared as no more than a collection of boulders on the horizon. Luis Váez de Torres has been mucked around by history. For 150 years his achievements in navigating the strait between Australia and New Guinea were ignored. But today, this remote group of islands he never saw are called by his name.

For the next three days to Indispensable Reef life at sea had a cyclical, premeditated quality. The same cracked-glass dawn lightened the sky each morning, followed by the same day, repeated almost move for move. The swells were unrelenting on the beam, sending the sloop into a pendulous roll. These heavy conditions determined the shape and scale of the life I led at sea. Preparing a meal required the time-consuming coordination of a hundred different activities. Between times, the days were filled with more detail, picking out points of focus and certainty in the cycle of dawns and sunsets, wind and waves. I greased the gimbals on the cooker and the flexible paraffin hose, and oiled the vane steering and its blocks, thus trying to ease the effects of motion on my little world by combating squeak and wear. I found things to scrub or re-secure, rope ends to tidy; I preferred simple tasks, things that couldn't go wrong, things that could be left off and picked up later while I searched out a change of scene, read more pages from a book, watched the horizon or tended the sails. At sea I sought to build my own world within the heaving confines of the boat, to create a culture of the ship. Behind me I had left the grass huts and centuries-old kinship of Tikopia. Somewhere ahead to the west were the glass and concrete towers of the Queensland coast. But on passage the sloop could belong to neither place. At sea the ship was its own cultural entity, entire and complete.

The same thing is apparent in William Bligh's account when, after months anchored at Tahiti, the plants were finally loaded and the *Bounty* was readied for the passage to Torres Strait. The ship's sails were taken ashore, aired and repaired. The anchor cables were hauled out and likewise aired in the sunshine. The ratlines were overhauled and tarred. The standing rigging of manila hemp was set up using billytackles. The blocks were dismantled and cleaned with tallow – a mixture of mud and fat. As the rigging was tight-ened and the cables creaked, the dangers of the beach were already diminishing. Bligh could now re-establish the insular culture of a sailing vessel under way, and his satisfaction is evident: 'I had a Ship in the most perfect order,' he wrote contentedly, 'and well Stored with every necessary both for Service and health . . .'.

I remember as a child reading an account of the mutiny on the *Bounty* in words of no more than two syllables. According to this simplistic version of history, the crew mutinied because Bligh had ordered that the ship would return to England by way of Cape Horn. In fact, this is quite untrue. It is also highly improb-able. The route from the South Pacific around Cape Horn would have involved running before the strong westerly winds in the

Roaring Forties across open ocean, just the sort of conditions that heavy, square-rigged sailing ships enjoyed most. By the 1780s the route south of the Horn was relatively well travelled. It was the most direct route home and the sailors would have welcomed the prospect.

Instead, Bligh's orders were to return via Torres Strait, a route that was almost unknown. Nineteen years earlier Captain Cook had weaved a course through the reefs and very nearly lost *Endeavour* in the process. *Bounty*'s crew knew all about the difficulties and dangers of this passage: her gunner, William Peckover, had been on board *Endeavour* with Cook. There is evidence that some of Bligh's seamen were terrified of the passage north of Cape York, which British sailors knew as Endeavour Straits after the channel pioneered by Cook.

In the years following the mutiny, as the various groups of survivors arrived back in England, Fletcher Christian's family began a campaign to clear his name. His brother, Edward Christian, Downing Professor of Laws at Cambridge University, wrote a pamphlet defending the mutiny based on interviews with several of those on board the *Bounty*, including the master, Fryer, and Midshipman Peter Heywood. According to Edward Christian, Bligh had abused his officers as 'scoundrels, damned rascals, hounds, hell-hounds, beasts, infamous wretches'. Furthermore, he had tormented them with the dangers of Torres Strait. Once the ship was among the racing tides and coral pinnacles Bligh apparently ranted that '. . . he would kill one half of the people, make the officers jump overboard, and would make them eat grass like cows'. *Bounty*'s crew '. . . were as much afraid of Endeavour Straits, as any child is of the rod'.

On the fourth day after the calm broke I cleared Indispensable Reef. The breakers were only three miles downwind, but I could see nothing of them. For days past the Coral Sea had been a grey mass ripped by driven spume. An austere cowl of rain and cloud still hooded the ocean. For four days the sloop had rolled west locked in the bubble of its own purpose, the same swells and dripping sky seemingly fixed in place, an inescapable, insular orbit. Indispensable Reef passed unseen, but still I felt a wave of tension lift from the boat. The reef had limited my sea room, preventing me bearing off the wind and sailing an easier course. Now, open water lay ahead. I shifted the vane on the self-steering system and bore nearly 30° further off the wind: a few seconds' activity were the culmination of four days' endeavour. In a moment the whole dynamic on the boat shifted. The seas and wind came round onto the quarter, the motion eased into the sluicing roll of downwind sailing, and I wondered why the Coral Sea had ever seemed such a menacing place.

Of Indispensable Reef itself I learned more from the man who first described it. In 1791, running west across the Coral Sea in a strong trade, Captain Edward Edwards wrote, 'At midnight between the 16th and 17th of August breakers were discovered ahead and upon our bow, and not a mile from us.' Edwards could not weather the reef so ran off to the north. Within an hour the lookout sighted more breakers on the dark ocean and in his log Edwards describes a double reef, each part enclosing a lagoon, extending far to the north-west: 'The sea breaks pretty high upon it in different parts.' Next morning the frigate was clear and Edwards continued his original course, west to Torres Strait.

Captain Edward Edwards commanded an expedition quite unlike any other to have sailed into the Pacific. HMS *Pandora* was a frigate of war mounting 24 guns.

The ship's company included no botanists, mathematicians or artists; Edwards's voyage had no scientific objective and his instructions made no mention of new discoveries. He was ordered to the Pacific to hunt down beachcombers. If possible, they should be captured and brought back to England; if not, he was to kill them. Now, as *Pandora* cleared Indispensable Reef, fourteen beachcombers who had been arrested at Tahiti were caged, shackled and naked, in a roundhouse built on the frigate's quarterdeck. All had been crewmen on Bligh's doomed *Bounty*.

I crossed the Coral Sea in August, the same month *Pandora* had made this passage 212 years earlier. At this time of year the cloud and rain can last for days. According to one of the men imprisoned on the frigate's deck the rain 'made our habitation very leaky'. With few clothes and no proper shelter the men 'applyd to the First Lieut. to have something done to remedy it to which he replyd, "I am Wet too and evry body on Deck and it will dry when the Weather Clears up."' The beachcombers had already been incarcerated for more than four months.

The writer was James Morrison, formerly boatswain's mate on the *Bounty*. Morrison describes the cage in which the fourteen men were confined as 11 feet in length and 18 feet wide (3.5m x 5.5m): 'This place we Stiled Pandoras Box . . .'. Buckets of salt water were hurled through the scuttle twice a week in the name of sanitation. As the frigate ran before the trade, rolling hard on the seas, the men were thrown together into a heap. Captain Edwards responded to their complaints by threatening to staple the beachcombers to the deck. Later, however, 'Mr. Cornor gave us some short boards to Check ourselves with which he made the Carpenters secure; and thereby prevented us from Maiming each other and ourselves.' A sentry paced the roof of the roundhouse; a midshipman patrolled the deck. The prisoners were kept in shackles and forbidden to speak to any member of the crew, except the Master of Arms, and even then only on account of provisions. Finally they managed to procure a copper kettle in which to boil cocoa laced with sugar 'and this with the Divine Providence kept us alive'.

The fourteen men shackled in Pandora's Box were a mixed bunch. Burkett and Sumner had both been actively involved in the mutiny and would certainly be hanged when *Pandora* reached England. Others, like Morrison and Heywood, occupied more questionable ground: they had not participated in the mutiny but neither had they tried to join Bligh in the open boat. By chaining these men in Pandora's Box Edwards was doing no more than obeying his orders. *Pandora*'s sailing instructions were issued by the

Admiralty on 25 October 1790 and signed by Lord Hood: 'You are to keep the Mutineers as closely confined as may preclude all possibility of their escaping, having, however, proper regard for the preservation of their Lives, that they may be brought Home to undergo the Punishment due to their demerits.'

But four of the prisoners had played no part in the mutiny, and Edwards knew it. Coleman, McIntosh, Norman and Byrne had been ordered to remain on the ship by Bligh for want of space in the open boat: '. . . you can't all go with me my lads [but] I'll do you Justice if ever I reach England'. True to his word Bligh wrote to the Admiralty from Coupang in August 1789 at the completion of the open-boat voyage stating that these four had been '. . . kept against their inclinations and are deserving of mercy'. They weren't shown any by Edwards.

In the eyes of Captain Edwards, the line separating mutineers and mere beachcombers was wafer-thin. When the men had been arrested in Tahiti, all were heavily tattooed, fluent in Tahitian, and most came with native wives and mixed-race children. *Pandora*'s surgeon, George Hamilton, wrote that '. . . many of the prisoners were married to the most respectable chiefs' daughters'. They came out to the frigate with the beachcombers' children, four girls and two boys. Several more of the women were 'big with child'. Their costumes were so bulky 'they were obliged to be hoisted on board like horn cattle'. The beachcombers were seen 'weeping over their tender offspring' while the women tore at their scalps with shells and 'smeared their breasts and shoulders with the warm blood, as it streamed down . . .' Captain Edwards soon grew tired of these visits. When he learned of a plot to cut *Pandora*'s anchor cable so the frigate would be washed up on shore the women were driven away and the sentry instructed to shoot any man heard speaking Tahitian. For Edwards, the part these men may or may not have played in Fletcher Christian's insurrection was irrelevant. All fourteen men were now guilty of beachcombing.

In the decades following Edwards's voyage the disdain which many ship's captains had for beachcombers only intensified. One colonial writer described Pacific beachcombers as sailors 'from the most revolting side'. Charles Wilkes, commander of the 1838 US Exploring Expedition, believed beachcombers to be '. . . worthless, dissipated, and worn-out vagabonds'. When Reverend John Williams reached Samoa in 1832 he vowed in his journal never to let another beachcomber on his ship. This was more than missionary prudishness. Williams was an experienced ship's captain and like others in the profession, he felt he had very practical reasons to distrust those who lived on the beach. Some of this antipathy can be traced back to events in Tonga in the early 1800s.

The privateer and whaler *Port au Prince* reached Ha'apai in central Tonga on 29 November 1806. In the preceding four years two other ships, the *Duke of Portland* and the *Union*, had been attacked in this same anchorage, but the *Port au Prince* traded peacefully with the islanders for two days. Captain Duck had died earlier in the passage and been replaced by an unpopular man named Brown. When Brown insisted that the sailors work on a Sunday, 19 men deserted after a heated altercation. Nonetheless, the *Port au Prince* still had a substantial ship's company of 77 men and was defended by 24 twelve-pound cannon and 8 twelve-pound carronades mounted on the quarterdeck.

Shortly after dawn on the third day the Tongans began boarding the ship in such numbers that some of the officers became concerned. Soon there were more than 300 islanders on the ship, most of them in the rigging. The ship's 14-year-old clerk, William Mariner, was blissfully unaware of this development as he was working on some papers below decks. When the clerk's pen failed, however, he came to the light beneath a hatchway to effect a repair. Looking upwards into the light he saw a Tongan raise his ironwood war club above the head of Mr Dixon, the supercargo, then dash his skull to pieces. With that the Tongans leapt down from the rigging and began a general attack.

Mariner ducked back down the hatchway. As he raced through the ship he bumped into the cooper, who was panic-stricken. Both men agreed the magazine would be the safest place to hide.

From inside this locked cabin they could hear the awful progress of the massacre being carried out on the ship's deck. William Mariner was evidently a young man who approved of decisive action and quickly 'came to the resolution of blowing up the vessel' and destroying themselves and their enemies together. The cooper must have been wishing he'd never bumped into Mariner and flatly refused, suffering 'great distress from the apprehension of his impending fate'. Undeterred, the youthful Mariner came up with an alternative: the two men should go on deck at once while the Tongans 'were still hot with slaughter, rather than, by greater delay, subject themselves to the cruelties of cooler barbarity'. The miserable cooper eventually agreed, but only 'if Mr Mariner would lead the way'.

Mariner was paralyzed with shock by the scene that greeted his eyes as he climbed onto the deck. 'Upon the companion a short squab naked figure, of about fifty years of age, was seated, with a seaman's jacket soaked in blood thrown over one shoulder; on the other rested his iron-wood club, spattered with blood and brains . . . On another part of the deck there lay twenty-two bodies perfectly naked, and arranged side by side in regular order, but so dreadfully bruised and battered about the head, that only two or three of them could be recognised.' As the Tongans already had control of the ship, together with its stores, muskets and ironwork, one of the chiefs ordered that Mariner and the cooper were to be spared.

On shore William Mariner was adopted by the young warrior king Finau for whom he performed many of the common beachcomber roles. In particular he worked as an armourer, servicing the muskets and cannon plundered from the ship, which was subsequently burned. Partly through the assistance of Mariner and the *Port au Prince*'s firearms, but also by manipulating a web of customary alliances, Finau became one of the most powerful chiefs in the group.

The attacks on the *Port au Prince* and the other two ships at Tonga were widely believed to have been 'at the instigation of aliens'. Beachcombers were condemned as traitors who had sold the secrets of the ship ashore. The islanders learned to attack ships in heavy rains when the guns would be least effective; to climb into the rigging where the sailors would be loath to fire for fear

William Mariner in the costume of the Tonga Islands. Frontispiece to John Martin, *An Account of the Natives of the Tonga Islands in the South Pacific Ocean*, 1817

of damaging their own ship; to cut the anchor cable in onshore winds so the ship would be driven aground. None of this, it was believed, would have been possible without beachcombers acting as guides; only with inside help could the islanders have learned how men armed with clubs and spears could overrun ships defended by muskets and cannon.

Around a dozen crewmen from the *Port au Prince* survived the massacre and were forced to live ashore. These men were stripped naked and lost their identity papers. The process of adoption and assimilation began which they were hardly in a position to refuse. Soon they had Tongan wives, wore native dress and were tattooed; they became indistinguishable from those men already living on the beach at the time the *Port au Prince* had been attacked. Ships called at Tonga regularly but such was the distrust of beachcombers that many of the *Port au Prince* castaways struggled for years before any captain could be persuaded to give them passage. William Mariner himself lived ashore for four years before he found a ship that would take him off. Captain Chase of the inappropriately named *Hope* refused to have Mariner on board, saying he had 'hands enough'. Another beachcomber in Tonga, George Vason, experienced the same thing. When an English ship came into the anchorage he launched a canoe and eagerly paddled out from the beach. 'When we came near, I called out, "How do you do, countrymen?" But the sailors only laughed at me . . .' On board the ship there was a missionary named John Harris. 'He remonstrated with me on my unbecoming appearance in the native dress.' Vason was dismissed by the missionary and the ship sailed without him. 'I now appeared to myself to be a deserter for ever. My powers of mind were scarcely able to support me.'

In fact, the evidence linking beachcombers to the attacks in Tonga is largely circumstantial. European sailors consistently overestimated the superiority of their weaponry. In other parts of the ocean, where there were no beachcombers, the islanders quickly learnt the limitations of muskets. At Ile Maré in 1858, three of James Paddon's sandalwooders gave chase to a group of Melanesians who had stolen some goods. Unable to catch the canoe in their longboat, the sailors opened fire. The islanders then knew that the muskets would take time to reload. They turned the canoe around and killed the three sailors with tomahawks.

Furthermore, in a humid, maritime environment, the sailors' guns were unreliable, being highly susceptible to damp. It's ironic that the first Spanish sailors in the Pacific were probably as well armed as those who came two centuries later. Quiros's sailors at Big Bay in 1606 were equipped with heavy shields, swords and pikes with which to defend themselves; their arquebuses were found to have a shorter range and be less accurate than Melanesian bows and arrows. Captain Cook's sailors were armed with flintlock muskets, similar to the 'Brown Bess' of the Napoleonic Wars, and this was the weapon used by most of the traders who followed in his wake up until the 1830s. The flintlock was quicker to load and slightly less susceptible to damp than the old arquebus, but in terms of range and accuracy was barely superior. The French navigator Philip Carteret lost three sailors to arrow wounds in an ambush while attempting a landing in Melanesia in 1767. Carteret reported that the islanders could shoot off three to four arrows in the time it took to load a flintlock musket.

The efficiency of muskets depended partly on the situation in which they were being used. Generally, muskets were far more effective as a weapon of attack than of defence. When sailors – and especially beachcomber mercenaries like Charlie Savage – were on the offensive, with the benefit of surprise and in fine weather, their muskets were often tools of wholesale slaughter. But in situations of ambush, where sailors were required to defend themselves, usually at close quarters, flintlocks proved to be slow and cumbersome. Trading voyages required extensive contact with the islanders; they were needed to cut sandalwood, collect bêche-de-mer, and bring out provisions in the form of pigs, coconuts, fruit and vegetables. Anchored ships were often surrounded by scores of canoes and a sudden attack was difficult to guard against. Sailors in open boats were particularly vulnerable. A favoured means of ambush was for a group of islanders to crowd around an open boat as it approached the beach, apparently offering a warm greeting. The boat was then capsized, rendering the muskets useless. In practice, throughout the first half of the nineteenth century, sailors were often dependent on their cut-lasses for self-defence.

In the 1840s and 50s traders tended to be armed with various types of percussion musket which, although better than the flintlocks, still suffered the same basic problems: slow to load, inaccurate, and unreliable in wet conditions. It wasn't until Colt revolvers became common in the Pacific from the 1860s that sailors enjoyed an unassailable advantage over indigenous means of warfare for the first time.

Nonetheless, many ship's captains were lulled into a false sense of security by their possession of firearms. When heavily defended ships were attacked and seized, beachcombers were often blamed for teaching the islanders the shortcomings of European technologies. Among the journals and accounts written by sailors, there are many examples of the distrust those on board ship felt towards those living ashore. In the most extreme cases, castaways making signals of distress were simply ignored. In May 1819 Captain Freycinet's French corvettes reached the island of Pilstaart (Ata, in Tonga) where he had no intention of stopping, correctly believing it to be uninhabited by Polynesians. But the lookout hailed from aloft to report an open boat putting out from the island's rocky shore. The expedition's draughtsman, Jacques Arago, observed that the boat was '. . . manned by three persons who are rowing with all their might: they are coming towards us: they wave a piece of white cloth on the end of a paddle . . . perhaps they are persons unfortunately shipwrecked, to whom providence sends unexpected succour'. Freycinet plainly observed the open boat, then ordered the corvettes to sail on westwards, without picking up the castaways. 'How many days may elapse,' the draughtsman lamented, 'before such another opportunity offers itself to those unfortunate men!'

Today, mariners are required by law to render assistance to those in distress and it's easy to forget this wasn't always the case. A further example concerns the wreck of the *Independence* on Starbuck Island in December 1835. The ship was a total loss and most of the crew set sail in three open boats to seek help, leaving a small group on the uninhabited island. As luck would have it, the sail of a passing whaler was soon sighted on the horizon and the castaways lit fires as a signal of distress. The whaler closed the shore, but no boat was lowered. Finally, one of the castaways swam off through the surf, but the captain refused to allow any of the men on board unless they could provide some identity document or ship's papers to prove they were not mutineers. The crewman then swam back to shore and returned with a bottle containing an account of the shipwreck signed by the captain of the *Independence*. Yet even then, the captain of the whaler was reluctant to take the men. First, he liberally supplied himself from the wreck, taking sails, spars and rigging, before the men were taken off. This, he said, was compensation against future trouble the castaways were likely to cause.

By the middle of the nineteenth century, the rejection of beachcombers was commonplace. When E.H. Lamont reached the Marquesas in 1852 he met a beachcomber named George living in an out-of-the-way part of the group. 'As he had little the appearance of that class of runaway sailors common amongst the islands, I asked him how he came to isolate himself in that retired spot. He told me he was a native of Ireland, had emigrated to America, and not being successful there, had left it in disgust, shipping, as a raw hand, on board a whale ship. Such a life was naturally uncongenial to him, and, on arriving at this bay, he had requested the captain to put him on shore, with his chest. Though the natives, of course, at first stole most of his things, he soon got on a good footing with them, and took to himself a wife, with whose family he lived some time . . . I expressed my astonishment that he had not come down to the vessel, as white men invariably do. He said that at first he had gone on board every vessel that had arrived, but being apparently looked on with suspicion by the officers and crew, he never went now . . .'

A short time later, while engaging in trade, Lamont's ship the *Chatham* was boarded by a chief who was rowed out from the beach by four servants – all white men. When the chief later took his departure '. . . one of his crew, an Englishman, came aft and begged the captain to take him from the island, as he was living in a miserable state, "a complete slave to this black nigger," as he most irreverently called the king, "and in momentary fear of his life". The captain refused. The "beach-comers," he said, "were a bad lot, and the first to turn against you, no matter how much they were indebted to your kindness."'

For some ship's captains the distinction between genuine castaways, deserters and mutineers began to fade once they had lived on the beach. Any man who had become separated from his ship, for whatever reason, was treated as suspect.

The waters immediately west of Indispensable Reefs were disturbed. Twice that night the sloop was hit by squalls and I ran blindly west through the rain under bare poles.

Early the next morning I saw a ship between the showers to the south. On the deep ocean swell only the superstructure was visible, a cluster of towers, derricks and cranes rising and dipping. Nothing could have looked less nautical. The ship most resembled a building site struggling to stay upright in the buckling seas.

Soon it fell calm for several hours with heavy rain and a sad, wilting sea. In the afternoon a murderous-looking cloud formation scaled the windward horizon. It appeared as a black arrowhead advancing over the ocean, a shard of precipitation with the apex above the masthead while bolts of lightning cracked in the east. I pulled down the sails as the first rain started to drum on the canvas and a bore of wind swept over the ocean. For 20 minutes I ran west before a gale-force squall, then a slit appeared in the cloud to windward. For a moment before night fell the dusk twilight was reversed as patches of lighter sky displaced the cloud.

Throughout that night a pair of boobies circled precariously around the wheeling rig. In the gusty wind they hovered and receded overhead, making endless approaches to the boat, deftly avoiding the mast and rigging as it slashed back and forth through the sky.

Their cry was a comfort at first, but grew ever more lugubrious as the night wore on. From my bunk I listened to their insistent squawk clashing with the quieter creak of the steering lines on the tiller until I finally dozed off to sleep. An hour later I was climbing sleepily through the companionway but froze rigid in mid-step when a mad flapping erupted above my head. One or both of the birds – I could never see – had finally settled on the sprayhood. Now they disappeared into the night, offended that their nest had been disturbed, but for several hours the cockpit was ingrained with a rank, birdy odour.

By dawn the wind was steady at 15 knots. The sun rose in a clear sky and beat down unobstructed on the ocean for the first time in days. I hoisted the light-weather headsail and threw the hatches wide to air the boat.

That afternoon I passed a strange milestone in my voyage. At 3:30 the sloop crossed an impression on the chart that I had made 11 years earlier. It was the faint mark of a pencil line I'd drawn in 1992 while planning the passage I intended to make that year to Torres Strait. The line described a north-westerly course, passing Fiji, swinging through the central islands of Vanuatu, then heading direct across the Coral Sea into the approaches to Torres Strait. I'd planned to make the passage in 1992 but never sailed that course. Only a few months later I decided to spend another year in the Pacific and put off the passage to Torres Strait. I'd been putting it off ever since.

The islands became a home rather than simply a constellation of waypoints to be ticked off on a journey to another place. I had rubbed out the pencil line on the chart now, but the indent in the thick paper was still just visible. I felt it as an odd little disturbance in the ocean that afternoon – a personal hiccup in the otherwise placid swells. This was, perhaps, the closest I would ever get to the original beachcombers. They too had never intended to stay in the Pacific. Their home had been a ship, until the course of their lives was diverted by chance and circumstance. A few of the beachcombers, years later, had made this passage west across the Coral Sea to Torres Strait. But most had never left the islands. Their bones lay bleached by the equatorial sun at the water's edge.

For days on end now the sky was a pure, crystalline blue, the colour normally only seen from an aircraft window flying high above the clouds. The weather was settled, the seas small and regular, and the passage assumed an easy gait towards the Australian coast. I set all three sails and ambled down the folding swells into the west. For four more days I lay in the sunshine on the cockpit bench reading the beachcombers' accounts. Most of these texts were bulky photocopies, gleaned from various libraries over the years. The only sound now was of pages crackling in the following wind, chattering white caps, and an occasional snap from aloft as the edge of a sail collapsed and reset in the trade. I read, watched the sea and glanced at the weather horizon, waiting for something to change. It never did, and in time I began to doubt it ever would.

Four hundred miles off the Australian coast I was shaken from my reverie by a roar building in the sky. At first it seemed part of some unimportant background activity. Only slowly did I understand its insistent proximity was directly focused on me. It was a boom now, close and loud, familiar but strangely unrecognizable after eleven days alone at sea. As I sat up on the cockpit bench I saw a silver glint in the sky. With a piercing rude shudder a twin-engine Bombardier de Havilland Dash 8 aircraft screamed beside the sloop. It sported red and white livery, the colours crisp and distinct above the ocean's seamless frieze. 'CUSTOMS' was boldly printed on the plane's swollen quarters. An Australian flag was tucked beneath the cockpit windshield. An official seal emblazoned the tail. I waved lamely and went below to turn on the radio. The speaker immediately crackled into life.

'Australian Coastwatch aircraft calling the single-masted sailing yacht. Do we have you now sir?' I could almost see the flyboys grinning from behind their mirrored shades, smell the aftershave on their chins and the starch in their collars. It was there on the radio waves, the levity of speed and height.

I gave details of the boat and voyage. He then read a set text outlining regulations for vessels approaching the Australian coast – proceed direct to a port of entry, no one to board the vessel before a quarantine officer – the usual routine. 'I have to ask you to confirm you heard and understood that message sir.'

I asked if I was permitted to anchor once inside the reef so as to sleep.

'Affirmative. You can anchor but not go ashore and you should proceed to a port of entry without unnecessary delay.'

I switched off the radio and scanned the blue skies above the boat but the aircraft was already out of sight.

Next day the plane was back, circling at altitude, checking my progress. And the next day it was back again, updating my ETA, counting down the miles as I closed in on the Great Barrier Reef, an airborne shepherd mustering this stray towards the coral enclosures that guard the coast. I heard the drone of the plane's engines as a reflection of the crowded waters up ahead, and the rumbling breakers on the first reefs and cays which now lay only just below the horizon.

It was somewhere here, a day or so out from the Barrier Reef, that I crossed another invisible track on the ocean. The message in a bottle I had thrown from the boat on the fourteenth day of the voyage would have drifted north-west through the Coral Sea and crossed these same waters. It was washed by the breakers over the outer barrier and then continued to drift north-west through the shallows for about 80 miles, before being cast up on the sand cay at Meiu Reef.

A bottle adrift in almost any part of the tropical South Pacific would inevitably come this way. Captain Schoone, cruising the Pacific coast of Ecuador aboard *J.H. Leibkin* in 1892, threw a MIB from the ship. Over the next 2½ years the bottle drifted 8,000 miles across the Pacific and was found on Australia's Cape York

Peninsula. South Pacific drifts are more predictable than many, being governed by the south-east trade winds, one of the most reliable winds in the world. The effects of the trade, coupled with the south sub-tropical current, determines that flotsam in the South Seas, unless it is stranded on one of the islands, will be swept into the eastern approaches to Torres Strait. In May 2000, Randi and Laura Durbin threw a MIB from their yacht near Tonga. It was found 2 years later on the Cape York Peninsula by Mark Tischler after a drift of 2,700 miles. The bottle had covered the same route that Captain Bligh sailed in the open boat after the mutiny on the *Bounty*.

Today, the coast of tropical Queensland is a beachcomber's heaven. The most common items to be washed up are thongs (flip-flops), the floating footwear ubiquitous in the South Pacific. Russell Doig, a panel beater from Ayr, has collected more than 4,000 thongs on his local beach and nailed them to his garden fence. Elsewhere in Queensland there is a 'thong tree' at Cowley Beach and a 'thong pole' on Yorke Island. Torres Strait and its adjacent coastlines are the final resting place for an ocean's flotsam.

The strait is shaped like a funnel into which the trade wind blows, and the current flows. Sailing boats seek to follow the line of least resistance, tracing the winds and currents. In the end, negotiating the reefs of Torres Strait becomes an inevitable part of the Pacific voyage. I'd felt the same thing for more than 1,000 miles sailing west across the Coral Sea. Even if I had dropped the sails and allowed the sloop to drift, I would have reached Torres Strait. The Coral Sea was a maritime conveyor, travelling to the north-west. Here, Torres Strait guards the Pacific's endpoint and exit, its arms thrown wide to greet the coming ships. But the strait's embrace turned out to be a stranglehold. When they reached the narrows, beyond the point of no return, sailors found the way barred by hundreds of miles, layer after layer, of coral reefs awash in shallow seas. This is the fundamental paradox of Torres Strait: it was both attractive and deadly at the same time.

Square-rigged sailing ships, their sails spread wide to harness the trade, were drawn into Torres Strait like moths to a flame.

Before beginning the voyage I had gone to talk to one of my relatives about Torres Strait. My cousin Marsden Hordern is a maritime historian whose books on the voyages of Phillip Parker King and John Lort Stokes to chart the waters of Australia's eastern seaboard had always inspired me to sail among the shoals of the Barrier Reef and Torres Strait. I met Marsden in his home on Sydney's north shore. He's in his eighties today, but his eyes still sparkle when he talks about his own passage to Torres Strait, 58 years ago, to fight the Japanese.

Late in 1944 the Royal Australian Navy gave the then 22-year-old Lieutenant Hordern command of a Fairmile harbour defence motor launch, number 1347. *ML 1347* fitted out in Sydney, then steamed north up the coast. At the Brisbane Naval Depot the launch developed a mechanical fault and he was ordered to carry out 100 hours of engine tests making day cruises around Moreton Bay. On each of these cruises Marsden took a group of WRANS (women naval personnel), and also an 'aquaplane', today called a 'wake board'. At 12 knots the Fairmile kicked up a steep wake and the WRANS rode the aquaplane over the waves behind the ship while a crewman sat on the flybridge with a rifle watching for sharks.

On 1 June 1945 *ML 1347* entered the waters in the lee of the Great Barrier Reef and next day anchored at Lizard Island. In Watson Bay Marsden decided to test *ML 1347*'s gun, as the launch would soon be entering hostile waters. A rock ashore was selected as a target, then riddled with 800 rounds of 20mm explosive shells from an Oerlikon automatic cannon. This story illustrates the speed and scale of tourist development on the Barrier Reef. In 1945 remote Lizard Island was uninhabited. Today, Watson Bay is thronged with game-fishing boats, ski boats, jet skis and windsurfers. An exclusive resort marks the spot where Marsden tested the cannon.

ML 1347 crossed Torres Strait from south to north, an unusual passage in the sense that historically most ships have passed through the strait from east to west, from the Pacific to the Indian Ocean. Marsden took on fuel at Thursday Island, then set a course up the Great North East Channel, the route through the strait first charted by William Bligh on the second breadfruit voyage in the *Providence*. At Port Moresby Marsden saw a Norton motorbike. It had been captured by the Japanese at the fall of Singapore and brought to New Guinea, where it had subsequently been captured back again by the Australians. Marsden bought it for £20, hoisted it onto the ship with the depth-charger davit, had a canvas cover made to protect it from the elements, and stowed the bike on the quarterdeck. *ML 1347* cleared New Guinea's East Cape then headed north-west up the coast. While berthed at Alexishafen, Marsden and the First Lieutenant decided to ride the Norton to Madang to have lunch and a cold drink in the wardroom. The area was supposedly under the control of Australian forces, but they had been warned there might still be Japanese snipers in the bush. The Norton was cruising down a jungle track with tropical forest close on either side when Marsden felt a little puff of wind as a bullet whizzed in front of his throat, then a split-second later heard the crack of a rifle above the engine. He accelerated down the road for a mile, then stopped. The two sailors held a terse conference. If they went ahead there might be more ambushes. If they went back there was at least one sniper. To stay still was worst of all. Marsden turned the Norton round, the First Lieutenant drew a .45, and with a throaty roar the Norton sped back down the jungle track at 60 mph. *ML 1347* continued her passage along the north coast of New Guinea almost to the equator where the remaining days of the war were spent defending the US Naval base at Hollandia (Jayapura, Irian Jaya) from Japanese midget submarines.

The route that *ML 1347* took along the north coast of New Guinea was once simply known as the Northern Route. Before Torres Strait was charted this was the orthodox course for ships sailing west out of the Pacific. The French navigator Louis Antoine de Bougainville had sailed the Northern Route in 1768 and found it to be a wretched undertaking. Bedevilled by equatorial heat and calms, his scurvy-ravaged seamen were forced to eat the leather sacks, or *cueros*, that had once contained their food. 'There have been many arguments over where Hell is situated,' Bougainville wrote. 'Truly, we have found it.' The French finally found relief at the Dutch settlement at Buru in the Spice Islands after a passage of 3,000 miles. Had Bougainville sailed through Torres Strait the distance to Buru would have been halved.

A glance at the atlas reveals the strategic importance of any strait between Australia and New Guinea. Torres Strait is the most direct sea route between the Pacific and Indian Oceans. The strait itself is 100 miles wide and, all other things being equal, would present few obstacles to navigators. There are only a handful of islands in the strait, most of them high and easily seen. The complicating factors are that the strait is shallow and lies in tropical latitudes: coral polyps thrive in warm, shoal water. The result is a network of coral formations stretching for 1,250 miles from Torres Strait down the Queensland Coast. Sailing ships approaching from the Pacific found the strait was guarded by 80,000 square miles of shoaling studded with thousands of reefs, coral pinnacles and sand cays.

Captain Cook was the first European to repeat Torres's passage through the strait. It was the most difficult navigation of Cook's career and nearly cost him his ship when *Endeavour* struck a reef on 11 June 1770 and was seriously damaged. Peaks on the mainland adjacent to the reef are named Mt Sorrow, Mt Poverty and Mt Misery. Cook named this whole coral fringe, from the 23rd parallel as far north as Torres Strait, the Labyrinth. So complex is the geography here that parts of the Labyrinth have still not been charted today.

On the afternoon of 30 August I was approaching the Great Barrier Reef. The trade had freshened and a long, deep swell was running, what Captain Cook had described as a 'well growen Sea rowling in from the SE' when he crossed these waters. Dry, fast-shifting cloud scudded overhead. The sloop surfed north-west across seas little more crowded than in Cook's time. Today, most shipping uses the inshore route, inside the reef, so these were safe, deep waters, leaving me free to make my preparations at the chart table. Tomorrow promised to be the longest day of the voyage. I planned to come through the Barrier Reef at dawn using the Raine Island entrance. Then the course lay north-west for 90 miles between the reefs and cays to reach Cape York. The wind was in the east, fresh at 30 knots which was all to the good. Next day I needed to sail as far and fast as possible to get beyond the worst of the reefs before nightfall. I worked at the chart table much of that afternoon, drawing up a list of waypoints, distances and courses to steer between the Great Detached Reef, Jukes Reef, Shadwell Reef, Risk Reef, Maclennan Cay, Turning Point Patches, Onslow Reef, Wilds Shoal, Collette Reef, Parsons Reef, Monsoon Reef, McSweeney Reef and the Arnold Islets. Before dinner I went through the numbers again, checking each one. Shortly before midnight I hove to 15 miles to windward of Raine Island, in the open waters of the Coral Sea.

Fifteen miles was probably overkill. I hoped so. I had read too much about this shore to leave it to chance. I could see these texts now as the sloop slowly rose over the swells, the torn photocopies of Cook, Bligh, Morrison, Edwards and Hamilton that had been my companions for weeks, lying on the bunks and stuffed into the shelves of the sloop's cramped cabin. The last three of these texts all spoke of the dangers of heaving to in these waters.

When a sailing boat is hove to it is effectively stopped, or greatly slowed, in the water. This is normally done by backing one of the sails so it acts as a brake against the other(s). Different boats have different characteristics, though, and in my Twister it's not necessary to back a headsail. I turned the sloop into the wind, hauled the mainsail in hard, disconnected the steering vane and lashed the tiller to windward. The boat was forereaching at less than half a knot, heading very slowly out to sea.

There shouldn't be any problem with heaving to in these conditions – provided that the water itself isn't moving. And that's the difficulty immediately east of the Barrier Reef. The south subtropical current coupled with an incoming tide sets the sea flowing towards the breakers. The boat might be stopped in the water, but the water itself is moving towards the reef.

The night was almost black, the cloud cover complete. In the darkness the sea was only sound and motion: I heard foaming crests all around and felt a staid pitching beneath my feet. I checked the numbers at the chart table one more time. Then I set the alarm for 30 minutes, but couldn't sleep. I climbed to the deck several times and stared out into the impenetrable night. I kept picking at the calculations at the chart table, running the parallel rule yet again between the reefs, checking to see that the crease in the chart hadn't allowed the rule to slip and give a bogus bearing. It was difficult to rest in these waters. Two hundred and twelve years earlier, almost to the day, *Pandora* hove to 20 miles from my present position, only to be pulled by the tide and current onto the reef.

Like all British sailors, Captain Edwards knew well the difficulties that Cook had experienced picking a passage through the Labyrinth. This knowledge '. . . determined me not to follow his Track, at least until I had searched for a safer or more commodious opening . . . to the Northward'. Edwards is sometimes scorned for his decision not to use the chart drawn by Cook. But from a sailor's perspective, his decision was perfectly sensible, given what was known at the time. By approaching the strait in about latitude 10° south, he hoped that the distance to be sailed among the reefs could be minimized. His bad luck was that exactly the opposite was the case. The shoals here are at their widest extent.

On 25 August 1791 Edwards made landfall on the reef close to a group he called Murray's Islands (now often known as Mer). He could find no passage through the barrier here and was forced to '. . . haul upon the wind in order to pass to the Southward'. By sunset no passage to the west could be discerned and the following day's search proved equally fruitless: 'I ran to the Southward along the reef with the intention and expectation of getting round it, and the whole day was spent without succeeding in my purpose and without seeing the end of the reef, or any break in it that gave the least hopes of a channel fit for a ship.'

Late in the afternoon of 28 August *Pandora's* lookout finally saw an entrance in the reef. Lieutenant Corner was sent in the yawl to examine it and Edwards ordered that the frigate be hove to. Night was approaching. The lead was heaved, no bottom was found, so it was assumed the ship was safely surrounded by deep water. What Edwards didn't know was that the tide that day was low at 5:30 pm. Thereafter, the incoming tide, in conjunction with the ocean current, would cause the water to pour in through the reef passage that Corner was investigating at speeds which have today been measured at up to 10 knots.

At 5:00 pm Corner signalled that there was indeed a passage fit for the ship. *Pandora* in turn signalled the yawl to return. Corner, however, made poor progress beating back to windward for the tide was beginning to run. Darkness fell but Edwards was determined to retrieve the yawl, having already lost two of the frigate's boats on the passage from Tahiti. Fires were burnt on *Pandora's* deck so Corner should have a guide. In return the flash from muskets showed that Corner was finally closing the frigate. The lead was heaved again and this time found the seabed at 50 fathoms. Corner brought the yawl under the frigate's stern while Edwards made sail, but before the boat was on board or the sails trimmed *Pandora* struck the Barrier Reef with such force the rudder and part of the sternpost were beaten away.

Within five minutes there were 18 inches of water in the hold. After ten minutes the depth had risen to four feet. The surgeon observed, '. . . we baled between life and death; for had she gone down before day-light, every soul must have perished'. All hands were turned to the three pumps and to bailing from the hatchways including three of the *Bounty* men, Coleman, Norman and McIntosh. Edwards always knew that these three had played no part in the mutiny and, at the end, gave them a chance for their lives. The fourth innocent man, Byrne, was partially blind and of no use to Edwards. He remained shackled and locked in the cage with the other beachcombers. Morrison wrote that two extra sentinels were stationed to guard Pandora's Box with orders to shoot 'if we made any Motion . . . there was no remedy but prayer'.

Within 1½ hours the ship beat over the reef into ten fathoms of water and was anchored amid chaotic scenes on deck. Two men were crushed to death, one by a gun which broke loose during an attempt to heave it overboard, one by the spare topmast which fell down from the booms. Shortly before dawn the captain and officers conferred on the quarterdeck and agreed that nothing could be done to save the frigate as 'The water was now coming in faster at the gunports than the pumps could discharge.' According to Surgeon Hamilton's account, the order was given to abandon ship and release the prisoners.

However, James Morrison has a different version of events. The beachcombers begged the Master at Arms to be allowed out of the cage to which came the reply 'Never fear my boys we'll all go to Hell together.' Then the Master at Arms together with all the sentinels and the captain jumped overboard. The forward end of the frigate was now under water as far as the main mast and seas were flowing into Pandora's Box '. . . when Devine providence directed Wm. Moulter (Boatswain's Mate) to the place'. Moulter unlocked the scuttle and the beachcombers began to climb out as the frigate sank. Hamilton records that 'The cries of the men drowning in the water was at first awful in the extreme.' Thirty-one of the ship's company were lost in the wreck, but as Morrison put it sourly, 'all the Officers were Saved'.

James Morrison found himself floating in the water as the sun rose over the scene. '. . . the Boats were now so far off that we could not distinguish one from the other'. For the second time in his life, Morrison crossed the cultural divide: '. . . throwing away my trousers, [I] bout my loins up in a Sash or Marro after the Taheite Manner'. He grabbed a short plank for buoyancy and swam for his life.

Ninety minutes later he reached the blue yawl and 'was taken up by Mr Bowling, Masters Mate'. But four of the other beach-combers died in the wreck. Midshipman Stewart and Able Seaman Sumner were killed by the gangplank violently resurfac-ing as the frigate sank. Skinner drowned with his limbs still shack-led. Hillbrandt never got out of Pandora's Box.

7

The Labyrinth

'. . . no space of three and a half degrees presents more dangers than Torres Strait'.

Matthew Flinders, 1814

THE ALARM SOUNDED for the last time at 3:30 the next morning. It was clipped to my jacket collar and had been set for 30-minute intervals since midnight while I catnapped on the cockpit bench.

I stood up stiffly in the cockpit. It was warm and close. The wind had eased over the last few hours but a big sea was still running. I shook out the reefs in the mainsail, unlashed the tiller and set the sloop running downwind. Sitting on the foredeck I rigged a pole to windward, then hauled out the genoa so the boat was running wing-and-wing through the night. It was pitch black: the sea and sky had merged to form one seamless void. The void, though, was alive: I could hear the birds overhead, hundreds of them, filling the dark night with their cries. Ahead, the Great Barrier Reef stretched for 1,200 miles across the sloop's track.

In the moments of sickly light before the upper limb of the sun broke the horizon I saw that the whole sky was filled with birds – masked boobies, red-footed boobies, brown boobies, black noddy terns, sooty terns. They appeared as dark flecks, like claw marks in the dawn's greasy canvas, filling the skies from an ocean eyrie up ahead.

Raine Island was two miles in the distance, a hazy step above the sea that was quite featureless except for the squat tower. The Raine Island tower was the first structure of any sort to be built on the outer fringes of the Barrier Reef. It marks an entrance that is seldom used today, but which was once the principal gateway to Torres Strait.

The problem for sailing ships approaching Torres Strait had always been finding a suitable passage through the Barrier Reef. For today's sailor equipped with detailed charts and GPS navigation this is relatively simple, but in the nineteenth century when navigators did not always know their position with any accuracy, finding the passage was far more problematic. HMS *Pandora* was the first ship to be wrecked searching for a passage through the Barrier, but not the last. The *Flora* was wrecked in these waters in 1832, *Charles Eaton* in 1834, *Ferguson* in 1840, *Martha Ridgeway* in 1842. If nothing else, the wrecks served as grim marker beacons around the reef entrances. When Captain F.G. Moore came in through the reef in 1851 he described how '. . . on either side of the passage through the Great Barrier there was a wreck lying'.

The reef entrance at Raine Island was, by general consensus, the best of a very bad bunch. As a landmark, Raine Island is the most dismal example. Only a few metres high, 800 metres long by 400 wide, it is a coral platform devoid of trees or even scrub. In May 1844 the cutter *Prince George* arrived from Sydney with 20 convict masons. On Raine Island they built a tower 45 feet high with walls 5 feet thick. A domed roof made of timbers from the numerous wrecks was completed by September. I could see the remains of the tower now, like a crumbling Martello, its height much diminished. The tower was anyway of questionable value as a beacon. More than twenty ships were wrecked in the vicinity of Raine Island over the 15 years following the tower's completion including the *Enchantress, Rio Packet, Bourneuf, Stata, Fatima, Island Queen, Cornelius, Frances Walker, Sultana, Chesterholme, Constant, Sapphire,* and *Marina*. The tower had its uses though. Survivors frequently took shelter within its three-storied accommodation and Raine Island's bird population provided a ready source of food for castaways. The convicts who built the tower ate 3,000 terns and 17,000 tern eggs in six months.

As steam power replaced sailing ships the Raine Island entrance fell from favour. Powered vessels invariably preferred the inshore route, hugging the coast, and today Raine Island is a forlorn and forgotten outpost on the reef. It is also a bird sanctuary where landing is prohibited.

Twenty dolphins surrounded the sloop as the sun broke the horizon. Their pumice-coloured bellies streaked through the bow wave for the next 1½ hours, from the 400-metre contour through to the first 5-metre shoal. Brown boobies circled and plunged continuously round the rig. The deck was drenched in the sound of breaking water, blowing mammals and crying sea birds. The reef entrance was a riot of wildlife and glancing sunbeams. But the seas were falling away with every passing mile. The rig was almost still in the sky now: the roll had ceased. This was what seafarers had always liked about the Raine Island entrance. The ship sailed under the lee of the Great Detached Reef and into calm seas before the first shoal was reached. So long as they could find the entrance, it was safe. I never saw the Great Detached Reef, only felt its imprint on the water all around. The ocean swells subsided and the sloop was surfing down the short, steep seas of confined waters. By the time I reached the first shallows the sun was well above the horizon. The water ahead was a turquoise film stretching into the west. This was the Labyrinth.

The Labyrinth here was at its widest. The direct distance between the outer barrier and the mainland is 64 miles but some of this area still isn't surveyed. The charted passage is about 10 miles wide, heading north-west for 92 miles to Cape York. My course lay down this swathe of surveyed water, picking between the reefs and cays. The trade was blowing directly down this passage, which meant I'd have to gybe downwind across its full extent. Worse, the wind had eased since midnight. A gale would have been preferable so as to push the sloop as far through the reefs as possible before nightfall.

I hoisted the light number one genoa and the sloop ran west under three sails, the wind on the quarter. At Jukes Reef I gybed and ran north for two miles under the lee of a series of coral outcrops, getting closer to the *Pandora* wreck site so I could follow the route taken by *Pandora*'s open boats into Torres Strait. Forty false killer whales (*Pseudorca crassidens*) joined the dolphins all around the boat. The largest were about five metres long; they came barging in from windward, smashing through the white caps, before pulling up centimetres from the bow. False killer whales were given their name by the Danish zoologist Johannes Reinhardt after a mass stranding in 1860. He concluded that the rotting remains he had observed were those of a marine mammal which resembled the orca, or killer whale. In fact, at sea, they are quite different to orcas; more slender and almost uniformly black in colour with no white patches. False killer whales are fast-swimming animals that revel in the company of vessels. I watched them surfing in the waves beside the sloop, the front portion of their bodies momentarily clear of the water before diving with shallow, arched backs. They crammed the sea beneath the bows until the sloop appeared to be pushing a squirming black mass north-westward through the shoals. From inside the cabin I could hear their song resonating through the hull. Not the lugubrious tune that people listen to in the bath, but an urgent, hectoring squeak. I gybed again and ran west into clearer water, then once more altered course, now northwards for Shadwell Reef.

It was mid-way through this run that I crossed the track of *Pandora*'s boats. Four boats had been saved from the wrecked frigate, the pinnace, blue yawl, red yawl and the launch. In the hours after the wreck the survivors had come ashore on a sand cay four miles distant which Surgeon Hamilton describes as 'about thirty paces long . . . the heat of the sun, and the reflection from the sand, was now excruciating'. I had passed a couple of these sand cays already and would see several more in the course of the day. They were all much the same: silvery mounds of sand rising from green seas. They looked like they would be fun to explore for about half an hour early in the morning; after that they would be a burning hell. Eighty-nine of *Pandora*'s company reached the cay, and ten of the beachcombers. For the beachcombers, whose skin was now pasty after being shackled in the perpetual gloom of Pandora's Box for five months, the sand cay was a torment. James Morrison describes how the sun was so strong 'our skin flea'd off, from head to foot; tho we kept our Selves Covered in the Sand during the heat of the Day, this being all the Shelter that the Island affoards'. It wasn't much better for the regular crewmen. The surgeon records that in the night they were 'disturbed by the irregular behaviour of one Connell, which led us to suspect he had stole our wine, and got drunk; but, on further inquiry, we found that the excruciating torture he suffered from thirst led him to drink salt water; by which means he went mad, and died in the sequel to the voyage.'

The four open boats were prepared for the passage ahead by cutting up the floorboards to form uprights, around which they stretched canvas so as to raise the gunwale '. . . to keep the water from breaking into the boats at sea'. Captain Edwards took command of the pinnace with a compliment of 25 men. One of them was Lieutenant Thomas Hayward, who must have taken his seat with a sense of dread: as a midshipman Hayward had been in the open boat with William Bligh. The red yawl was commanded by Lieutenant Larkan and carried 23 men; the same number were crammed into the launch, under Lieutenant Corner. The master, Passmore, took the blue yawl with 21 men on board. The boats were so overcrowded the survivors sat in two tiers. Among the beachcombers squeezed into the boats was John Millward, who had been an able seaman aboard the *Bounty*. As Bligh had been cast adrift Millward had jeered from the *Bounty*'s taffrail: 'Go and see if you can live upon a Quarter of a Lb. of Yams per day'. Millward now had to live off considerably less than that. Although the frigate had sunk slowly, Edwards's preparations for the increasingly inevitable boat voyage had been few. The rations amounted to just '2 Musket balls weight of Bread &

hardly a Jill [¼ pint] of water & Wine together for 24 Hours'. Each boat commander was given the latitude and longitude of Timor, 1,100 miles distant. All four boats pushed off from the cay on 31 August 1791 at 10:30 in morning.

I ran north-west throughout that day, following the route towards the mainland taken by the four *Pandora* boats. The wind was lighter than I had hoped, and easing closer to the coast. By early afternoon I had gybed the sloop six times, each time swapping over the whisker-pole to keep the boat running under best advantage with three sails set. The sun was intensely strong. From the crosstrees my view in every direction was a scalded seascape of cloudy shoals, a turquoise wasteland. It was a beautiful but frightening place. There was more space than I had imagined: the chart made the Labyrinth look more cluttered. It was the emptiness and the silence that made this an unnerving sea. The sloop was behind was largest reef in the world, but I'd barely seen it, apart from distant breakers. Ahead was the largest island in the world, out of sight, its desert shores strangely reflected in the dusty, sediment-laden waters about the boat.

This blue continental fringe between reef and beach was a fine moment of sea travel, the boat poised between two worlds, lineal, suspended in opaque waters composed of both sand and sea. On that long, lonely run through the Labyrinth there was a sense of being in both places at once: the memory of the ocean only just behind, the expectation of the land always written into the horizon ahead. These waters were saturated with the whole gamut of Pacific sail: splinters from *Endeavour*'s keel and the corpses of the *Bounty* beachcombers. The murky border-world between ocean and land has always been the true danger area for ships, more so than the open sea.

By evening I was on a westerly tack, sailing into the setting sun. The sky was almost completely clear, a blue-grey wash overhead. Only a few wisps of high cloud were visible distant on the windward horizon. The breeze had died to ten knots. The sea was slight. I considered anchoring, perhaps behind a cay, but decided to remain underway through the night and close the coast while there was still any wind at all.

At 6 o'clock I passed Monsoon Reef. The chattering surf broke benignly at the drop off. The only visible feature was a tiny sand cay at the centre of the formation, a golden dome catching the last sun in a blackening sea. Half an hour later, as the setting sun dissected the horizon ahead, a snippet of the mainland coast was exposed. I saw a stretch of low, pale land in the vicinity of Shadwell Peak trailing northward into the sea.

I gybed twice more and by 11 p.m. had cleared the Arnold Islets. Ahead lay a stretch of open water. The shipping lanes were eight miles to the west; the nearest reef was five miles distant. There was room here to rest. I hove to, the sloop stemming the north-setting tide, and lay down in the cockpit, the alarm set for 20-minute intervals. Prawn trawlers were working far to the south, picked out by their own deck lights. Two freighters used the lanes to the west. Otherwise there was no traffic. When the tide turned I hove to on the other tack, to hold position against the ebb tide. At five the next morning I got underway, the sloop having drifted half a mile in the night.

Broken lengths of the coastline to the west were visible at first light. The land was low and drab in the grey dawn, the sky cloudy but for occasional fracture lines of blue. Sunrise appeared as tiers of light visible through dark cloud. I passed close to the west of Shortland Reef, a thin strip of rock above limp seas from which there came a powerful stench of kelp. Mount Adolphus Island faded and reformed in the cloud. Land here was fragile, forever a false horizon, as if the great continent had exhausted its sense of self on this final dusty reach towards the equator.

I gybed just east of Turtle Island as the sun broke through the cloud. To the west the dunes and sandhills had been eaten up by the vast mangrove-lined mouth of the Kennedy River. In the approach to Albany Passage tidal eddies caused the sea to break as I ran beside orange dunes leading north to Fly Point. Two of *Pandora's* boats had made a landing here. After a night among the shoals they reached the mainland on the morning of the second day, 'a very barren aspect,' according to Surgeon Hamilton. Later that morning they met two canoes 'with three black men in each . . . They stood up in the canoes, waved, and made signs for us to come to them. But . . . having heard an indifferent account of the natives of that country, we judged it prudent to avoid them'. At the Entrance to the Albany Passage the two yawls approached the beach 'to ground and look out'. An excellent spring of fresh water was found in the sand and they filled two small casks before making sail after the pinnace and launch in the direction of Bligh's 'Mountainous Island', today called Mount Adolphus.

In the decades following the wreck of HMS *Pandora* the tally of wrecks in the eastern approaches to Torres Strait was appalling. Mathew Flinders, who was first to circumnavigate the Australian continent in 1802, likened navigating Torres Strait to 'threading the needle'. In 1804, after the *Mersey* was wrecked in the strait, the captain and 12 crew reached Timor in a long boat; 56 others died. 1814: the *Morning Star* was wrecked in the strait; some survivors were rescued from Booby Island; others reached Timor in the long boat; about 20 more men were drowned. 1816: the *Lady Elliot* under Captain Stewart disappeared on the Great Barrier Reef bound from Sydney to Batavia; there were no survivors among the 54 crew, most of them Lascars. 1818: the *Frederick* was wrecked on Cape Flinders; although the master and four men were rescued by another ship, 24 other crew left for Timor in an open boat and were not seen again. 1826: the *Sun* was wrecked in Torres Strait; two boats were launched but only one was seen again. 1829: the crew of the wrecked *Governor Ready* made Timor in three open boats. 1832: the *Flora's* crew sailed to Timor in an open boat. 1833: the *Agnes* sank in Torres Strait. 1835: the *Jane and Henry* was wrecked on the Barrier Reef; the crew voyaged to Timor in the longboat.

Captains Bligh and Edwards did not so much make unique boat voyages to Timor as pioneer an open-boat route to the Dutch East Indies that over the next 50 years would become a thoroughfare for castaways.

Between 1841 and 1864 at least 31 ships were wrecked in the Torres Strait.* These are the documented cases. There were possibly many more. One later casualty was the *Bluebell*, the old sandalwood schooner that had once belonged to James Paddon and the ship which introduced measles to Erromango. The *Bluebell* was wrecked at night on a reef north of Cape Melville in 1867. By dawn the schooner was a total loss but the crew came ashore in the boats in good order on 5 January.

In response to this epidemic of castaways the colonial authorities decided to establish a station in Torres Strait so that shipwrecked mariners might find some European outpost closer than Timor. The site chosen was the Albany Passage, a half-mile wide channel between the mainland and Albany Island.

White caps were breaking on either side of the entrance to Albany Passage as the sloop approached, but in the channel itself the water was calm. I ran under the mainsail alone, making only two knots, but the flood tide set the brown waters of the channel flowing like a river. Rolling, dun-coloured hillsides rose on both sides while the shores of the channel were cobbled with numerous small bays. I gybed beneath a rocky buttresses where tendrils of bush were tugged downtide on the swirling flow. On the south side, behind a magenta beach, were the few tumbled down remains of Somerset, the station established in 1867 by HMS *Fly*. Over the next ten years castaways from ten wrecked ships found refuge here. When the government station was shifted north to Thursday Island in 1877, Somerset was taken over by the Jardine family who ran a fleet of pearlers with beachcomber crews.

A four-knot tidal stream flushed the sloop from Albany Passage. I hauled up on the wind and set a course north-east across the

---

*Including the *Maryts, Two Sisters, Clifford, Queen Victoria, Oriental, America, Coringa Packet, Hydrabad, Maid of Athens, Elizabeth Brown, Duroc, Tasmania, Ann, Druid, Gibson, Victoria, Mahaica, Fatima, A.L.Johnstone, Aerd van Nes, Phoenix, Lightening, Aleyia, Valient, Zwartz-Zwaan, Pauline et Victoire, Lady Kinnaird, William Kirk, Equator, Delfshaven,* and *Diana.*

trade. This basin of water was ringed by islands, small, barren, craggy, some of them little more than rocks. There was a stark, comfortless beauty to the abrupt alternations of water and rock. The whole place was run through with the drama of land's end. To the west I finally saw Cape York, a flinty peninsula reaching north, shaped like the outstretched paw of some desert dog, its claws sunk into the green seas of Torres Strait.

Under Mount Adolphus Island's lee there was a fine bay. Small, gritty beaches lined the shore, divided by slabs of rock running down into the sea. *Pandanus* trees and anthills covered the island's flanks. The milky lagoon and rich mangroves were the most visually nourishing things in sight. Above the water, the earth was red and the grass burnt a friable brown. As I climbed the hillside a goanna, a forked-tongued monitor lizard, scuttled away through the crumbling leaves. To the west the sea was pierced by the silhouettes of islands, and the jagged outlines of two ships steaming through the lanes off Cape York.

Captain Edwards brought *Pandora*'s open boats to this island searching for food and water. Hamilton watched alarmed as '. . . natives flocked down to the beach in crowds. They were jet black . . .'. The four boats pulled into the shallows, but none of the crew dared go ashore. The islanders filled one container with water, but then '. . . we observed the women and children running'. As the sailors heaved at the oars, pulling for deep water, the sky filled with a shower of arrows, one of which split the pinnace's planking. The castaways could expect little sympathy in Torres Strait. The islanders believed that shipwreck victims had been rejected by the sea. Even those of their own race whose canoes had foundered were sometimes killed as the price for being cast up on the shore.

Next morning the sun was strong. The haze that had smothered this coast for days past had burnt off. As I heaved up the mainsail the blue sky overhead was deep and hard. A dry 15-knot trade was coming from the Coral Sea. It funnelled through the Adolphus Channel and spread hungrily across the open waters beyond. As the sun passed behind the Lacey Islands their jagged spines formed a silhouette as black and shiny as liquorice. The sea was piebald with shadows and shoals. Cape York was beside my course now, a rocky spur dappled in shade. By mid-morning Endeavour Strait was open to the south-west, its entrance scattered with tiny isles shaped like droplets. Endeavour Strait looked wide and inviting, the trade wind would be on the beam: Captain Cook had taken the most obvious course. But Edwards led the four open boats on before the wind, towards a gaggle of islands on the north-western horizon. The castaways desperately needed to try again for food and water before beginning the passage to Timor.

I followed Edwards's course and by noon was coasting Horn Island. Plains of sun-drenched yellow grasses climbed to the island's apex, like a vast thatched roof above cobalt seas. Shoals appeared as brackish stains in the vibrant waters. Green turtles were awash in the choppy fetch as I ran into the Flinders' Channel. Despite the name, Edwards and his fleet of boats were the first Europeans to sail this way, inching uncertainly round in the dead of night into the basin of water sheltered by Horn, Wednesday and Thursday Islands. At dawn Edwards marvelled at the scale of this protected anchorage. Surgeon Hamilton speculated that '. . . were a little colony settled here, a concatenation of Christian settlements would enchain the world'.

That little settlement was indeed built in 1877 on Thursday Island. Today it is known throughout the region simply as T.I.

I ran before the wind down a channel of breaking water and anchored off the township in a pool bounded by reefs. Much the grandest building ashore was the Customs House. It stood as solitary and upright as a flagstaff planted on the foreshore, painted gold with emerald shutters. These rich colours reflect the long dead aspiration that Thursday Island would become a thriving entrepôt, an Austral Constantinople on the cusp of the Pacific and Indian Oceans. It was hard to picture this in today's sleepy settlement of tin and timber.

*

There was an autumnal feel on the waterfront at T.I. Almond trees lined the shore, their scorched, ruddy, leaves clattering down the road before the wind. Dark clouds raced diagonally across the sky. In the shade it was cool, as if the season had changed. The south-east trade was remorseless in the narrows. It coursed through Torres Strait, crashing between the islands like a run of bulls through the alleys of the old Basque town where Luis Váez de Torres himself had been born.

Thursday Island was full of symbols from its history. Boats were everywhere. On T.I. boats must have outnumbered cars ten to one. They littered the beaches and foreshore. Beneath the almond trees piles of aluminium runabouts were stacked up like trays. Even the streets were full of boats, parked on trailers, propped on blocks, lying on the cracked and arid verges. Like the Inuit sensitivity to snow, the Torres Strait Islanders have eighty words to account for the different tides. A new tide is likened to a feeble infant; it grows through the stages of childhood, adolescence, and adulthood; in the final quarter of the moon the tide is equated with frail old age and death.

At the centre of Thursday Island, on a grassy hilltop sunburnt to the colour of toast, are two huge wind turbines. They are geared very low, so that even in 30 knots of wind they turn only slowly, the individual blades always easy to define. The trade wind in Torres Strait is recognized as one of the most consistent winds in the world. The turbines are visible from just about everywhere in this central part of the strait, a response to the forces that brought ships here from all over the Pacific. Their painstaking but elegant motion spins a tribute to a township born as a waypoint for journeys made under sail.

Along the waterfront a row of old weatherboard trade stores with narrow verandas faced the sea. Some were now boarded up, their latticework frayed by the constant action of wind and dust. The main street climbed gently inland up the hillside. On the east side I walked past the offices of an organization whose name conjured those first European voyages into the Labyrinth with its unlikely mix of so-Spanish and so-English: The Torres Shire Council.

Today, Thursday Island is the administrative centre for the wider Torres Strait region. The street was rather quiet and empty. There were a couple of cafés, a gallery and bookshop. It took less than an hour to wander through the town. Then, after so long on the boat, I stretched my legs along the stony trails that twist through the gum trees. But when I returned to town next day the few people I met smiled in recognition. The lady in the bookshop greeted me by name.

In the garden outside the small cathedral I met Bishop Saibo Mabo. He was pacing up and down the driveway beside the church in a crisp linen suit, a sprig of frangipani pinned to his lapel, occasionally stopping to drum both hands on the car roof, his lips pursed. He was already late for a function, he told me with the ease that island churchmen have for addressing total strangers, but was still waiting for his wife to appear from the residence. 'Have you seen our cathedral?' Bishop Mabo asked. I had been roaming the lawns, taking photographs, but had not yet been inside. 'Oh well, you must. Come with me now.' His voice became a trifle sharper: 'I'm sure I still have a moment or two longer to wait. As a sailor you will want to see this, our church is dedicated to a ship.' Bishop Mabo led the way through the creaking double doors.

Perhaps appropriately in Torres Strait, the Quetta Memorial Church was dedicated not only to a ship, but a shipwreck. History here was spiked with something similar to the absurdity of trench warfare: the ships just kept coming over the top of the Pacific horizon, piling up on the reefs, their remains rotting in the waterlogged no-man's-land of the strait. The *Quetta* was a 3,500-ton steamer plying the Brisbane to London route. On 29 February 1890, under a full moon and in calm seas, an uncharted rock tore out the steamer's bottom and she sank in three minutes. The *Albatross* picked up 160 castaways from Muri Island, most of them Lascars returning home. One hundred and thirty-three passengers died, the majority Europeans en route to the tropics after spending the wet season further south.

On one wall of the cathedral was a large-scale Admiralty chart, 'Torres Strait from Bramble Cay to Glamis Castle Shoal'. The chart had been given pride of place, as if it were a sacred text. In a sense, it was. The slaughter among the reefs had only been brought to an end once the chart was completed, drawn up from the cumulative experience of generations of seafarers. 'The church was consecrated in 1890, the same year as the *Quetta* wreck,' Bishop Mabo said from behind my shoulder, 'and is now the cathedral for my Diocese of Carpentaria.'

He pointed out various relics from the doomed ship that adorned the cathedral's walls and pillars: a life ring marked 'S.S. Quetta, Glasgow'; a bronze porthole crusted with barnacles and rime. It is cruel the way genuine nautical artefacts can so closely resemble the tat sold in seaside souvenir stores. A few minutes later the Bishop's wife appeared at the doorway in a boater draped with fresh flowers, and the two took their leave.

The Admiralty's vision for Thursday Island when it was established in 1877 was that it should become a British outpost guarding the crucial seaway through the strait, not unlike Gibraltar or Singapore; the harbour would be bustling with European trading ships and Malay *praus*. But the legacy of shipwreck and castaway sailors was nonetheless a better icon for the settlement. Rather than a European satellite, Thursday Island has more in common with the beach communities that grew up in the Pacific basin in the nineteenth century.

In 1800 there were only four port towns around the Pacific rim to service trading voyages into the islands: Sydney, Valparaiso, Manila and Canton. Over the next decades, however, beach communities developed among the islands themselves. They emerged organically at the places where ships called in order to meet the numerous needs of trading vessels, notably at Papeete (Tahiti), Apia (Samoa), Levuka (Fiji), Honolulu (Hawaii) and Kororareka (Bay of Islands, New Zealand). All these sites were determined by the needs of western ships: all had deep-water anchorages easily accessible under sail yet protected from the prevailing weather. None had previously been an important location for the indigenous peoples, whose canoes could be dragged up the beaches almost anywhere. Thus the arrival of the first ships changed the local political dynamic ashore as the sometimes lowly tribes living close to the main anchorages enjoyed an elevation of status.

These settlements became centres for beachcomber artisans and all the trades associated with ships: shipwrights, pilots, coopers, sail makers, carpenters, blacksmiths, provisioners, grog-sellers and brothel keepers. Beachcomber tradesmen originating on trading vessels founded these towns, which became supply and refit bases for ships. As such, they were usually denigrated by visitors. Kororareka (now renamed Russell) was known as the 'Hell-hole of the Pacific' on account of the number of beachcombers living there. One visitor in 1837 described the town as a 'filthy looking miserable place', and there were riots in 1839.

The fate of the beach towns has been mixed to say the least. Papeete and Honolulu were both taken over by the colonial authorities when Tahiti and Hawaii were annexed. Both have become modern cities and few traces of their beach origins remain. But Kororareka (Russell) and Levuka were bypassed when the colonial administrations moved to Auckland and Suva respectively. Russell and Levuka are often regarded today as among the most atmospheric towns in the Pacific, full of old-world charm, museum pieces where time has stood still. Visitors adore Russell for its 'Englishness', its quaint weatherboard cottages and their rose-covered trellises. But in its heyday English visitors hated Kororareka. Charles Darwin, visiting in the *Beagle* in 1835, described the residents of Kororareka as 'the very refuse of society'. After the authorities moved to Auckland six years later, another visitor 'was struck with the apparent solitude of the place . . . silence had usurped the place of noise, bustle and activity'.

This description could have applied equally well to Thursday Island at the time of my visit. The autumn here had really begun long ago. But in its prime T.I. had been a booming anchorage, though perhaps not of the sort the Admiralty had originally envisaged. In the age of sail, Thursday Island was known as the 'Sink of the Pacific', cluttered with deserters, beachcombers, castaways, Japanese pearl-shell divers, failed traders, Kanakas, Polynesians, Norfolk Islanders and Malays. The anchorage was full of trading ships, while on shore beachcomber artisans provided all the usual services and professions that visiting sailors required.

Few buildings on Thursday Island better reflected the settlement's faded glory than Number 16 John Street. At first glance it looked similar to most of the other houses in the dusty grid of back streets. Only the aerials gave it away. The rusty iron roof boasted three VHF antennas; an HF mast rose from the garden supported by a seaman-like lash-up of cables and warps. This weatherboard villa built in 1911 was one of the oldest surviving buildings on Thursday Island. It was now considerably dilapidated, but still home to the Reef Pilots. I climbed the wooden steps to the front door with some trepidation. The Reef Pilots had the reputation of inhabiting a closed and insular world, suspicious of those not inducted to their clan.

In the foyer I introduced myself to Andrew Hurry, a senior Reef Pilot with 18 years' experience. 'So you're a WAFI are you?' he said looking me up and down. I had a vague memory of what this meant, the third letter was inevitable, but pretended not to understand. 'That's right a WAFI,' he said again. 'A yachtsman. A wind-assisted fucking idiot. Most yachts are a pain. They come wandering into the middle of the two-way route as if they own the sea. A few weeks ago I was off Restoration Rock doing 18 knots in a container ship. It was a dark night and this WAFI suddenly decided to turn on his navigation lights 300 metres under the ship's bows. I altered course and missed him by 20 metres. Next thing, the galah is on the radio blaming me!' A 'galah' is a colourful, but stupid, Australian bird.

The pink faded from Pilot Hurry's cheeks with the venting of this spleen and he invited me through into the living room. As we sat he said in a conciliatory tone, 'Most WAFIs are all right. Ninety-five per cent are responsible. The other five live up to their name.'

Ship's pilots are distinct from other seafarers in that they are not tied to one particular ship, but to a stretch of coast they know intimately. A pilot works on numerous ships which ply that coast and his local knowledge compliments the expertise of the ship's officers to ensure a safe passage.

Inevitably then, the first Pacific pilots were beachcombers. As the first white settlers in this ocean, they were the first to acquire detailed local knowledge. And since most of them were runaway sailors, beachcombers also understood the world of ships.

The first recorded instance of beachcomber pilotage I found dates from the 1790s. Edward Robarts jumped from the whaler *Euphrates* in 1798 and lived on the beach in the Marquesas for eight years, marrying into a chiefly line and fathering three children. Robarts eventually settled on the shores of Taiohae Bay where he spied an opportunity for employment '. . . as ships frequently pass by, being unacquainted with the harbour and no one for a pilot'. Robarts set to work, 'surveying the harbour and rocks and observing the different sets of the current − being the most valuable Knowledge that I could gain to assist the weary Navigator in the time of need'.

Pilotage was one of the services offered in most of the Pacific beach communities that emerged in the early 1800s. In Levuka, Fiji, the beachcombers William Cary and David Whippy organized pilots for the Salem trading ships that came for bêche-de-mer. When the French navigator Dumont d'Urville arrived at Levuka in 1838 he found that all the pilots had 'certificates' of recommendation from previous skippers and were competing for business. Pilotage was one way that castaways and beachcombers sometimes rejoined the world of ships: first they proved themselves in the role of pilot so as to win the confidence of ships' captains who might otherwise distrust them. In Hawaii the beachcombers John Young, Isaac Davis and John Harbottle all worked as pilots in Honolulu Harbour. Jonas Coe was pilot in Apia Harbour for many years. But it was in New Zealand, with its extensive coastal geography and sometimes belligerent

Dicky Barrett, a trader and beachcomber in New Zealand who worked as a pilot in Cook Strait. Barrett also served as a warrior; for four weeks in 1832 he helped 250 Te Ati Awa tribesmen hold out against 1,600 attackers, employing three ship's cannon and a swivel gun which killed 350 of the besiegers

weather, that beachcomber pilotage was particularly common. Richard Driver, a whaleman who was captured by Maori when his boat crew were massacred in Otago Harbour in 1838, was later appointed official pilot for the same harbour by Governor Grey.

Likewise the beachcombers Lewis Acker, Dicky Barrett and Charles Marshall all served as pilots, in Foveaux Strait, Cook Strait and the Waikato River respectively. Pilotage became one of the classic beachcomber roles, being one more form of agency between ship and shore.

I started by asking the Torres Strait pilot Andrew Hurry to clarify the relationship between the captain (or master) and the pilot on the bridge of a modern ship. 'The pilot is there to give the benefit of his advice. He has the conduct or control of the ship – what we call the "con" – but not the responsibility. The master could take the con at any time.'

Andrew Hurry was misnamed. He had a cool, slow ticking voice that would acknowledge no urgency. He looked, as many true seamen do, very tired; above the tender, inky bags poised over his cheekbones, his eyes were drawn and fraught. This was a man who shepherded oil tankers through the Great Barrier Reef, the jewel in the coastal crown of the land 'girt by sea'. Tension and irritability ran through 16 John Street, as if the piles themselves were stressed, and sleepless anxiety was eating through the timbers like shipworm. 'We've had the Greens on our backs for 20 years,' he said. 'In fact, the threat to the reef doesn't come from ships. It's fertilizer run off from the sugar cane plantations during the wet season that's killing the coral.'

Photographs of the pilot's house from 1935 show the veranda laid out with card tables, white linen and vases of cut flowers. Heavy slat blinds could be rolled down to provide shelter from the wind and sun. This was a building devoted to rest and renewal, a haven from the sea. Until the 1970s the pilots slept in an open dormitory on the cool, wide, southern veranda, each bed fitted with a mosquito net. Once, a neighbour complained that the pilots did not deserve their exalted status in the local community because, as far as he could see, all they ever did was sleep on the veranda, play billiards and have barbeques.

'I came through Torres Strait for the first time in 1964,' Andrew Hurry told me. 'I was a lowly third mate but I knew then that my ambition was to be a Reef Pilot. As a professional mariner, this is as far as you can go. There's nothing else like this in the world.' For most of history Torres Strait has not been water at all but a land bridge between Australia and New Guinea. The first sea channels were formed about 6,500–8,000 years ago, the result of earth movement to the west and volcanic activity to the east. The strait was finally 'drowned' about 3,000 years ago to become a shallow shelf, separating two oceans with quite different characteristics. Indian Ocean tides are mostly diurnal (high water every 24 hours); Pacific tides are semi-diurnal (high water every 12 hours). In the Torres Strait these out-of-phase tides meet in a myriad of channels, shoals and coral lagoons. The resulting tidal streams are chaotic. The Prince of Wales Channel has some of strongest tide/current combinations in the world reaching four metres per second at times. But when the tide and current are opposed, slack water may occur for several hours.

'Don't think of Torres Strait as a sea,' Andrew Hurry said. 'Think of it as a tidal river with limited depth, full of coral and granite pinnacles. Pilots are trained to bring deep-draught ships through here without electronics, at full speed, at night, in a gale. The maximum draught of ships we bring through is 12.2 metres and the controlling depth in the Varsin Passage is 10.6 metres so you have to work the tides. It's a three- to four-day steam from here to Brisbane, the longest single-handed stretch of pilotage in the world. You can leave the bridge on some of the easier stretches. I'm off the bridge for about 30 per cent of each passage.'

Later he asked, 'So what about you? You've come up the coast from Brisbane, have you?' I explained that I'd come in through the reef at Raine Island. He paused a moment, stared at me, and the frown almost disappeared from his face. 'Really? You used the old Raine Island entrance, by yourself? No one goes that way anymore.'

The cloud in the pilot's face resulted from more than simple tiredness. Pilotage itself was on the rocks. The Reef Pilots had enjoyed a monopoly since the first licences were granted by the Queensland Marine Board in 1884. But ten years before my visit the industry had been deregulated and a competitor organization established, known as the Torres Pilots. I asked Andrew Hurry where their headquarters was; I'd seen no sign of it around the town. 'They operate out of the local pub,' he said wearily. 'Competition in pilotage is a nonsense. Price is the only issue for shipowners. So long as they have a licensed pilot on the bridge they've met the requirements of their insurance. In the end standards will be cut.'

Ships themselves have obviously been revolutionized by technology over the last two centuries, but the human societies on board them have echoes of the past. Today's trading ships are still melting pots and there are traces of the old Lascar and Kanaka seamen. 'If it goes on like this,' Andrew Hurry said, 'they'll soon be taking pilots from the [Indian] sub-continent. That's not racism – it's only that their standards are lower than ours. Racism is one brush you can't tar the Reef Pilots with. In this job you have to get on with every nation on earth. You eat their food, you're a minority of one on their ship. Some of them don't speak good English – they're supposed to, but they don't. We use a sort of bridge patois to communicate.

'It's a dying profession. Today I'm paid 65 per cent of what I got in 1993. I'm paid less than the master of an Australian or New Zealand ship. The satisfaction of the job is the only reason to do it now.' Once, there had been a queue of eager mariners aspiring to call themselves a Reef Pilot. Not any longer. 'One day they'll be taking people off the beach,' Andrew Hurry said gruffly.

The first Pacific pilot, Edward Robarts, eventually tired of life on the beach. Despite his marriage to a chief's daughter, he realized he would never be fully accepted into Marquesan society. The beach was a place of divided loyalties and identities. Robarts protected the Marquesans from the swindles of visiting sailors and persuaded some captains not to punish minor thefts by explaining the islanders' non-existent notion of private property. On the other hand, when the Russian navigator Krusenstern visited the group Robarts told him '. . . not to place any confidence in these islanders; to be always on our guard, and, when any of them offended us, to shoot them immediately'.

Robarts is unique among Pacific beachcombers because when he quit the Marquesas aboard the privateer *Lucy* in 1806, he took his Polynesian wife and children with him. The family travelled on various ships to Tahiti, New Zealand, Fiji and New Ireland. They then went on board the *Frederick* in order to make the passage through Torres Strait, or 'Dorris Straights' as Robarts called them. In the Labyrinth the *Frederick* was nearly lost. The ship struck the reef twice, the second time so seriously on a shoal immediately north of Cape York that Robarts believed the *Frederick* might have to be abandoned. In anticipation of following the open boat route pioneered by Bligh and Edwards, the longboat was prepared in order 'to carry all hands to the Island of Timor'. As the crew worked frantically to save the ship Robarts 'was very faint, having eat no food the whole day and spit a deal of blood'. In the evening they were rewarded when the *Frederick* floated clear on the flood tide. Robarts, however, lived up to the reputation of beachcombers as troublemakers and the captain of the *Frederick* dumped him and his family in Penang in 1808 after the two men had fallen out. Here, he worked as butler to the sister of Thomas Stamford Raffles until her death in 1810, after which the family continued their shipboard wanderings as far west as Calcutta.

In the course of his 53-year life Edward Robarts worked in an extraordinary variety of roles. He was a true beachcomber, typically pragmatic. As well as a whaleman, deserter, pilot, interpreter, trading agent and butler, Robarts was a builder, tailor, moonshiner, overseer at the Botanical Gardens in Calcutta, midwife, teacher, storekeeper, slave trader, police constable and warrior. But if in the Marquesas he had never been fully accepted into Polynesian life, in Calcutta, where the family lived in the native quarters on the margins of European life, he realized he could never now be wholly reintegrated into European society. With his tattoos, a Polynesian wife and mixed-race children, he was trapped on the beach in perpetuity. For beachcombers, the passage out of the Pacific was doubly difficult. The physical dangers of navigating through the reefs of Torres Strait were mirrored by an equally tortuous and uncharted journey back to their original cultures. Many failed to find safe passage and were forever caught between worlds. In his final years in Calcutta Robarts was reduced to begging.

Of all the beachcombers who sailed through Torres Strait and returned home, none did so with greater success than Peter Heywood. As a midshipman, Heywood was the youngest, but also the highest ranking, of the ten *Bounty* men who survived the wreck of HMS *Pandora* on the Barrier Reef. Bligh always loathed Heywood, being convinced that he and Christian had plotted the mutiny together. Heywood had been one member of Christian's infamous shore camp at Point Venus in Tahiti, established so the Kew gardeners, David Nelson and William Brown, could pot up the breadfruit seedlings ready for the voyage home.

Heywood made the open boat voyage through Torres Strait in August 1791 together with the other *Pandora* castaways and reached Timor two weeks later. At the eventual court martial in England he was convicted of mutiny, but granted a free pardon by King's Warrant. He returned to service in the navy and became a distinguished cartographer making contributions to Horsburgh's 1807 sailing directions to the Indian Ocean and to Flinders' 1814 atlas of the Australian coast. According to Lady Belcher, a close friend of Heywood's, Lord Melville offered him the post of Hydrographer of the Navy, but he turned it down on account of ill health, and on his recommendation the job went to Captain Francis Beaufort (of wind scale fame). Heywood was physically frail for much of his adult life. Lady Belcher put this down to the privations he endured in Pandora's Box. From the time of his arrest in Tahiti until he finally reached England Heywood spent 17 months continuously in chains. After his retirement Captain Heywood often went to court, where he was a friend of the Duke of Clarence, a man who enjoyed poking fun at seamen and nautical language. On one sultry day the Duke pulled a handerchief from his pocket and as he wiped his face observed, 'Obliged to swab, Heywood, 'bliged to swab.' That an aristocrat like the Duke of Clarence would even stoop to speak, let alone joke, with a man with a tattooed backside illustrates Heywood's success at rehabilitating himself into English society. Uniquely, Heywood managed to portray beachcombing as somehow exotic. His experiences in the Pacific, both on the *Bounty* and on the beach at Tahiti, helped bring him to prominence. Family connections didn't hurt, either.

Heywood was a remarkable exception. No other beachcomber rose to such heights. Of the other *Bounty* men, James Morrison was also pardoned, but was later lost at sea when the *Blenheim* sank with all hands in a gale off Madagascar in February 1807. Coleman, Norman, McIntosh and Byrne, the four men who had always been cleared by Bligh, were acquitted of mutiny. Musprat got off on a technicality. Ellison, Burkitt and Millward were convicted of mutiny and publicly hanged aboard HMS *Brunswick* in October 1792.

Those other beachcombers who managed to return home met equally mixed fates. George Vason reached England after five years on the beach in Tonga, most of which had been spent indulging in pleasures of the flesh with several teenage wives. Vason returned to his native Nottingham where he married Miss Leavers, 'a woman of eminent piety and unaffected humility'. His first employment was as Keeper of St Mary's Workhouse. Later, he was appointed Governor of Nottingham Gaol.

William Mariner, the boy clerk who survived the massacre on the *Port au Prince* in Tonga, finally reached Gravesend on the *Cuffnells* in June 1811 after four years on the beach. Mariner never went back to sea. For many years he worked in the office of Mr Edward Hancock, a stockbroker at 12 Copthall Court in the City of London, but drowned, aged 53, in the Surrey Canal.

Some sailors believed that tattoos, and facial tattoos in particular, amounted to an outcast's brand which made re-entering European society impossible. There are several reports of tattooed sailors being stoned and spat at on the streets of London. A handful of beachcombers, however, made a virtue of their tattoos. The Frenchman Jean Cabri showed off his full-body tattoos to the good and the great in Moscow and St Petersburg. Scientists studied his markings and he was initially rewarded by being appointed swimming instructor to the marine cadets at Kronstadt,

'John Rutherford, the tattooed Englishman.' Portrait by George Scharf, c. 1829

on account of his ability to swim like a South Sea Islander. Later, though, Cabri was reduced to trudging through the salons and provincial fairs of Europe exhibiting himself as a freak. At the Orleans Fairs in 1817 he found himself playing second fiddle to a performing dog named Munito. When Cabri died in Valenciennes the authorities initially proposed skinning him in order to preserve his extraordinary tattoos, but in the end he was buried intact between two other corpses, one above, one below, to deter body snatchers.

Cabri's experiences were shared by several others. A New Zealand beachcomber named John Rutherford who had a full facial tattoo, or *moko*, joined a troupe of travelling entertainers when he reached England and earned a living exhibiting his tattoos. Afterwards he was reported to be a London pickpocket operating in the character of a Maori chief. James O'Connell returned to the United States from the Pacific in 1835 and worked in circuses as 'The Tattooed Man' till his death in 1854. So popular was the attraction that rival circuses sometimes crudely 'tattooed' a man in order to set up in competition. When Archibald Campbell came home to Scotland from Hawaii, where he had been an advisor to the royal household, he found his circumstances much reduced. At home Campbell earned a miserable pittance playing the fiddle for the entertainment of steerage passengers on steam ships plying the Clyde.

The passage of sailing vessels through straits has long represented a voyage from the known to the unknown. In mythology the son of Zeus sailed between the Pillars of Hercules – the Straits of Gibraltar – in a golden chalice shaped like a lotus and so entered the Green Sea of Darkness. Beachcombers found that the passage through Torres Strait and the journey back to Europe took them to a place where they were now strangers. The streets or fields of home had become their own 'sea of darkness'. It was much easier to cross the beach and go to live among the islanders than ever to cross back again. For the majority, beachcombing was a one-way journey. Sometimes through choice but mainly through necessity, most beachcombers stayed on their islands till the sun bleached their bones.

Today, the shipping lanes through Torres Strait are busier than ever, but most of it is through traffic and very few ships stop at Thursday Island. For a time, however, in the nineteenth century the 'New Singapore' tag was not wholly unjustified. By the

1820s more than one hundred ships a year were passing through Torres Strait. In the boom years of the 1880s and 1890s all trade from Queensland and the Pacific to India and England came through the strait. The pearl-shell trade alone was worth £100,000 a year. The bêche-de-mer trade was almost as valuable. Thursday Island boasted seven hotels as well as numerous shipyards, workshops and provisioners. Never previously being an important centre for the Torres Strait Islanders, it was chosen as the site for the government station specifically because of its easy accessibility for deep-draught sailing ships. The magistrate, Chester, built a large bungalow on Thursday Island with verandas facing the cooling trade where captains of passing ships gathered in the evenings. As steam-powered shipping became ever more prevalent, Thursday Island developed as a significant bunkering depot.

One of the last trading ships to make the passage through Torres Strait under sail was the *Otago*, an iron barque built by Alexander Stephen and Sons on the Clyde in 1869. Some considered the *Otago* to be damned. In the Far East she was commanded by a Scot from Kirkcaldy named John Snadden. The officer who eventually replaced him described Snadden as '. . . a peculiar man – of about sixty-five – iron grey, hard-faced, obstinate, uncommunicative . . . [He] Would come on deck at night, take some sail off her, God only knows why or wherefore, then go below . . . and play the violin for hours . . .'

In November 1887 Snadden threw his violin overboard while on passage to Hong Kong. Within hours he was dead from fever. The crew buried him at sea in the Gulf of Siam, then brought the barque up the Meinam River to Bangkok. The chief mate, a German named Born, hoped to succeed to the captaincy as there was always a shortage of European officers in Bangkok. However, the British consul cabled Henry Ellis, the marine superintendent in Singapore, to find a new master for the *Otago*. At the Officers' Sailors' Home Ellis tracked down a 31-year-old unemployed Polish-born seaman. Whether he was the perfect candidate for the job is a moot point. His uncle had long mocked his ambition of going to sea, saying he looked more like a man who 'spends all his time in drawing-rooms'. He had lost 3,000 francs of borrowed money in a venture running guns to Carlists (reactionary monarchists) in Spain's Gulf of Rosas. In an effort to recoup his losses he took a further 800 borrowed francs to the tables at Monte Carlo and lost that as well. His powers of imagination seemingly exhausted he then attempted to shoot himself through the heart at his Marseille lodgings. He had no previous experience of command and had now been mooching around Singapore in a black dog depression for more than two weeks since quitting his last ship, the *Vidar*. Ellis immediately offered him the job. Originally christened Józef Teodor Konrad Korzeniowski, he would later be better known as Joseph Conrad.

Conrad went aboard the *Otago* at Bangkok in January 1888. He was, by his own admission, plagued by anxiety. Some of the crew, particularly Born, resented his appointment, and a minor navigational error while descending the Meinam River to the sea did little to win their confidence. The passage to Singapore was a miserable affair, thwarted by calms. The crew were sick with fever and for much of the trip the 31-year-old captain was assisted by a single healthy hand, the Dutch cook Veilom who had a weak heart. Conrad did not leave the deck for 17 days or sleep at all for the final 49 hours.

From Singapore the *Otago* sailed south of Australia to reach Sydney with a cargo of teak. Here the barque's owners, Henry Simpson and Sons of Port Adelaide, instructed Conrad to carry cargoes on the coastal run between Sydney and Melbourne. Two months passed repeating the same passage – a frustrating time for Conrad who found coastal sailing a bore. Finally, a reprieve came in the form of instructions to sail for Mauritius with a mixed cargo. The standard route for such a passage was to again sail south of Australia and so into the Indian Ocean.

In *Last Essays* Conrad wrote, 'Almost without reflection I sat down and wrote a letter to my owners suggesting that, instead of the usual southern route, I should take the ship to Mauritius by way of Torres Strait. I ought to have received a severe rap on the knuckles . . . in submitting such an unheard-of proposition.' However, Simpson agreed, provided this course did not 'endanger the success of your passage'.

The *Otago* cleared from Sydney on 7 August 1888. Nine days out the barque was in the eastern approaches to Torres Strait. This was, as Conrad put it, '. . . the strait whose existence for a century and a half had been doubted, argued about, squabbled over by geographers, and even denied . . . It was not without a certain emotion that . . . I put her head at daybreak for Bligh Entrance, and packed on every bit of canvas she could carry.' He passed the wreck of the *Honolulu* stranded on a reef, and ran west for 36 hours across wind-swept, sunlit, empty waters, half-veiled by a brilliant haze, believing that the spirits of dead sailors haunt the waters of their Earthly exploits. Of the passage through the shoals, from Bligh Entrance to Cook's Booby Island, Conrad wrote, '. . . what would the memory of my sea life have been for me if it had not included a passage through Torres Strait . . . along the track of the early navigators?'

For Joseph Conrad the passage of Torres Strait was a personal coming of age. He had been a novice when he first took command of the *Otago* in Bangkok eight months earlier. But by choosing to come through the reefs to Thursday Island he stamped his authority on the ship. The *Otago* was his first and only command. Piloting the barque through Torres Strait was the pinnacle of Conrad's short career as a seaman.

Torres Strait serves as a bottleneck at the ocean's end. Ships which have sailed a hundred courses through the islands here navigate the same shallows. Among the shoals and spits awash, lagoons, reefs and myriad channels, their stories intertwine. The words and waters mix where the out-of-phase tides collide. Conrad chose to associate with his heroes, the great navigators Cook and Bligh who pioneered the passage through the strait. But his experiences as a seaman exposed Conrad to the whole cross-section of life afloat on which he drew in his later career as a writer. Conrad also understood the nature of the beach and beachcombing. In his novel *An Outcast of the Islands*, Conrad's fictional trading skipper echoes the mindset of those earlier sea captains who refused to have beachcombers on their ships. Captain Lingard will not allow the beachcomber Willems to board his schooner. Instead, Willems is abandoned at a remote Malay island: 'You are not fit to go amongst people . . . You are neither white nor brown. You have no colour as you have no heart . . . You are my shame.'

When the trade was fresh the anchorage at Thursday Island was choppy for small boats, and on the second day I beat across the channel to the more sheltered waters under the lee of Horn Island. Early in the evening I paddled ashore. The tidal stream was setting hard around the piles of the wharf. Half a dozen pelicans came sailing past on the glittering blue seas, tail feathers puffed out by the wind like downy spinnakers. Their eyes were rigid and glassy, permanently staring up into the sky.

Behind the waterfront a row of plain, concrete houses stood back from the road. The trade was gritty, peppered with airborne dust. At the western end of the small settlement stood its principal feature, the Wongai Hotel. When the *Pandora* castaways came ashore on this coast in 1791 they gorged themselves on the fruit of the *wongai* tree which Surgeon Hamilton described as 'resembling a plum . . . As I discovered some to be pecked at by the birds, we permitted the men to fill their bellies with them'.

The Wongai Hotel was a typical, functional Antipodean watering hole, the tables at chest height to minimize the distance between glass and mouth. Round the back there was a cavernous restaurant and I pulled back the ranch slider and went inside. A large party of workers from the airport had arrived just before me, dressed in tight blue shorts and white shirts, their breast pockets bulging with pens and notebooks. The airport workers commandeered a table at one end of the barn-like room and I sat at the other end, in front of a small stage where 'Diver Dan' was adjusting a microphone ready to begin his evening performance.

Dan had been a diver in the pearl-shell fishery, once the principal industry in Torres Strait. Captain Cook had first noted the abundance of shell in the strait in 1770 and, as was usual throughout the ocean, his own voyage was followed by those of the traders. One hundred years later Captain Banner sailed the brig *Julia Percy* up from Sydney and returned with a cargo of shell worth £3-400 pounds a ton. Over the next decades traders and opportunists from around the Pacific flocked to Torres Strait to cash in. Profits were made not from the pearls themselves but rather from the shell, used for pistol handles, mirror frames and inlay for furniture. Its most important use, however, was in the manufacture of buttons.

Diver Dan's lyrics were simple and returned again and again to the same themes: the pearl luggers that had once pounded into the concave seas of Torres Strait; the polyglot crews with spray dripping from their faces; the reefs; the tides; the south-east trade. The airport workers were lost in their own boisterous exchanges and Diver Dan serenaded me alone while I chewed on steak.

At the end of his set I offered to buy Diver Dan a drink and he pulled up a chair at my table. I asked him where he was from. 'I'm from this place,' he said, 'the Torres Strait.' His ethnicity was impossible to determine but he was clearly mixed race. By the mid-twentieth century anthropologists were speculating that there would soon be no pure blood Pacific Islanders left, such was the impact of the beachcombers. One beachcomber named Connel in Fiji fathered forty-eight children; another in Melanesia, Jackson, thirty-eight. In the Torres Strait, diving for pearls was so dangerous that few whites were ever prepared to do it. The luggers were crewed by the Torres Strait Islanders themselves, or by Malays, Japanese, Maori, New Hebrideans, Aboriginals, Chinese, Norfolk Islanders and the mixed-race children of beachcombers who were most at home in the shallows. Fletcher Christian's grandson had been a pearl-shell diver in Torres Strait. Some skippers preferred to employ women as they could dive deeper. One of Diver Dan's songs mocked the racial hierarchy of the pearl-shell industry: 'England number one. Japanee number two. Malayo, Manila bloody fool. South Sea all same.'

When the supply of shell accessible to free divers was exhausted, the rudimentary diving apparatus used aboard the luggers made accidents more common still. Many divers were killed each year by shark attack or the bends.

'I worked on the *Triton* and then the *Winston*,' Dan told me. 'It was the oil that finished off them days.' I didn't understand. 'Plastic,' he said. 'They started making plastic buttons and that was it. In the 1960s you could see near thirty of the old luggers abandoned at T.I. Some of 'em was awash at high tide. Some had only their masts stickin out of the water.'

It was hard to say whether Dan had really been a pearl-shell diver. He was just about old enough and certainly full of yarns. But he also had a well-rehearsed wink and a showman's come-rain-or-shine grin. Maybe 'Diver Dan' was only a stage persona. I didn't really care. The next morning I'd sail west into the Arafura Sea. This was the first time on the voyage that I had heard beachcomber ancestry being celebrated.

8

In Shallow Water

'I was born to be unfortunate . . .'

Edward Robarts, beachcomber

THE TIDE RAN hard west of Thursday Island. A stream of coursing water was squeezed through the narrows. Eddies spun the sloop at 40° to its course. A Reef Pilots' launch steamed north for the rendezvous at Goods Island, half hidden in the perpetual fog of its own exhaust.

The rising sun revealed an incongruous scene ahead. Two images from quite different places appeared to have been crudely pasted together. Above the beaches the islets were brown and grassy. Homesteads with wide verandas stood in bare paddocks. It was a copybook scene of Australian pastoral life, a world of jackaroos, sweat-stained felt hats, merino sheep and shears.

But container ships lined the horizon. Beneath the beaches, azure waterways swirled with tide rips. The hulk of an old ship was rotting on the foreshore at Goods Island, its blackened frames like the ribcage of some beast that found the waterhole dry. As the tide reached its peak flow, the sloop was flushed down Normanby Sound faster than a galloping sheep.

I worked on the foredeck, rigging a whisker pole and setting both headsails as the sun rose above the islands. The sloop ran west beside Larpent Bank through water as green and still as a lawn. Two dugongs sported in the shallows, their creamy brown tails raised calmly as they dived. By mid-morning Booby Island was on the beam, the last guano-covered outlier before the open waters of the Arafura Sea. When I looked back over the wake now, the Labyrinth had already closed up. From ten miles offshore there appeared to be no channel here, only a continuous chain of land.

A short, worried sea came up from the Gulf of Carpentaria, throwing the boat into a twitching roll. The Gulf, 400 miles long and 300 wide, is a yawning chunk cut from the coast of northern Australia, and I would be crossing its mouth for several days to come.

In the mid-afternoon I sailed over the Hocking Patches, a nine-metre shoal where the water was pea green, full of weed and turtles. When they heard the sloop's bow wave the turtles stuck their heads from the water in a sad, prehistoric stare. Then they gasped and flippered out of sight. The castaway crews of open boats making this same passage had made a feast of turtle meat and slaked their thirst with blood.

Before midnight I passed the Carpentaria Shoal and set a course west, beside one of the shipping lanes that leads into Torres Strait. I sat up through the night but saw little traffic, only a cargo to the north, and a trawler to the south turning maddening circles on the dark, empty plains of the Gulf.

A rain squall heralded the dawn. An oozing, wet rainbow formed to the south-east. The wind was frail for a time and the sloop stalled in muddy, green waters. When the rain and cloud shifted, a waft of scalding wind flooded over the eastern horizon. The heaving roll of the Pacific swell was far behind now. The waves in the Arafura Sea barely formed crests. They broke with a light fizzing sound, an elated sigh that eased down the flanks of the boat. A butterfly came on board that day, little troubled by the trade. Deep brown with white markings on the tips of its wings, it hovered over the cockpit for a time, settling once or twice, before drifting off on the light airs. Fractured cloud cast a spider's web of shadow over the water. Dolphins were so frequent around the boat that I noticed it most when they left and the sea fell silent.

For three more days I ran west under all sail in winds of no more than ten knots. The hatches were thrown wide to the world as the boat dried out in the brittle, desert breeze. The tiny seas came in as regular as the corrugations in a sheet of iron, glittering and playful as they rose over the south-eastern horizon. Bonito fish took the lure at sunset. After dark the motion was so slight I might have been sailing across an inland lake. The air above the boat was soft and warm, filled with waxing moonlight and music from the stereo.

Five days out from Torres Strait I approached the Arnhem Land coast at Croker Island. The sun was playing on a chain of sand hills that terminated in a rocky point. The sea was dappled with the bold clarity of a chessboard: silver in the sun, inky blue in the shadows cast by passing cloud. Flying fish skimmed and spattered on the surface all around the sloop. A white trawler was working near Bramble Rocks to the south. Early in the afternoon I cleared Cape Croker and ghosted into the island's lee and an anchorage at Sommerville Bay.

Ashore, the landscape was as still and empty as the moon. I dragged the kayak up the beach across sand the consistency of flour. Rust-coloured sand hills stretched north to Croker Point where the cliffs were glowing crimson in the afternoon sun. I climbed inland up a crumbling bank until there was a clear view across the island. Savannah stretched away into the heat haze, dotted with bush, tussock and spinifex grass. The breeze was hot and heavy, like an animal's breath. I stared with watering eyes into the desert wind flowing over the wilderness and knew without doubt that the Pacific was now far behind.

An hour before dawn, I got up the mainsail and crept from under from the lee of Croker Island. In the cool gloaming I set both headsails for the passage west along the coast. From the foredeck, looking back down the length of the boat, the blunt summit of Croker Island was edged in gilt as the sun rose.

Although it was the clearest of days, the land remained stubbornly indistinct. Peacock Island, only a few metres high, faded into the sea just four miles away. Croker Island disappeared from view before I had sailed five miles. As the sun rose the sloop nudged its own intact shadow westward through the shoals, making only two knots in silent seas. On the chart I ticked off the coastal features to the south: Raffles Bay, Danger Point, Sandy Point, Sandy Island No.1, Sandy Island No.2. The shoals kept me seven miles from shore, and even from the crosstrees I could see almost nothing of the coast. Only occasionally the heat haze was punctured by fuzzy headlands trembling in the heat, minutely raised above the water. The coastline was uniformly low, an oily mirage, a place of promise so close but always beyond reach. The overwhelming impression of the day was of emptiness. Northern Australia was an unfathomable mix of vastness and invisibility. This was a huge, but unobtrusive shore. Thicker cloud over the land was the clearest indication of its presence. The immense continent slipped without fanfare beneath the waves to form the shallowest sea. Anaemic wastes stretched away to the north. Trawlers were almost continuous now along the horizon, distorted, glinting forms, as shapeless as car wrecks crunched into the skyline.

Early in the afternoon I rounded the reefs off Smith Point and hauled up on what was left of the wind. Ahead to the south the bay of Port Essington crawled laboriously inland for 20 miles between low wooded hills and sandy bluffs. The sloop wandered into the expanse of the bay through shimmering brown waters as sedentary as a village pond. Under the lee of Black Point the flow of air fell back to little more than a stale draught. The sails hung limp in the rig and the sloop was carried inland by the tide. Ahead, the harbour branched away to the south as a series of silver encroachments through a land of green and gold. Several times the boat lost way and drifted on the stream.

The wind was too light and I gave up hope of sailing to the headwaters of Port Essington. Late in the afternoon I anchored in a little bay under Turtle Point, only five miles inside the entrance. It was deathly still. There was no bird song, and not even a twig shifted ashore. As the sun went down no lights were visible on any part of the shoreline. The whole vast acreage surrounding Port Essington, from beach to hinterland, appeared as a black thread floating on the sea.

Sir Gordon Bremer arrived here at Port Essington on 27 October 1838 in the *Orontes* and the schooner *Essington*, equipped with supplies for eighteen months and five prefabricated buildings, including a church. This proposed British settlement was intended primarily to defend the western approaches to Torres Strait against French and Dutch incursion. But Bremer had also come in response to persistent rumours that child beachcombers were living in captivity on the shores adjacent to the Arafura Sea.

As soon as the monsoon was over in 1839 Bremer ordered the *Essington* to sail north 300 miles to investigate one particular report that English children were being held captive at the island of Timor Laut (Kepulauan Tanimbar, Indonesia). On arrival, Captain Thomas Watson anchored the *Essington* off the village of Louron and took a local rajah hostage until, after a tense standoff, a canoe approached in which 'we were able to distinguish the features of a European equipped as a native'. The man was 'received on board in a very lame and miserable condition'. He was presumed to be in his mid twenties and had been enslaved on the island for 14 years. His long blond hair was 'triced up after the native custom with a comb made of bamboo . . . His only garments were a sort of waistcoat without sleeves, and a blue and white dungaree girdle around his loins.' Watson noted an expression of agony in his countenance which 'from continued suffering had become habitual'. He was unable to walk and had 'almost entirely forgotten his native language'. Later the man 'was found to be much injured in the genitals, and on being questioned about it he said that it was caused by the bite of a pig'.

Watson learned that the man's name was Joseph Forbes. He had been a boy on the schooner *Stedcombe* which called at Timor Laut in 1825 to trade for livestock. Forbes, another boy named John Edwards and the steward stayed on board the schooner while the rest of the crew went ashore to trade. They watched the longboat reach the beach, but as the sailors walked up the sand they were attacked and every man was killed. The steward released the anchor cable and the two boys were getting up the sails in an effort to escape, but it was a futile task with so few hands and the canoes came alongside before the schooner was underway. The steward was beheaded and the two boys 'expecting to share the same fate, betook themselves to the rigging'. Inevitably they were captured and taken ashore. After ten years of enslavement and torture John Edwards died but Forbes lived on for another four years before being rescued by the *Essington*.

Bremer feared that Forbes would never recover from his ordeal as he was a 'perfect cripple, his legs being withered and contracted, and there is no hope of his ever recovering the use of them'. However Forbes defied these predictions. He not only made a fair recover but also went back to sea for many years. He eventually returned to Australia and settled at Williamstown where he died in 1877.

The rumours of child beachcombers to which Sir Gordon Bremer initially responded had several sources. The most notorious concerned the barque *Charles Eaton* which slammed into a reef near the Murray Islands (Mer) in Torres Strait in 1834. The Melanesians killed most of the crew in the aftermath of the wreck, but two children survived ashore for two years before being picked up by another ship. One was the captain's four-year-old son, William O'Oyley. The other was John Ireland, the ship's boy.

Child beachcombers were relatively unusual in the tropical South Pacific as few passenger ships had reason to sail among the islands. Some crew members on trading ships, however, were little more than boys. William Mariner was just 14 when the *Port au Prince* was seized in Tonga in 1806. Another survivor of that massacre was two-year-old William Stevenson, the son of a beachcomber in Hawaii. William's father placed him in the care of the *Port au Prince*'s sailmaker so that he could be taken to his relations in Scotland to be educated. The sailmaker was killed in the attack and William was adopted by a Tongan chief. Mariner believed that the boy never left Tonga.

In New Zealand there are several stories of child castaways living among Maori tribes. Two-year-old Betsy Broughton was captured in 1809 when Maori attacked the *Boyd* in Whangaroa Harbour. Betsy was the illegitimate daughter of the Deputy Assistant Commissioner in Sydney, William Broughton. Her mother was one of seventy European passengers and crew killed and eaten when the *Boyd* was attacked by warriors from two tribes, Ngati Uru and Ngati Pou. Betsy lived in captivity for six weeks on heavily fortified Ohaururu Island in Whangaroa Harbour, where she became the adopted daughter of a chief, Te Pere.

She was rescued by Alexander Berry, an officer on the *City of Edinburgh*, and a friend of her father's. Berry abducted a chief and held a loaded musket to the man's head saying he would kill him and everyone in the village unless the child was returned. Berry wrote: 'When at last she was brought to the boat she was crying in a feeble plaintive voice, "Mamma, my Mamma" . . . Her hair was combed and ornamented with a white feather in the native manner . . . She was tolerably clean but her only clothing was a linen shirt. From the marks upon it I saw it had belonged to the captain of the *Boyd*. The poor child was very emaciated after some weeks among the natives.'

Her troubles were far from over. The *City of Edinburgh* sailed from the Bay of Islands in January the following year, bound for the naval dockyards on the Thames with a cargo of kauri-tree timber. Off the Cape of Good Hope, however, the ship lost its rudder and drifted disabled for five months in the Roaring Forties, back east across the Indian and Pacific Oceans towards South America, finally limping into Valparaiso. Betsy was eventually returned to her father in Sydney aboard the whaler *Atlanta* in March 1812, nearly 2½ years after her capture. She later married a wealthy settler in Sydney, John Throsby, with whom she had seventeen children.

The anthropologist Trevor Bentley has estimated that fifteen white children were captured by Maori in the nineteenth century, eight of whom were girls. All the girls were later rescued, but some of the boys continued living among the tribes and were assimilated to play traditional beachcomber roles. James Caddell had been 13 years old when he survived the massacre of a sealing gang on Stewart Island and was adopted by Ngai Tahu. He married a chief's daughter and became a *rangatira Pakeha*, or white

Betsy Broughton survived the massacre on the *Boyd* and was adopted by a Maori tribe. Portrait by Richard Read, 1814

chief. In later years he became a successful intermediary between two worlds, working as an interpreter, guide and ship's pilot in Foveaux Strait. His name, Jamie, was rendered by Maori as *Hemi* – a reflection of his status as a living amalgam of two cultures, and two languages.

*

At two o'clock in the morning the surface of Port Essington was a blaze of darting shards beneath the full moon. It was dead calm. The telltale ribbons in the sloop's rigging hung vertically, dripping beads of dew. It was mid-September; the trade winds were coming to an end. This was the season of transition before the start of the north-west monsoon, the 'Wet' as the locals economically describe it. I had been lucky to carry a favourable wind this far along the Arnhem Land coast. It might take days or weeks now for a southeasterly to return. I started the engine and motored through the silvery darkness to catch the tide.

The water was still slack as I passed Allaru Island. But off Popham Bay the tide began to set hard to the south as it squeezed through the strait. I heard eddies crackling in the water and the slippery orb of the compass showed the boat slewing around its course. At Cape Don white caps were breaking on either side as the tide raced from the Arafura Sea into the great basin ahead – Van Diemen's Gulf.

In the early 1800s there was a legend that a huge river reached the sea somewhere on this north coast of Australia. When Philip Parker King in the *Mermaid* made the first survey of this entrance on 6 April 1818 he was buoyed by the vision of navigating an Austral Nile rising in high cordillera. According to one theorist, this was the 'River of Desired Blessing' which led to an inland sea, an oasis at the centre of this Antipodean Hell. King considered this opening so significant he named it Dundas Strait after no less a figure than the First Lord of the Admiralty himself. It was just one more expression of doomed optimism on this coast. The *Mermaid* spent two weeks in Van Diemen's Gulf, in burning breezes and shallow seas while King made hopeless attempts to navigate the muddy creeks along the south shore before concluding this was a 'dreary, low and uninterruptedly flat country'.

The dawn was red, heavy and still – an inland dawn of dust, bush and mirages shimmering along the horizon. Although by now there was land all around *Gordian*, still almost nothing of the continent could be seen. Van Diemen's Gulf resembled an aquatic dustbowl enclosed by the Cobourg Peninsula and Melville Island, the turquoise full of mud. Cape Don disappeared within an hour. Melville Island was only a few scratches of bush above the western horizon. To the south the mainland was 60 miles distant, the shore studded with mangroves, the air thick with flies, the creeks infested with crocodiles. The sloop plodded southwards at 4 knots, the one-cylinder diesel hammering at full revs. The noise, vibration and heat merged into one soporific buzz. At midday no land could be seen at all. Beneath a lank, exhausted grey-blue sky, it was a vast, empty, scorching, featureless day with not a hint of breeze.

I sat in the shade beneath the small awning over the cockpit. With no landmarks ashore I looked most often at the depth sounder as the most distinct point of reference. The seabed here had more presence than the land. In Van Diemen's Gulf, shoals were the clearest features to be found. I picked a course between the Hinkler Patches, Ommaney Shoal, Abbott Shoal, Wells Shoal, Giles Shoal, Mataram Shoal, Fitzpatrick Shoal. For the week since leaving Thursday Island *Gordian* had never been in water more than 50 metres deep. For the last two days the seabed had mostly been less than ten metres down. Charts of the waters north of Australia reveal this to be a uniformly shallow sea. The contours of the seabed are as gentle as those of a prairie. In cross section Torres Strait is not unlike a levee, with deep ocean on the Pacific side, but only a muddy puddle of saltwater to the west. Humankind has lived in Papuaustralia for around 25,000 years and for most of this time Australia and New Guinea were joined, often by the whole of the Arafura basin. Aboriginals walked, or waded, south from New Guinea and into the Red Centre. Over history this shallow scoop in the surface of the continent has been covered and uncovered several times; Torres Strait has served as a crossroads on the journeys made by two cultures, first by land, later by sea.

In a strange way European cartography has reflected these geographical changes. Confusion and misinformation about Torres's voyage resulted in contradictory charts. Sixteen years before Torres's voyage, Ortelius's world map showed a strait existing between New

Guinea and Australia. But Mortier's chart, completed in 1701, nearly a century after Torres's voyage, showed New Guinea and Australia as one landmass. Mortier was not so much wrong as a few thousand years too late. Today's charts of the Arafura Sea show a plateau, an ocean steppe covered in a film of water, the shallow seabed an extension of the continental landmass it abuts.

In the shallows there was a sense of journey's end. For the first time since leaving Auckland, I was feeling tired. On the passage up to Melanesia and through the islands I'd seen little traffic at sea. The ocean had been wide and deep and there had been time enough to rest. But for the week since leaving Torres Strait all this had changed. This was a shoal, constricted sea. The continent was often just beneath a horizon cluttered by ships and trawlers, the seabed was seldom far below, the radio regularly crackled into life as Coastwatch aircraft passed overhead. Usually I'd sat up on watch through the night and tried to catch up on sleep by catnapping during the day. Motoring south across Van Diemen's Gulf I moved heavily between the cockpit and chart table, marking my position, ticking off the shoals as the sloop went past. With heavy eyes I stared out to sea, trying to penetrate the heat haze ahead.

In these shallow waters there was also a sense of closing in on the beachcombers. Beachcomber narratives invariably begin in the shallows. One compelling paradox to emerge from beachcomber texts is that so long as the ship was in deep water, the sailors felt relatively secure. In their journals and letters the traders barely mention the deep ocean because it was eventless and safe. Their narratives begin in the sheltered lagoons close to land, in dangerous waters. Captain Cook weathered the gales and high seas in the Southern Ocean: 'Not only farther than any other man before me, but as far as I think it possible for man to go.' Cook survived all the extremes that nature could throw at him, but met his death on a picturesque beach in tropical Hawaii. The scenario of Cook's death was no aberration. Rather, it provides an only too tragic blueprint for the fates met by many of the sailors whose wakes I'd crossed on the passage to Torres Strait: Reverend John Williams at

Dillon's Bay; the crew of the *Oeno* in Fiji; Vernon Lee Walker at Steep Cliff Bay; two of the escaped convicts in Charles Stewart's stolen sloop; the crew of the *Antarctic* in Melanesia; *Bounty*'s quartermaster, John Norton, in Tonga; the crew of the *Stedcombe* at Timor Laut; and many others. All these sailors were killed landing from a longboat and walking up the beach. The obvious truth is that, for the most part, sailors were very good at sailing. They survived the gales and squalls, even the hidden reefs, but died in the process of making cultural contact on the beach, something for which they had no training and were often woefully ill-prepared.

The era of the classic Pacific beachcombers was relatively short-lived. They arrived in force from the 1790s, in the aftermath of Cook's three Pacific voyages which opened up the ocean for trading ships as never before. But by the 1820s in the main centres like Papeete, and by 1840-50 at the latest in most other significant anchorages, beachcombing in its original sense was in terminal decline. The commodities which had brought traders to the islands were becoming exhausted: sandalwood in the Marquesas, Fiji and New Hebrides; pearls in the Tuamotus; bêche-de-mer in Fiji; sealskins in the high latitudes. By the 1840s, bêche-de-mer traders like J.H. Eagleston found the reefs so denuded that it took months to harvest the same cargo that might have been found in weeks a decade earlier. Similarly, when Benjamin Morrell reached the sub-Antarctic Auckland Islands in 1829 he left the group 'without seeing a single fur-seal'.

Furthermore, the unique set of historical circumstances under which beachcombers had thrived began to disappear. The need for intermediaries to explain one world to the other was inevitably eroded as the pace and depth of contact between ship and shore increased. The islanders discovered that sailors weren't spirits but only too mortal. Despite the beachcombers' efforts to monopolize the skills on which their livelihoods depended, the islanders learned for themselves how to forge iron, administer western medicines, build frame-and-plank ships, distil alcohol, and service muskets; in the process many of the traditional beachcomber roles disappeared. Pidgin languages like Bislama developed, making interpreters redundant. Bona fide trading agents such as August Unshelm representing the Hamburg-based Godeffroy business were sent to the islands and usurped another role previously fulfilled by beachcombers. When the missionaries began to arrive in force in the mid-1800s they quickly won the confidence of the islanders, thereby making life on the beach increasingly untenable.

Some beachcombers retreated west to outer islands like Nauru, Rotuma and Ponape. Colonial governments, administrators and missionaries transformed the old beach settlements of Papeete and Honolulu into European satellites. Others, like Kororareka (Russell) and Levuka, were sidelined when colonial capitals were established in Auckland and Suva respectively. A few of the beachcombers assimilated back into European life, becoming keepers of modest trading stores, even missionary assistants. But most lived on the margins of settler communities and the term 'beachcomber' was used to describe poor whites in the islands generally, rather than transculturists.

By the 1880s the process of romanticizing life on the beach had begun. When the British traveller H. Stonehewer Cooper voyaged through the Pacific and wrote *Coral Lands* (1880), he described the beachcombers as 'hardy, healthy, powerful and bronzed. They have the strength to lift a kedge-anchor and to carry a load of perhaps 200 cocoa-nuts out of the forest in the heat of a noonday sun. They climb trees like apes, and can dive almost as well as the natives with whom they live . . . Some of these men have as many as twenty children with huge frames and gipsy countenances. Their intellect is of a low order, and their morals very lax.'

Cooper's beachcombers were still morally degenerate, but they were to some extent redeemed by being physically robust men, living healthy, natural lives. In fact, the evidence to support this is rather mixed.

One 1858 visitor paints a quite different picture of the beach-combers 'with their careworn faces and haggard looks [they] exhibit a wretched appearance'. Beachcombers tended to suffer all the usual complaints of white men transplanted to the tropics, being particularly susceptible to yaws, elephantiasis, boils, tropical ulcers and a range of pus-generating staphylococci infections. A common image of the beachcombers provided by their own literature is of physically frail men who were seldom enchanted with island life.

After the wreck of the *Eliza* in Fiji in 1808 one of the castaways, Samuel Patterson, wrote: 'I was nearly blind with soreness of eyes . . . I was an object of pity; the use of one leg entirely gone, so weak that I was not able to stand, and my body burned with the scorching sun in such a manner, that I was blistered from the crown of my head to the sole of my feet, even the rims of my eyes were blistered.' By the time he returned home Patterson was crippled: 'Deprived of the use of [my] limbs . . . the publick will at once perceive there are but few employments to which [I] can resort with any hope of being useful'. Likewise, when Archibald Campbell returned from the beach in Hawaii he was admitted to hospital in Edinburgh as his wounds from the Pacific had still not healed properly. He was, according to his editor James Smith, 'dismissed as incurable. [He] contrived to earn a miserable pittance, by crawling about the streets of Edinburgh and Leith, grinding music, and selling a metrical history of his adventures'.

William Mariner in Tonga enjoyed the protection of a chief but 'life was still not only uncomfortable, but often exposed to many dangers'. Another castaway sailor, this time in the northern Cook Islands in 1853, saw no romance in his lagoon-side life beneath the palms: '[I suffered from] fits of despondency which I could not avoid frequently indulging in, as my hopes of escape were daily diminishing . . . I had established friendly relations all round the group, and could command assistance from any quarter in time of danger; but this was a poor solace where, amongst a host of barbarians, life was of so little value to me.' Many beachcombers had seen their friends and shipmates either drowned at sea or killed on the beach; they were frightened and isolated; many were malnourished if not physically sick; and many others, even before they ever landed on the beach, were drunks.

It would be difficult to overstate the role played by alcohol on board trading vessels, in shipwrecks, and on the beach. If anything, the extent of drunkenness seemed to increase as the nineteenth century progressed: the better the sailors came to know the islands, the more they wanted to lose themselves in drink. William Bligh described *Bounty*'s surgeon, Thomas Huggan, as a 'Drunken sot . . . constantly in liquor'. Huggan died at Tahiti of an overindulgence and was buried close to the shore camp at Point Venus. Booze, together with violence, is a recurring theme in some beach narratives. When E.H. Lamont, joint owner of the *Chatham*, went aboard the brig in San Francisco harbour in 1852, he anticipated putting to sea straight away. However, the captain was nowhere to be seen and the sails were still furled. 'After waiting some time . . . [the captain] made his appearance, but in such a state of drunkenness that it was impossible for him to proceed to sea.' By evening the captain appeared to have sobered up sufficiently and the *Chatham* got underway, but even before the traders had cleared the Golden Gate the brig had collided with two other vessels, 'an accident by which part of our bulwarks and our taffrail were carried away'. The drunken captain of the *Chatham* was a retired Nankucket whaleman named George Snow, 'a short, stout little fellow, more like a Dutchman than a Yankee, except for the cut of his beard'. Lamont had so little faith in Snow's abilities that he could rarely sleep when the captain was on watch. This lack of confidence proved only too well justified. It was Snow who had the watch when the *Chatham* piled up onto the reef at Penryhn Island the following year, casting the crew away on the remote atoll for more than a 12-month residence. And while many ships had the misfortune to be wrecked on uncharted reefs, leaving the crew relatively blameless, Penryhn was, much to Lamont's disgust, 'laid down on every chart, and mentioned particularly by Wilks [Commander Wilkes of the US Exploring Expedition 1838].'

Like violence, drunkenness began on the decks of the trading ships but transferred to the beach as the sailors came ashore. Earlier in the same voyage, the *Chatham* had called at the Marquesas and taken on board a pilot, the successor to the first beachcomber pilot in that group, Edward Robarts. 'He was no sooner on our deck than he commenced his task in a masterly manner, though, as we were informed, he had such a love for strong liquors, when he could procure them, that he was seldom in a fit state to take charge of the ship. According to his own story he had at one time served as an officer in the British navy; but many years' residence among the savages, together with habitual intemperance, had left few traces of the gentleman about him.' Another beachcomber, Alexander Adams, guided ships in Honolulu harbour from 1816 to the mid-1840s, longer than any other pilot, but was eventually dismissed by the Hawaiian government for persistent drunkenness while on duty.

The picture that emerges of life on the beach, both from the accounts of the beachcombers themselves and also those who encountered them, is rarely one of health and happiness. Nonetheless, it was H. Stonehewer Cooper's image of beachcombers as 'hardy, healthy, powerful and bronzed' that came to prevail. Cooper began the process of sanitizing the beach, of taking it back to its literary origins, particularly Daniel Defoe's *Robinson Crusoe* (1719). Defoe chose to locate his castaway on an uninhabited island. This wasn't entirely without justification. Defoe based his story on the experiences of Alexander Selkirk who was marooned on the then uninhabited Juan Fernandez Islands off the coast of Chile from 1704 to 1709. Some other real-life sailors were also cast away on uninhabited Pacific Islands: the men seen by Freycinet at Ata in 1819; the crew of the *Independence* on Starbuck Island in 1835. However, in reality there were very few uninhabited islands in the Pacific. Most true beachcombers landed on islands that were densely populated. When Robinson Crusoe eventually found footprints on the beach, Man Friday became his willing slave; but in true castaway stories the slaves on the beach were the white sailors.

Similarly, in Johann David Wyss's classic children's story *Swiss Family Robinson* (1812), the ocean has been cleansed of native peoples. Wyss was rector of the Protestant Cathedral in Bern, and a keen student of the voyages of Captain Cook. His story was inspired by the experiences of 250 Swiss emigrants who sailed for the Carolinas in 1735. Their leader, Sam Jenner, had recruited the colonists with a pamphlet titled 'New Found Eden'. But their ship was wrecked off the coast of Carolina and all the emigrants were presumed to have drowned. Wyss's fictional island in *Swiss Family Robinson* was supposedly near both Tahiti and New Guinea, though these two islands are more than 3,500 miles apart. The family of Swiss castaways must battle the natural world in order to survive; the island contains fantastical flora, together with exotic wild animals which they must master and tame. On the beach they embody the Victorian imperial virtues of courage, self-reliance, steadfastness in the face of adversity, and daily Christian worship. 'Little Mother' rears four blond sons who grow into resourceful men but are otherwise barely changed by their experiences – their skin bronzed but unblemished by tattoos.

As a European fantasy, the beach was purged of drunken degeneracy, violent bloodshed, terror and alienation, pagan cere-monials, polygamous sex and numerous mixed-race children: all those things that defined the experiences of true beachcombers and castaways, and so offended Victorian observers. If H. Stonehewer Cooper began this process of returning real-life Pacific beaches to their literary origins, then the task was willingly taken up by later writers, notably the Australian E.J. Banfield and the New Zealander Tom Neale. Banfield's *Confessions of a Beachcomber* (1908) describes his life on tiny Dunk Island on the Great Barrier Reef. Neale's *An Island to Oneself* (1966) is an account of his solitary life on Suvarov Atoll in the Cook Islands. Though five decades apart, the themes of both books are similar. The beaches where Banfield and Neale lived were far removed from the place where Cook was killed or the metaphorical tidal strip between cultures where beachcombers in Samoa once led sailor cults. In earlier times the beach had been an alternative to the ship, or perhaps the penal colony. But for Banfield and Neale the beach was a refuge from industrial, urban life; a haven for escaping to, not a place to escape from. The books written by both men encapsulate the beachcomber of popular myth, enjoying an idyllic, simple lifestyle in a pristine paradise, lapped by invigorating surf, and literally 'combing the beach' for articles of value from which to make a living. Here the beach has lost its status as the threshold dividing two cultures, and so living on the beach has lost its power to shock and repel.

The speck of land on which Tom Neale cast himself away was virtually all beach. In the 1950s and 60s Neale spent six years living alone on a tongue-shaped coral islet half-a-mile long, part of the uninhabited Suvarov Atoll that was more than 200 miles from the nearest inhabited island. The ship which landed him there had to be specially diverted to call at Suvarov and it was unclear when, or even if, he would ever be taken off the islet. He came ashore with little more than a pile of books by Defoe, Stevenson, Conrad and Somerset Maugham, and wore only a *maro*, the traditional loincloth of Polynesians and beachcombers. But here any similarity with the original beachcombers ends. For Tom Neale, life on the beach was a 'yearning'. Suvarov was his 'island of desire'. He wanted to live 'very close to nature'. These themes are never found in the accounts of the first beachcombers. In order to survive, all of Tom Neale's negotiations take place with the natural world: cyclones, sharks, drought, starvation. But from the journals of Morrison, Mariner, Vason, Cary, Patterson, Lamont and many others, it's clear that these true castaways survived by negotiating with Polynesian tribes and foreign cultures. For them the beach was more akin to a nightmare than a dream. Many beachcombers, like Edward Robarts, considered themselves to have been damnably unlucky: victims of cruel fate which saw them trapped at the water's edge, perpetually caught in the cultural limbo between worlds, unable to truly belong.

One irony of Tom Neale's story is that he had more in common with the original beachcombers before he went to live on Suvarov. For many years prior to his self-imposed exile, Neale lived in the thick of a Polynesian culture, working as an itinerant storekeeper in the Cook Islands. He distributed European goods to the islanders: needles, cloth, spectacles, brightly coloured tin trunks, lengths of rusty chain, fishing hooks and line. He became a jack-of-all-trades: doctor, moneylender, village counsellor, and guide to European products. His store was a portal between the island and foreign technologies.

The term 'beachcombing' might still be in use but the nature of the activity itself has changed almost beyond recognition. Today, beachcombing books are either field guides, or they are found on the 'Spiritualism' and 'New Age' shelves of bookshops. Rarely does a brown or black face feature in their pages.

Late in the afternoon Cape Hotham was visible to the south-west. In the heat haze it could have passed for Manhattan from 30 miles distant: a disk of land, the towers forming a jagged skyline. But it was a fleeting distortion of scale. The cape was only four miles ahead and the scrub that had seemed like skyscrapers proved to be just a few metres high. As the sun set I motored round to its western side and anchored in shoal water north of Escape Cliffs.

It wasn't a good spot. The tide would run hard and the anchorage was open to the west. But it had been calm all day and I only intended to stop for a few hours to wait for the tide to turn. The last obstacle on the voyage lay directly ahead, the Clarence Strait, where the spring tide would set at four knots between the reefs.

Northern Australia had defied three attempts at British settlement in the early 1800s. This was a heartbreak coast of iron gravel shores and stagnant malarial airs. Port Essington, where I'd anchored the previous night, had been the third proposed outpost here. It was conceived by the Admiralty as another 'New Singapore', the promise of rich, spice-laden islands always hanging above the northern horizon. The reality of the north Australian coast proved time and again to be crushingly different from the rose-tinted image. Like its two predecessors, Essington had been thwarted by cyclones, fevers and crippling isolation. One visitor to the fledgling Port Essington was T.H. Huxley, Aldous Huxley's grandfather, who branded it 'the most useless, miserable, ill-managed hole in Her Majesty's dominions [which deserved] all the abuse that has ever been heaped upon it. Port Essington is *worse than a ship*, and it is no small comfort to know that this is possible.' Seven years later Port Essington was 'by unanimous consent condemned'.

The city that was eventually founded on this coast was Darwin, 120 miles west of Port Essington, and 45 miles west of my present anchorage at Cape Hotham. Darwin was where I would end the voyage. I planned to leave the boat there, fly home to New Zealand to work, and return at a later date to sail among the islands and archipelagos of South-East Asia. So this anchorage at Cape Hotham was only a pit stop. I intended to stay here for six hours, eat a meal and get some sleep. Before midnight the tide would turn in my favour. By dawn I'd be through the Clarence Strait and approaching the city of Darwin. The only spoiler would be a westerly wind, a headwind blowing through the strait against the tide.

The westerly wind set in very quickly. I was siphoning diesel from a jerry can into the main fuel tank when I first felt it on my face. Within 10 minutes it had risen to 15 knots. It was dark by now and the sloop was pitching heavily at anchor, the wind blowing directly on shore. I got up the mainsail and started the engine with little choice but to put back to sea. As I knelt at the windlass, the boat was snubbing and yawing on its anchor chain and seas slopped across the foredeck at the bottom of each pitch. When the anchor came smashing up into the stem-head I gunned the engine to push the boat away from this lee shore. Soon the outgoing tide took hold and the sloop was swept back to where it had been a couple of hours earlier off Cape Hotham. I unfurled the genoa as the moon rose above the marshes at Aralaij Beach. Under full sail I stemmed the outgoing tide for five hours, the boat stationary just north of Cape Hotham, the short seas crashing past in the darkness.

An hour before midnight the tidal stream went slack and I started beating south-west. I passed the green can buoy at Rooper Rock as the moon came out from behind cloud and the seascape turned a frosty white. There is a sectored light on Vernon Island: a white beam shines down the navigable channel. It took six hours to clear the Clarence Strait, short tacking through steep overfalls in the Howard Channel. Several times the sloop lost steerage as the transom and tiller were buried in the troughs.

At five o'clock next morning I cleared March Shoal and set a course south-west. Twenty miles ahead the loom of light from Darwin city appeared as a watery stain in the sky. I sat on the cockpit bench, dumb with released tension. Every few minutes I glanced at my mobile phone, waiting for a signal, the first one on the Australian coast. As the sky lightened in the east the phone came within range and I called my girlfriend Helen in New Zealand.

'You sound terrible,' she said. 'What's wrong with your voice?'

There was a 3½-hour time difference. Helen was at home on Waiheke Island, getting ready for work, walking around the kitchen on the cordless phone, pouring coffee, eating toast. 'Are you drunk?'

'I've been up all night.'

'I can tell that. Is that safe?'

Helen was not a sailor. She had worried about me many times since I'd left home. After leaving Port Vila I'd been unlucky with the telephones and often failed to get a connection. In the Banks Islands two weeks had elapsed after the time I'd promised I would call. When I was finally put through I heard the sound of crying coming from the receiver. That sound followed me all across the Coral Sea; even above the shriek of squalls in the rigging, those cries from home had a different timbre that the ocean could never cover up. But from Helen's point of view, once I had reached the Australian coast, it was all over. For her, the open sea was dangerous, but shallow, coastal waters were safe. Now all I had to do was follow the coast round to Darwin. Why was it taking so long? When I'd kissed her lips on the beach at Rocky Bay, before taking the sloop up to Auckland for a clearance at the start of the voyage, I had promised I would be back in four months. That was five months ago. The voyage had been a succession of broken promises.

Sea travel under sail is almost impossible to tie down. I can never make it fit a timetable, give fixed dates of when I will be at a certain place from which I can call home, as I can rarely be sure when I'll make landfall or what I'll find when I do. Few things are certain. The winds will fail, or I'll follow a sidetrack, or arrive to find the phones are down. Pacific Island states like Vanuatu are slippery and elusive; places like Lamap, which had been towns 30 years ago, hardly exist today.

Yet this is what I love about it, the daily negotiation with uncertain winds, seas and islands. Sea travel operates in denial of anything outside this mix. It has its own insular dynamic of preparations, passage making and landfalls. Day to day, little is required from beyond the boat's rail, except a steady breeze. In this respect it is a selfish thing to do. The boat is tied to nothing and no one, except those on board.

For me, this constant state of flux gives sea travel its spice. But for Helen, I'd simply disappeared over the horizon towards Torres Strait, and failed to keep in touch. In the end a sea voyage is dependent on more than favourable winds and currents. Mine would have been impossible without her accepting that I should go.

'So where are you now?' she asked.

'I can see the lights of Darwin up ahead. I'll be there in a few hours.'

'About time. When are you coming home?'

'It'll be a few days. I've got to organize the boat and book a flight.'

'I've got to go to work. I'll call you this evening when you've sobered up.'

*

At dawn the sky was crimson, the sea the colour of pumice. From ten miles offshore the city of Darwin made almost no impact on this coast. It was only a series of harder lines and specks on the dusty, rusty plains. The wind fell ever lighter and the sloop slowed to two knots through turgid seas. At 9 o'clock that morning I finally anchored in Fannie Bay and collapsed into my bunk.

When I woke early in the afternoon the sea breeze had built and the sloop was gently pitching on small swells. As I climbed dazed into the cockpit I heard the clickety-click of a rope being pulled through a block. With a whoosh of wind and wake a catamaran slid past. The female crew was suspended from a trapeze, her head completely bound in an Arab *keffiyeh* against the sun, dark glasses like a fly's eyes staring inanimately ahead.

A couple of hours later I was met by Ian and Sue Frood aboard *Tinkerbell*. Ian and Sue managed the marina where I planned to leave the sloop over the wet season. They had been out fishing for the day and offered to pilot me up Sadgrove Creek to the marina lock gate. *Tinkerbell* was a whimsical name for a rust-stained, grunty, plumb-stemmed trawler with an exhaust like a bulldozer. Sue Frood was gutting fish beneath an awning, a baby on her hip. I followed them up the harbour, past Stokes Hill Wharf. In the oozing tidal reaches of Sadgrove Creek we zigzagged from mangrove shore to mangrove shore, tracing the course of the deep-water channel. Without a local boat to act as pilot it would have been easy to go aground in the otherwise shallow waters of the creek.

Among the mangroves on the west shore there was a substantial lock of concrete and steel. *Tinkerbell* inched through the open gate and I followed, then tied up alongside the trawler. The tomb-like vault of the drained lock fell startlingly silent as Ian cut the trawler's engine. Slowly the heavy steel barrier closed behind us. The walls were thick with slime, the sky an oblong slot high overhead.

We had to wait here, tied up side by side. I'd come from offshore and my boat had to be inspected by the Fisheries Department for black striped mussel (*Mytilopsis*), an invasive marine pest that clogs ships' cooling systems and storm-water drains ashore. Sue was talking on the mobile. Then she stuck her head through the wheelhouse door: 'Fisheries will be down in 15 minutes,' she said, and took the baby down below.

'That's all we need,' Ian muttered and ripped the ring from a can of beer. 'You been to Darwin before?' he asked.

'No, never.'

'Nothing like Darwin. When you've been thrown out of every other town in Australia you come up here to Darwin.' Presumably, both Ian and Sue had been thrown out of every other town in Australia as they had both sailed their own boats up here to Darwin. They now ran fishing charters on *Tinkerbell* and had taken over management of the marina a few weeks earlier. As part of the job they offered an informal pilot service to visiting boats, just as the beachcombers of old had done when ships arrived from offshore.

'You like jackhammers?' Ian asked. 'Shame. They start around here before it gets light. It's a funny place. It's a development – cafes, apartments, houses, with a boat harbour in the middle. It's a building site right now. That's why it's half the price of any-where else. We've got quite a little community in here.'

I climbed the ladder recessed into the lock wall to have a look around. The concrete shells of half-built apartment blocks rose uncertainly from the landscaped surrounds. A muddy brown basin of water stood at the centre of the development. The boats moored there flew the flags of half a dozen different countries. Some of them looked like they had been here a long time, stained with rust, a thick frill of growth around the waterline, the deck covered in pot plants, air-conditioning units built into the fore-hatches. I guessed that many of these boats would never leave Darwin now. Almost everywhere I've ever been in a boat there are fragmentary pieces of the beachcombers' memory. Sailors who had been heading somewhere else are now living behind the beaches, around the bays, up the estuaries and creeks. It's no more than a resonance with the past, but it's there among the frangi-pani, the tree ferns and the mangroves. There was a distinct whiff of the same thing up that muddy creek round the back of Darwin.

The woman from the Fisheries Department arrived and we climbed back down to the boats in the lock. 'Waterline looks okay,' she said. 'When did you last anti-foul?'

'About six months ago.'

'I need to see the receipt for the paint and the slipping.'

I didn't have either.

'You must have a receipt for slipping.'

'I used a public grid. There was no charge.'

'Well the paint then, I need a receipt for the paint.'

'I don't think I've got one. I don't keep things like that.'

'Course you do. No one would throw away something like that.'

'I think a lot of people–'

'Course they wouldn't. I've got to see a receipt for the paint or you're not going past this lock.'

I was beginning to get worried. 'Well, I suppose I might have the receipt somewhere at home,' I said. 'I could call my girlfriend tomorrow and ask her to look for it.'

'So you'll fax it to me tomorrow?'

'Well . . .'

'That's settled.' She signed the form, then scaled the ladder back into the sunshine overhead, the clipboard held in her teeth.

'She was officious,' I said to Sue.

'Aw, it was sweet. She said on the phone there would be no problem. Just a formality. That's what people are like up here.'

Ian fired up *Tinkerbell*'s engine with an explosive roar and signalled the keeper to start flooding the lock.

As soon as the boat was tied up to the dock I started work. I'd been restless and fidgety all afternoon, unable to relax, impatient to get the boat packed up and start the journey home. I stripped the sails and running rigging, slackened the backstays. A man was working on the boat tied to the next pontoon, completing similar tasks but in reverse, evidently getting the boat ready for sea. It was an old, much-travelled 30-foot catamaran. 'She's been round the

world twice,' he said. 'Don't tell me, looks like it too,' he added
with a chuckle. His name was Marty, from Queensland. He was
a delivery skipper he told me. He'd worked on scores of yachts
over the years and sailed many thousands of miles. He would be
leaving in a couple of days, taking the catamaran east to Thursday
Island and back down to Queensland, where the owner lived.
Marty was every inch the seaman, thick grey beard, strong,
confident fingers that handled ropes and knots with accomplished
ease. He was squatting next to the tiller, eying it up. The tiller was
a mess. The cross bar connecting the two rudders must have
broken at some point and had been replaced with a length of
bamboo which was roughly lashed in place. 'I'm not going to sea
until I've got this sorted out,' he said, rubbing his fingers over the
bamboo and picking at the frayed lashings. 'What a botch-up.
Looks like something the bloody coons up in Torres Strait would
have thrown together.' He seemed to have found his theme now.
'You're from New Zealand, eh?' He looked at me pityingly. 'I hear
the Maoris own everything down there now. You mugs! You'll
have given away the whole bloody country before you realize
what you've done.'

A few minutes listening to Marty was enough to convince me
of the difference between Australia and New Zealand. I'd lived in
New Zealand for ten years but never heard anything like this.
Coons. There are people in New Zealand who would share
Marty's sentiments. The difference is that they wouldn't come
straight out and say it to a stranger. They just wouldn't be
sufficiently sure that you'd be of like mind. They'd be frightened
of the possible consequences of getting it wrong. For many out-
siders, Australia and New Zealand must seem to be chips off the
same block. Following the initial convict settlements in Australia,
both countries were colonized by similar groups of people – pre-
dominantly Anglo-Celtic. But on matters of race the prevailing
cultures in the two countries are different.

I was still working at twilight, doubling up the mooring lines,
when my mobile phone rang. Helen and I talked for more than

an hour, the first real chance we'd had since she'd left Port Vila over three months before. She had time for trivia now, the day-to-day details of life on the island that I'd blotted out during the course of the voyage: the window that had blown out in a gale, the floods in the basement, the chickens she'd been given that were now roosting in the trees. I sat listening in the thickening dusk, my cheeks still smarting from the sun, while she filled my head with images of the green hills and cool coastal breezes of home.

The next day I finished packing up the boat. Marty was at work on the catamaran next door all day. He made a good job of the steering, replacing the rickety length of bamboo with an aluminium tube, through-bolted onto the short tillers coming from each rudder with neat backing plates. I gave him the remains of the food from the sloop's lockers. His passage back east through Torres Strait was going to be long and hard in that worn-out old boat. In the evening I went through the two shelves of books in the sloop's cabin, picking out the narratives and letters of the beachcombers who had been my companions for the last five months. The sandalwooders James Paddon and William Lockerby; James Morrison, boatswain's mate on the *Bounty*; the whalemen Edward Robarts and William Cary; the ship's clerk William Mariner; the lapsed missionary George Vason; the traders Peter Dillon, Samuel Patterson, Benjamin Morrell, Leonard Shaw, E.H. Lamont and Vernon Lee Walker. They came with me, stuffed into the top of a holdall, on a midnight flight back into the Pacific.

The beachcomber settlement on the remote Pacific Island of Pitcairn has been in the news recently. Just forty-seven people comprise the island's population. Most of them are descended from the *Bounty* mutineers led by Fletcher Christian. Late in October 2004 courtroom verdicts were handed down against a group of Pitcairn men.

In all, prosecutors named thirty-one men as abusers of women and children on the island over the past half-century. The charges included gang rape, incest and indecent assault on girls as young as 12. Evidence was given by women still living on Pitcairn, but mostly by the descendants of the beachcombers now living in New Zealand, Norfolk Island, Australia and England. Three judges, along with lawyers and court officials were shipped to Pitcairn from New Zealand. Seven women testified by video link from Auckland.

Six men were found guilty, including Steve Christian, who claims to be a direct descendant of Fletcher Christian and was, at the time of writing, still mayor of Pitcairn Island. The court heard that Steve Christian raped one 12-year-old girl under a banyan tree while two friends held her down. He was sentenced to three years in jail for four rapes and five indecent assaults. In court Steve Christian was described as the island's patriarch, assuming the right to initiate young girls who subsequently became members of his personal 'harem'. His son, Randy, was sentenced to six years having been found guilty on four charges of rape and five of indecent assault.

The oldest of the accused men was Len Brown, aged 78. He was convicted of committing two rapes in a watermelon patch and sentenced to two years in jail, though he was given leave to apply for home detention. His son, Dave, was found guilty of nine indecent assaults and sentenced to 400 hours of community service. Both Len and Dave Brown are descendants of William Brown, the Kew gardener sent by Joseph Banks to assist the principal gardener, David Nelson, in overseeing the shipment of the breadfruit plants on board the *Bounty*.

Supporters of the accused men condemned the prosecutions saying that sex with young girls was a culturally accepted norm on Pitcairn Island. There's an element of truth in this. Many of the *Bounty* mutineers had been introduced to the Polynesian institution of *taio*, or 'bond friendship', of which one manifestation was the frequent occurrence of casual sex, sometimes with young girls. And on isolated Pitcairn it appears that little has changed over the intervening 214 years. The violence began almost immediately after Fletcher Christian kidnapped a group of Tahitian women (and some men) and took them to the island in 1790. No ship called for the next 18 years, until Matthew Folger in the sealer *Topaz* sighted Pitcairn on 7 February 1808. Of the nine original mutineers who reached the island, Folger found only one, John Adams, now calling himself Alexander Smith, was still alive. The others had all been killed according to Adams. But Adams's testimony is unreliable as he gave contradictory versions of what happened on Pitcairn after the *Bounty* was burned in 1790.

A more reliable account of the massacres on Pitcairn was provided by the Irish navigator Peter Dillon, whose Pacific voyages brought him into contact with several of this ocean's more notorious beachcomber episodes. Dillon was returning to the islands from Valparaíso in the *Calder* in 1825 and stopped at Tahiti for provisions. Anchored in the lagoon off the beach settlement of Papeete he interviewed a woman whose name he transcribed as Teehuteatuaonoa, or 'Jenny', one of the Tahitians kidnapped by Fletcher Christian and taken to Pitcairn 35 years earlier. Jenny had lived on Pitcairn for 27 years as the wife of Able Seaman Isaac Martin – the man who fed Bligh segments of pamplemousse during the mutiny as his throat was so hoarse from screaming. After her husband's death she was finally taken off Pitcairn by a passing ship in 1817 and returned to Tahiti. Peter Dillon translated Jenny's testimony, which was given in a jumble of Tahitian and pidgin English – the language of the beach. It's clear from her account that Pitcairn was never a paradise. Relations between the Tahitians and the Europeans quickly began to deteriorate into brutality and bloodshed, a process ending with the deaths of all but one of the white sailors. The conflict was, essentially, about which side should 'possess' the women.

One problem with the story of the mutiny on the *Bounty* and its aftermath is that it is usually told in isolation. Sea voyages make such effective, linear narratives that writers have been reluctant to put the *Bounty* story into any kind of context. In fact, one of the few truly unique things about the *Bounty* voyage was the plants; the whole saga took place against a backdrop of tropical foliage bursting from the Great Cabin. Otherwise, similar forces were at work on countless other ships which sailed through the tropical Pacific in the nineteenth century. The islands and the islanders were never passive in the process of European voyaging. The cultures of the islands infiltrated many ships. The sailors were fêted by young women. Their skin colour was changed with tattoos. They learned to speak Pacific languages, or pidgins like Bislama, and came to question the old shipboard hierarchies. The Polynesian concept of *taio* proved an overwhelming motivation for many sailors to mutiny or desert, and go to live on the beach. The Gloucestershire sailor William Marsters reached Polynesia in 1862 and never left. He took three wives and established himself as patriarch on tiny Palmerston Atoll, which he ran as a personal fiefdom. His descendants, like those of Christian, Brown and their confrères from the *Bounty*, are now scattered through the tropical islands, New Zealand, Australia and England.

The recent events on Pitcairn Island represent one legacy of the beachcombers, but there is more to the beach than the *Bounty* story. Part of the fascination with beachcomber narratives lies in the breadth of the experiences they describe. Beachcombers witnessed almost every aspect of life in the Pacific Islands. They led war parties and lived in fear of being attacked. They were variously caged, tortured, starved, or fattened up for the pot. Some were seized as young children; others haunted the beach as old men. They mediated, traded, interpreted, guided, piloted and explained; a few rose to the ranks of chiefs and achieved a higher status on the beach than they could ever have dreamt of in the societies from which they came; collectively they wrote accounts that were adventure stories, polemics against racial intolerance, and works of amateur anthropology.

Given this range of roles and outcomes it is difficult to generalize about the nature of the beach. The characteristics of any one beach were a negotiation between sailors and islanders. Neither group was homogenous: the sailors ranged from emissaries of the Enlightenment like the crews of Bougainville and Cook, to alienated illiterates and convict seamen, while island cultures across the great span of the South Pacific were varied and diverse.

But looking back at the beachcomber literature it's apparent that many of these texts share one particular feature. The degree of warmth and respect some beachcombers came to express for the peoples among whom they lived was seldom shared by the wider community of sailors, who considered the islanders to be 'savages' – *coons*. A beachcomber named O'Connell in Micronesia said of his hosts: 'After five years residence with them I pronounce them hospitable, sagacious and benevolent.' When Lockerby finally escaped from Fiji he records a fond parting with the chief who had treated him as a son: 'From the good old King I had received kindness which I should remember while I live with gratitude.' Similarly, James Morrison's account of the beach in Tahiti is touched by affection for a people whose lives he shared, whom he knows intimately, '. . . their Breath sweet and perfectly free from taint'. In Tonga, George Vason remembered listening to the islanders speculating about the 'men from the sky': 'I have been delighted, for hours, in listening to these nocturnal confabulations, and often very much surprised and improved, by the shrewdness of their observations, and the good sense of their reasonings . . .' In Hawaii, Stephen Reynolds wrote on the death of his Polynesian wife that she would '. . . ever be Remembered with feelings of tenderness & Respect'.

Beachcombers also played a perhaps unlikely role in nation building. The Hawaiian chief Kamehameha united that group of islands and did so partly with the assistance of beachcombers acting as guides, advisors and mercenaries. Similar forces were at work in several other parts of the ocean. In Tahiti, the *Bounty* beachcombers, and later a group led by the Swede Peter Hagerstein who deserted from Vancouver's store ship *Daedalus* in 1792, helped bring the house of Pomare to prominence. In Fiji, Charlie Savage worked for the Bau chiefs who became the dominant force in that part of the group. Likewise, in Tonga both George Vason and William Mariner assisted the warrior king

Finau to fight his rivals. The beachcombers' participation in these wars was motivated only by pragmatism; by allying themselves with up-and-coming chiefs they won status and security in their host societies. Nonetheless, the result in some island groups was that genuine paramount chiefs emerged who bound together previously fractious tribal entities under a single governance.

Across much of the ocean beachcombers served to soften the impact of the arrival of European ships. Most beachcombers came ashore alone or in small groups; in themselves they posed no direct threat to the tribes among which they lived. But their presence ashore helped ease the Pacific peoples' transition into a new world where western technologies would have a permanent presence.

I knew I was never a beachcomber in this original meaning of the term. The beachcombers had been a product of a specific set of historical circumstances that were now long gone. I could not resurrect their ghosts, and given the violence of those times, which is still manifest in places like Pitcairn, perhaps that was a good thing.

But the spirit of the beachcombers lives on, and it does so in New Zealand more than in any other group of Pacific Islands. When I'd first arrived in New Zealand in 1992 I knew almost nothing of the country's history. I sailed here because its shores lay at the ocean's western periphery and I'd run out of space; because it was outside the tropical cyclone belt; and because I needed to work to refill the coffers. I only learned later that modern New Zealand's origins lie partly in a beachcomber society.

I arrived home at Waiheke Island late in September – spring in the southern hemisphere. I made my final landfall, but without a boat, and at first it didn't seem to matter. I climbed down the steep stairs – almost a ladder – to the basement where my office is in the old laundry room. When I opened the door, the first thing I saw lying on the desk was a copy of John Martin's account of William Mariner's life on the beach in Tonga, first published by John Murray in 1817. The frontispiece showed Mariner, bare-chested, clasping a spear, a displaced sailor amid the landscape of a Pacific Island, and I immediately felt at home. The office is no bigger than *Gordian*'s cabin, though with a little more headroom. I unpacked the beachcomber texts I'd brought from Darwin and placed them on the shelves around the walls, recreating the trappings of my floating home here on land.

The writer Janet Frame, who lived on Waiheke for a time, called it the 'Skid row of the South Pacific'. Beach and ex-beach settlements have long attracted such epithets. Russell was the 'Hell-hole of the Pacific'; Thursday Island was the 'Sink of the Pacific'. There was never a 'Paris of the Pacific'.

Waiheke is a sailor's island. Ocean-going boats are moored in most of the island's bays. Sailors from many parts of the world have long made their homes here. Others were returning from offshore all the time. Tim and Ginny Le Couteur had just got back from their circumnavigation. There was an easy nonchalance about seafaring on the island, an acceptance of sudden departures, and unannounced returns. 'How was your trip?' people would ask. 'Did you see Gary and Ingrid in Vila?'

Each morning and evening I sat with Helen on the commuter ferry going to and from the city. I saw the sea now, beyond the ferry's rail, when I looked up from the newspaper, or the pile of homework I was marking. I'd gone back to my old job teaching English to foreign students at the university. My students were mostly from China, Korea and Japan. They asked me why I was tanned and I told them about my trip to Torres Strait.

'How long did it take?'

'Five months.'

They stared dumbstruck. 'Five months! All alone! What did you eat?'

There was a map of the Pacific on the classroom wall. I showed them the way I'd gone, the many islands along the way, names they'd never heard before. I explained that this was a peopled ocean, voyaging didn't take place in isolation, and that I'd never been on my own for more than two weeks. I pointed out the configurations of the different island groups: Micronesia, Melanesia and Polynesia. They seemed surprised by the notion that culturally New Zealand was among the Pacific Islands, part of Polynesia. They had supposed it was simply a detached section of Australia.

After a month at home I was restless to get back out on the water and a friend lent me his Laser sailing dinghy. Helen and I repeated the same car journey down to Rocky Bay that we'd made six months earlier at the start of my passage to Torres Strait. We drove through the lanes early one Saturday morning, the car's headlights cutting through the tunnel of bush overhead, with the Laser lashed on the roof rack. I rigged the dinghy on the stony beach and headed out into the Tamaki Strait. Six months earlier in the sloop I had turned west and sailed 11 miles up the harbour to Auckland in order to clear customs. This time I turned east towards the haze of green islands and farmland beneath the rising sun.

Waiheke's orientation has been completely reversed in the 234 years since the first European ship arrived here. The island is 11 miles long and 5 miles wide at the widest point. Today, the main villages are all at the western end of the island facing Auckland, where the commuter ferry docks. But when Captain Cook sailed HMS *Endeavour* into these waters in 1769 he made landfall at the eastern end of Waiheke, and the traders and beachcombers who came in his wake all made their base in the bays, islands and coast-lines around Waiheke's eastern shores.

The south-west wind was picking up and I sailed south-east on a powerful, wet reach. It was still early spring and the spray thrown up by the dinghy was chill. I gripped the tiller with bloodless fingers, the mainsheet in my teeth, the white caps at chest height, struggling to recall the almost forgotten skills of balance and agility required to handle this skittish little boat after the five-ton sloop I had lived in for most of the last six months. The sun was catching the oyster groins in the bays to the north and playing on the vineyards and olive groves that cover Waiheke's hillsides. On the headlands I could see the remains of terraces and trenches that had once been Maori *pa* sites, or fortified settlements. Waiheke's

60 miles of coastline and numerous shallow, sheltered bays and inlets had long provided abundant fishing, especially for snapper. Maori settlement dates back ten centuries when the island was known as Te Motuarui-roa, or 'long, sheltering island'.

After five miles I turned north-west up the protected waters of the Waiheke Channel which had provided both easy access and countless anchorages for the first square-rigged ships. Behind the beaches ashore were the iron roofs, curved verandas and brick chimneys of the first colonial houses built on the island. Four miles to the north in the muddy shallows of Man O' War Bay I beached the dinghy beside the stream where Captain Cook had taken on water. I swapped the wetsuit for some clothes and hiked up the gravel road to the hilltop at Stony Batter which dominates this end of the island. Fifteen miles to the east Cape Colville and the Coromandel Peninsula formed a bold, blue mole of land protecting these waters from the Pacific Ocean.

Captain Cook had rounded Cape Colville and sailed into the Hauraki Gulf on 18 November 1769 in HMS *Endeavour*, six months before he piloted the barque through the Labyrinth and Torres Strait. Cook named the whole of this gulf the 'River Thames' believing it to be the seaward arm of a great river. It was shallow and sheltered affording 'good anchoring in every part . . . being defended from the Sea by a Chain of large and small Islands'. Its shores were 'Cover'd with Woods and Verdure'. One part of Cook's instructions from the Admiralty on the first voyage required him to look for trees suitable for ship's spars. Supplies of Baltic pine, on which sailing ships of that time were dependant, were dwindling, and the naval dockyards of England were crying out for a fresh resource. Cook took a long boat and together with Joseph Banks navigated some distance up Waihou River where he found 'immence [sic] woods of as stout lofty timber as is to be found perhaps in any other part of the world'. With a quadrant he measured one tree as being 89 feet to the first branch and 'straight as an arrow' with little taper – just the type of timber the Admiralty was seeking.

Cook's report of timber in the Hauraki Gulf prompted the first trading voyages to these waters, a similar pattern to that seen throughout the tropical islands. And with the traders there inevitably came the first beachcombers. The *Fancy* arrived first in 1795 and loaded kauri timber at Waiheke Island and Coromandel. Four years later the *Hunter* loaded a cargo of the kahikatea trees that Cook had measured beside the Waihou River. Four of her crew deserted and went to live ashore as beachcombers. When the *Royal Admiral* arrived at the mouth of the river in 1802 one of these men, Thomas Taylor, boarded the ship. He now had a Maori name, Tararoki, a Maori wife, and was fluent in the language. Taylor told the crew of the *Royal Admiral* he had travelled 300 miles into the interior of the North Island and enjoyed the protection of a powerful chief, to whom he served as *mokai*, which translates roughly as 'pet'. As in the tropical islands, some chiefs used beachcombers as curiosities to be shown off in order to enhance their own status. But Taylor's role was also practical: on the *Royal Admiral* he served not only as pilot, guide and interpreter, but also initiated trade between ship and shore, orchestrating cargoes of timber to be transported from the plains down river to the waiting ship. Boatloads of flax were also shipped for the manufacture of rope, netting, canvas sails and sacks. Taylor was taken off by the *Royal Admiral*, although the fate of the three men who had deserted with him is unknown.

In the event, the kahikatea timber reported by Cook actually made poor quality spars but the kauri tree, having no knots or flaws, was better and also made excellent decking material. The kauri taken from Waiheke Island in the early 1800s stocked naval dockyards in Britain and is said to have been one factor that gave Nelson an advantage over the combined French and Spanish fleets at the Battle of Trafalgar.

Early in the afternoon I started walking back down the hill to Man O' War Bay. A punt was working at the oyster beds and as the tide receded in the bay the warm spring sunshine had turned the mudflats a brilliant gold. The remains of an old iron slipway running down from the beach occasionally broke the surface of the mud. Ships started calling frequently at Man O' War Bay in the early 1800s. Almost all were whalers and sealers who came in to the sheltered anchorage to repair and re-provision. A Scot named Thomas Maxwell moved ashore and married Ngeu Ngeu, the daughter of the Maori chief Tara Te Irirangi. Maxwell built several houses, set up his forge, and established a small shipyard, not unlike the beachcomber shipyards at Levuka, Kororareka (Russell) and elsewhere in the Pacific. On the beach in Man O' War Bay he built a trading schooner from Waiheke kauri, the

Between worlds: beachcombers left children throughout the Pacific Islands. Caroline *(left)* and Sarah Barrett, daughters of the beachcomber pilot, trader and warrior Dicky Barrett

Sarah Maxwell, but both shipwright and schooner were lost in a gale leaving Wellington Harbour in 1842. Ngeu Ngeu refused offers of marriage from several other European settlers and returned to her tribal village with Maxwell's six mixed-race sons.

The pattern of white settlement in New Zealand was quite different from that seen in other parts of the ocean. The penal colony at nearby Port Jackson (Sydney) was established in 1788 and came complete with a governor to oversee the convicts and a conscious programme of settlement. But for the next five decades New Zealand had no comparable form of colonial government. Commercial activity was lawless, untaxed, unregulated and unplanned. The seas around New Zealand were the realm of trading sailors, and the first whites to come ashore were beachcombers. The huge seal colonies reported by Cook in the South Island started to attract ships to the high latitudes in the 1790s. Sealskins, like sandalwood and bêche-de-mer, were one of those commodities the Chinese would trade for tea. Almost immediately, sailors began to defect to Maori tribes. At the same time, in the north, the Bay of Islands became a significant centre for the burgeoning whaling industry. The beach settlement of Kororareka developed to meet the needs of shipping and was peopled partly by runaway sailors, beachcombers and castaways. In the 1830s Kororareka became the principal base for whalers in the South Pacific where oil could be transhipped or exported, repairs could be made, and supplies of yams and pigs bought. Gilbert Mair ran one of the principal refitting and ship's chandler's outfits just south of the town, employing fifteen skilled beachcomber artisans.

Among the beachcombers in New Zealand there were undoubtedly many escaped convicts. These islands were the closest landfall to all three penal colonies, at Port Jackson, Van Diemen's Land and Norfolk Island. And with these escapees there came the first female beachcombers. When the sealer *Endeavour* was wrecked in the South Island in 1795 an astonishing forty-six convict stowaways were found on board, two of them women.

The first female beachcomber of whom anything is known was Charlotte Badger, formerly a London pickpocket and prostitute. Charlotte then moved to Worcester in the English Midlands, the town where I was born and grew up. At the Worcester Assizes in 1796 she was convicted of housebreaking and sentenced to seven years' transportation. Reportedly, she 'leered at the judge from the dock'. Charlotte Badger spent the next four years confined in English prisons and prison hulks. She then made the nine-month voyage to Port Jackson where for five years she was incarcerated in the Parramatta Female Factory. In 1806 she gave birth to a daughter, Anne. In June of that year she was transferred to Van Diemen's Land but on the passage south, together with some male convicts, she mutinied and seized the brig *Venus*. One account describes Charlotte as dressed in men's clothing during the mutiny, holding a flintlock pistol in one hand and a length of rope in the other, with which she flogged the captain. He, together with the rest of the loyal crew, was subsequently cast away on shore. In the Tasman Sea the *Venus* attacked another vessel and seized supplies. Now a pirate ship with a convict crew, the *Venus* set off into the Pacific. At the time of the mutiny Charlotte was described in the official record as '. . . very corpulent; had an infant child'.

In New Zealand Charlotte moved ashore in the Bay of Islands where in 1807, according to Captain Birnie of the brig *Commerce*, she was living with the Maori tribe Ngapuhi. The following year Captain Bunker reported that Charlotte had moved in with a *rangatira*, or chief, and had refused to accompany him back to the ship, saying she preferred to live among the Maori, which is unsurprising given that she was now an outlaw who would have been hanged if captured. In about 1815 she went back to sea, probably on board a New England whaler. In 1818 the whaler *Lafayette* reported that Charlotte was living at the Vava'u group in Tonga as the wife of a Polynesian chief with whom she had had at least one child.

According to the anthropologist Trevor Bentley, in the early 1800s several thousand beachcombers settled in the harbours and anchorages around New Zealand and a few penetrated inland. They were known as Pakeha Maori, a name which sums up the duality of the beachcomber experience. Most were Anglo-Celtic, a few were continental Europeans and there were a handful of Lascars and Africans. Almost all were runaway sailors who now made a permanent landfall in this ocean. The Pakeha Maori displayed the same characteristics as beachcombers in the tropical islands. They took Maori wives, spoke their language, were tattooed, and lived according to local customs and taboos. They fulfilled the same diverse range of roles as beachcombers elsewhere in the Pacific: intermediaries and interpreters in trade, mercenaries, armourers, slaves, artisans, smiths, boatbuilders, innovators, ship's pilots, gardeners, grog-sellers, and guides to missionaries and explorers.

New Zealand's beachcomber origins flavoured the course of its social development. In Australia it was always the Aboriginals who had been expected to assimilate into the Crown Colony. Beachcomber settlement was exceptional because it was the sailors who had to do the assimilating: their lives were always dependent on the goodwill of their hosts. At the same time, some Maori chiefs grew accustomed to being in positions of authority over whites. Still today, children of mixed marriages in New Zealand often identify as being Maori, not European. When the Treaty of Waitangi was signed in 1840, modern New Zealand was founded on a concept of bi-culturalism that is unique in colonial history.

Beachcombers were the first whites to live in New Zealand, so these sailors turned settlers were my distant forebears. At the start of my voyage I had wondered whether this beachcomber ancestry was for better or worse. A typical, but also telling, encounter with beachcombers occurred in Tonga when the mission ship *Duff* arrived in the anchorage in 1796. Two beachcombers were living ashore at the time, Benjamin Ambler from London and an Irishman, John Conelly, from Cork. More than thirty mostly young, fresh-faced missionaries were lined up behind the *Duff*'s rail and they certainly expressed all the usual scorn for the men of the beach: 'They soon showed themselves to be base and wicked creatures,' one of the missionaries wrote, '. . . [who] swore with the fluency of abandoned seamen'. Ambler had three wives, Conelly had four, and both men '. . . treated the women with brutish indecorum and cruelty'. But the missionaries would say none of this to the beachcombers' faces: '. . . however, we thought it prudent to engage their influence with the chiefs in our favour'. The writer has neatly summed up the essentially antagonistic relationship between vessel and shore; the beachcombers were despised, but they were also useful.

Most beachcombers came from the ranks of ordinary sailors. On board ship they had been men of little account, but through the turbulence of shipwreck, mutiny or desertion they found themselves on the sand where they learned something of value. Of all the sailors, beachcombers understood the islands best; they knew the customs, animist beliefs, taboos, tribal politics, languages, tides, currents and uncharted reefs. On shore they became wise men and their wisdom was the currency with which they traded. Ultimately, many ship's captains, even some missionaries, came to appreciate the roles played by beachcombers. Knowledge of the sea was all very well, but without knowledge of the islands, their voyages would end in failure, and possibly death.

Beachcombing should never be romanticized; in reality it was a clandestine, piecemeal, often violent and highly imperfect process. It was also an inseparable part of seafaring. Beachcombers arrived in the islands with the first voyages of discovery. As the numbers coming ashore increased, their places on board ship were taken by indigenous deckhands. In the end, the experiences of sailors in the Pacific for more than four centuries has been a journey towards co-existence.

By the time I arrived home at Waiheke Island I had made my peace with the men of the beach. The beachcombers themselves often considered their plight to be marked by misfortune. This might be so, but my great good fortune has been to sail in their wakes and make a permanent landfall, by accident rather than design, in a country that is the finest product of European voyaging in the Pacific.

In the mid-afternoon I saw Helen on her way to pick me up. A plume of dust was rising from the black fleck of the car as it twisted down the switchback road that leads to Man O' War Bay.

I glanced at my watch and saw with a moment's relief that she was rather late; this had been my own prerogative for so much of the previous six months. I gathered up the dinghy's sail, dagger-board, rudder and sheet, then climbed slowly up the shingle beach to the road.

Glossary

I have tried to keep the text as free from 'nauticalese' as possible but the use of some technical terms has proved unavoidable. Nautical language, particularly relating to types of boat and rig, can be extremely difficult to gloss as usage is constantly evolving. Many terms have meant different things in different countries at different times. A detailed account of the various meanings of some individual terms would run to several pages. The explanations offered here are intentionally simple – no doubt simplistic – and relate specifically to the ships sailing among the Pacific Islands in the eighteenth and nineteenth centuries. Purists will be horrified, but my hope is to make some of the quotations and other descriptions in the text accessible to the general reader. For definitions of boat types I have relied on that exemplary reference book, *A Dictionary of the World's Watercraft. From Aak to Zumbra*, Compiled by The Mariners' Museum (Chatham Publishing, London, 2000).

Atoll	A ring-shaped reef enclosing a lagoon. Small islands usually form on the reef, sometimes a continuous ribbon of land, rising no more than a few metres above sea level.
Backstays	Wire rigging from the masthead to the back of the boat.
Brig	Used here as an abbreviation for Brigantine: a relatively small two-masted ship once commonly used as a trader in the Pacific Islands.
Billytackle	A block and tackle used on board ship, usually with three parts.

Capshroud   Wire rigging from the masthead to the side deck.

Casuarina   A common tree in the Pacific and South-East Asia, with slender branches and very small leaves.

Cay   A low bank or reef of coral, rock or sand rising above the sea.

Coachroof   That part of the cabin roof raised above the deck.

Companionway   Steps leading from the deck down into the cabin.

Corvette   An armed vessel mounting up to 30 guns, usually three-masted, sometimes used for reconnaissance and exploration.

Crosstrees   A pair of horizontal struts attached to the mast to spread the rigging, also called 'Spreaders'.

Davit   A small crane or hoist.

Flybridge   An open deck above the main bridge of a vessel, usually equipped with duplicate controls.

Genoa   A large headsail.

Gybe   Change course by swinging the sail across a following wind.

Jolly boat   In the nineteenth-century British navy, a general-purpose open boat, equipped with oars, single or double-masted.

Kanak   The indigenous people of New Caledonia. In the nineteenth century the term 'Kanaka' was often used to describe any Pacific Islander, particularly those working as deckhands on European ships or as indentured labourers on plantations.

Kedge anchor   A smaller anchor, often rowed out by boat and used to manoeuvre the ship.

Lascar   A sailor from India or South-East Asia.

Launch   Usually the largest and sturdiest of a ship's open boats, used as a workboat for transporting water and provisions to the ship. Equipped with oars and sails, often double-masted.

Lee cloth	A piece of sailcloth attached to the side of a bunk to stop the occupant falling out at sea.
Longboat	A ship's boat on a man-of-war or merchantman, generally the largest, mainly used to lay out anchors, carry drinking water and stores, and as a lifeboat. Equipped with oars and sails. Generally superseded by the 'launch' in the nineteenth century.
Lugger	A generic term used to describe any working sailboat, regardless of rig or hull type.
Marae	A sacred ceremonial space in Polynesian cultures comprising land and buildings, or just an open area.
Mizzen mast	A second mast behind the ship's mainmast.
Ni-Vanuatu	The people of Vanuatu.
Overfalls	Waves created by wind against tide conditions, or a current or tide flowing over a shoal.
Pandanus	A tropical tree or shrub whose fibrous leaves are often used for weaving. Also called the 'Screw Pine'.
Pinnace	A ship's open boat, especially on a naval vessel, generally assigned to the lesser officers; equipped with oars and, typically, two equal sized sails.
Prau	A generic term for an indigenous vessel in South-East Asia.
Ratlines	Short, horizontal lengths of rope fastened in the rigging, used as a ladder for climbing aloft.
Rudder pintels	Pins or bolts on which the rudder turns.
Schooner	Typically a two-masted vessel, though in the nineteenth century the number of masts increased, ultimately reaching seven. On two-masted vessels, the rear mast was the taller. Commonly used for trading voyages to the South Pacific.

Sloop	The term has had a variety of meanings, depending on the era and place of usage. Typically today, a single-masted boat with two sails.
Soursop	A large acidic custard apple with white fibrous flesh.
Sprayhood	A canvas hood over the main hatchway to protect it from the elements.
Stem-head	The pointed front of the deck, where the anchor is stowed.
Supercargo	The owner's representative on a trading ship, responsible for the supervision and trading of the cargo.
Taffrail	The rail around a ship's stern.
Tapa	Cloth made by pounding the bark of the paper mulberry tree, used especially in Polynesia for clothing, bedding and decoration.
Taro	A staple plant in the Pacific Islands; both the tubers and leaves are edible.
Transom	The flat surface forming the stern of a boat.
Whisker pole	A light pole used for holding out a headsail for downwind sailing.
Wing-and-wing	The sails held out on either side of the boat for downwind sailing.
Yawl	The smaller open boats carried on naval ships in the eighteenth century. While most depended on their oars, a number also carried up to three masts.

Acknowledgements

If my passage to Torres Strait was powered by the winds and currents, the writing of this book has been no less dependent on the hospitality and guidance of those I met along the way. The people of Vanuatu welcomed me into their lagoons, villages and homes with a generosity I shan't forget: *Tangku tumas, evriwan*. Other than those mentioned in the text I would particularly like to thank Ralph Regenvanu and Abong Thompson at the Cultural Centre in Port Vila for fielding my endless requests and queries with patience and good cheer. Also: Joel Iau, Meleun Erna, Roch Luan, Jean-Claude Tambe and Romain Batick.

Professor John Lynch at the University of the South Pacific in Port Vila (*Yunivesiti blong Saot Pasifik blong Port Vila*) checked much of the Bislama that appears in this book although, of course, any errors, either of analysis or translation, are my own. Marsden Hordern was an inspiration throughout and led me to several manuscripts I would not otherwise have discovered. Judy MacDonald's passion for the remarkable Tikopia was infectious. Tom Ludvigson opened my mind to an interpretation of boats and sea travel I had not heard before. My father Chris Hordern is not a sailor but has always watched over my voyages from afar, sometimes with concern, but always with love and support; in this instance he also provided information from the family archives. I must also mention Guy Hordern, Clyde Binfield, Professor Hugh McLeod, Jean Robinson, Bernard Rhodes, Tania Thomas, Valerie and Dennis Crompton, and Kit Nelson at the Waiheke Island Historical Society.

ACKNOWLEDGEMENTS

The staff at various museums and libraries were most helpful, in particular: Peter Gesner (Museum of Tropical Queensland, Townsville) who shared with me his own research into the route taken by *Pandora*'s boats through the Labyrinth, Linda Groom (National Library of Australia, Canberra), Martin Beckett (State Library of New South Wales, Sydney), Betty Moss (Alexander Turnbull Library, Wellington, NZ), Christine Whybrew (Taranaki Museum, New Plymouth, NZ), Matthew Sheldon (Royal Naval Museum, Portsmouth) and Monica Petraglia (Newberry Library, Chicago).

I'm lucky to have among my friends so many willing readers, especially Clare Strack van Schijndel, James Magrane, Darren Conway, Natasha Hay and Pete Atkinson. My agent Judith Murray has always been an irrepressible source of enthusiasm and support. I'm very grateful to Gail Pirkis who commissioned the book and got me under way. The text has benefited enormously from the scrutiny and counsel of my editors at John Murray, Gordon Wise, Andrew Maxwell-Hyslop and Caro Westmore.

Most of all I owe a debt to Helen, my true anchor before, during and after the voyage. This book is dedicated to you with love and thanks.

Sources

Principal Sources

Arago, *Jacques, Narrative of a Voyage Around the World in the* Uranie *and* Physicienne *Corvettes Commanded by Captain Freycinet*, 2 vols, Treuttel & Wurtz, London, 1823

Beaglehole, J.C. (ed.), *The Journals of Captain James Cook on his Voyages of Discovery*, 3 vols, Hakluyt Society, Cambridge, 1967–69

Bligh, William, *A Voyage to the South Sea, undertaken by Command of His Majesty, for the Purpose of Conveying the Bread-fruit Tree to the West Indies, in His Majesty's Ship the* Bounty, George Nicol, London, 1792

The Log of the Bounty. *Being Lieutenant William Bligh's Log of the Proceedings of His Majesty's Armed Vessel* Bounty *in a Voyage to the South Seas*, 2 vols, Golden Cockerel Press, London, 1937

Bougainville, Louis Antoine, *A Voyage Around the World. Performed by Order of His Most Christian Majesty, In the Years 1766, 1767, 1768, and 1769*, Translated from the French by Johann Reinhold Forster, J. Nourse, London, 1771

Calkin, Milo, *The Last Voyage of the* Independence, privately published, San Francisco, 1870

Campbell, Archibald, *A Voyage Round the World, from 1806 to 1812 . . . with an Account of the Present State of the Sandwich Islands, and a Vocabulary of their Language*, Archibald Constable & Co., Edinburgh, 1816

Cary, William, *Wrecked on the Feejees. Experiences of a Nantucket Man a Century Ago, Who Was Sole Survivor of the Whaleship 'Oeno' and Lived for Nine Years Among the Cannibals in the South Seas*, Inquirer & Mirror Press, Nantucket, 1928

Cooper, H. S., *Coral Lands*, 2 vols, Richard Bentley & Son, London, 1880

Diapea, William, *Cannibal Jack: the True Autobiography of a White Man in the South Seas*, Faber & Gwyer Limited, London, 1928

Dillon, Peter, *Narrative and Successful Result of a Voyage to the South Seas, Performed by Order of the Government of British India, to Ascertain the Actual Fate of La Perouse's Expedition*, 2 vols, Hurst, Chance & Co., London, 1829

Edwards, Edward, *Papers, 1789-1792, re Mutiny on the* Bounty *and HMS* Pandora, unpublished manuscript, Mitchell Library, Sydney, [viewed on microfilm]

Captain's Letters, 'Pandora', *1792*, Public Records Office, London, ADM/1 No.6963

Edwards, Edward and Hamilton, George, *Voyage of H.M.S. 'Pandora', Despatched to Arrest the Mutineers of the 'Bounty' in the South Seas, 1790-91*, ed. Basil Thomson, Francis Edwards, London, 1915

Erskine, John, *Journal of a Cruise Among the Islands of the Western Pacific, Including the Feejees and Others Inhabited by the Polynesian Negro Races, in Her Majesty's ship 'Havannah'*, John Murray, London, 1853

Geddie, John, *Misi Gete. Pioneer Missionary to the New Hebrides*, ed. R. S. Miller, Presbyterian Church of Tasmania, Launceston, 1975

Jacobs, T. J., *Scenes, Incidents and Adventures in the Pacific Ocean . . . During the Cruise of the Clipper* Margaret Oakley, *under Captain Benjamin Morrell*, Harper Bros., New York, 1844

Lamont, E. H., *Wild Life Among the Pacific Islanders*, Hurst & Blackett, London, 1867

Lockerby, William, *The Journal of William Lockerby, Sandalwood Trader in the Fijian Islands during the Years 1808-1809: with an Introduction and Other Papers Connected with the Earliest European Visitors to the Islands*, Sir Im Thurm Everard & Leonard C. Wharton (eds.), Hakluyt Society, London, 1922

Martin, John, *An Account of the Natives of the Tonga Islands in the South Pacific Ocean . . . Comp. and Arranged from the Extensive Communications of Mr. William Mariner*, 2 vols, John Murray, London, 1817

Morrell, Benjamin, *A Narrative of Four Voyages to the South Sea*, J & J Harper, New York, 1832

Morrell, Abby Jane, *Narrative of a Voyage to the Ethiopic and South Atlantic Ocean, Indian Ocean, Chinese Sea, North and South Pacific Ocean in the Years 1829, 1830, 1831*, J & J Harper, New York, 1833

Morrison, James, *The Journal of James Morrison, Boatswain's Mate of the Bounty Describing the Mutiny and Subsequent Misfortunes of the Mutineers Together with an Account of the Island of Tahiti*, ed. Owen Rutter, Golden Cockerel Press, London, 1935

Moyle, Richard (ed.) *The Samoan Journals of John Williams*, Australian National University Press, Canberra, 1984

O'Connell, James, *A Residence of Eleven Years in New Holland and the Caroline Islands*, B.B. Mussey, Boston, 1836

Orange, Rev. James, *Life of the Late George Vason of Nottingham*, John Snow, London, 1840

Patterson, Samuel, *Narrative of the Adventures and Sufferings of Samuel Patterson Experienced in the Pacific Ocean and Many Other Parts of the World, with an Account of the Feegee and Sandwich Islands*, Palmer Press, Rhode Island, 1817

Pritchard, W. T., *Polynesian Reminiscences*, Chapman and Hall, London, 1866

Robarts, Edward, *The Marquesan Journal of Edward Robarts 1797-1824*, ed. Greg Dening , Australian National University Press, Canberra, 1974

Rutter, Owen (ed.), *The Court-Martial of the Bounty Mutineers*, William Hodge & Company Ltd., Edinburgh and London, 1931

Thomas, N., and Eves, R. (eds.), *Bad Colonists. The South Sea Letters of Vernon Lee Walker and Louis Becke*, Duke University Press, London and Durham, 1999

Turner, Rev. George, *Nineteen Years in Polynesia: Missionary Life, Travels and Researches in the Islands of the Pacific*, John Snow, London, 1861

Twyning, John, *Shipwreck and Adventures of John P. Twyning among the South Sea Islanders: giving an account of their Feasts, Massacres, &c &c.*, privately published, London, 1849

Vason, George, *An Authentic Narrative of Four Years' Residence at Tongataboo, one of the Friendly Islands, in the South Seas, by George Veeson, Who Went Thither in the Duff, Captain Wilson in 1796*, Longman, Hurst, Rees, Orme, L.B. Seeley & Hatchard, London, 1810

Williams, John, *A Narrative of Missionary Enterprises in the South Sea Islands*, John Snow, London, 1838

Other Sources

Baker, John, *Man and Animals in the New Hebrides*, George Routledge & Sons, London, 1929

Banfield, E. J., *Confessions of a Beachcomber*, T. Fisher Unwin, London, 1908

Barrow, Sir John, *The Eventful History and Piratical Seizure of HMS Bounty and its Consequences*, John Murray, London, 1831

Bentley, Trevor, *Pakeha Maori*, Penguin Books, Auckland, 1999

—— *Captured by Maori. White Female Captives, Sex and Racism on the Nineteenth-century New Zealand Frontier*, Penguin Books, Auckland, 2004

Bonnemaison, Joël, *The Tree and the Canoe: History and Ethnography of Tanna*, University of Honolulu Press, Hawaii, 1994

Bresnihan, J., & Woodward, K. (eds.), *Tufala Gavman. Reminiscences from the Anglo-French Condominium in the New Hebrides*, Institute of Pacific Studies, University of the South Pacific, Suva, 2002

Cameron, J. (ed.), *Letters from Port Essington 1838-1845*, Historical Society of the Northern Territory, Darwin, 1999

Campbell, Dr John, *The Martyr of Erromanga, or, the Philosophy of Missions Illustrated from the Labours, Death and Character of the Late Rev. John Williams*, John Snow, London, 1842

Chappell, David, 'Indigenous Beachcombers in the Pacific Islands', *Pacific Studies*, vol. 17, no. 2, June 1994

David, Andrew, 'Peter Heywood and Northwest Australia', *The Great Circle*, vol. 1, no. 1, 1979

Desmond, Ray, *Kew. The History of the Royal Botanic Gardens*, Harvill Press, London, 1995

L'Estrange, Rev. A., *Lady Belcher and Her Friends*, Hurst & Beckett, London, 1891

Firth, Sir Raymond, *We the Tikopia. A sociological study of kinship in primitive Polynesia*, George Allen & Unwin, London, 1936

Forster, Johann R., *Observations Made of a Voyage Around the World*, N. Thomas, H. Guest, & M. Dettelbach (eds.), University of Hawaii Press, Honolulu, 1996

Fletcher, Robert, *Isles of Illusion. Letters from the South Seas*, Constable, London, 1923

Foley, J., *Reef Pilots. The History of the Queensland Coast and Torres Strait Pilot Service*, Banks Brothers, Sydney, 1982

Freeman, J. D., 'The Joe Gimlett or Siovili Cult: An Episode in the Religious Life of Early Samoa', in *Anthropology in the South Seas,* J. D. Freeman, & W. R. Geddes (eds.), Thomas Avery & Sons, New Plymouth, 1959

Fryer, John, *The Voyage of the* Bounty*'s Launch. John Fryer's Narrative*, Genesis Publications, Guildford, 1979

Gajdusek, Carleton, *Journal of a Trip to the Shepherd, Banks and Torres Islands and to Espiritu Santo and Efate in the New Hebrides*, National Institute of Health, Bethesda, Md., 1965

Gardiner, Margaret, *Footprints on Malekula. A Memoir of Bernard Deacon*, Salamander Press, Edinburgh, 1984

Gutch, John, *Beyond the Reefs. The life of John Williams*, MacDonald, London, 1974

Heywood, N. & Heywood, P., T*he Heywood Manuscript*, unpublished manuscript, Newberry Library, Chicago, POS.2072 [viewed on microfilm]

Hordern, Marsden, *Mariners are Warned! John Lort Stokes and HMS Beagle in Australia 1837-1843*, Melbourne University Press, Melbourne, 1989

—— *King of the Australian Coast. The work of Phillip Parker King in the Mermaid and Bathurst 1817-1822*, Melbourne University Press, Melbourne, 1997

Johnson, Martin, *Cannibal Land*, Constable, London, 1922

Jones, John D., *Life and Adventures in the South Pacific by a Roving Printer*, Harper Brothers, New York, 1861

Kele-Kele, K. M., Stevens, J., et al. *New Hebrides: the Road to Independence*, Institute of Pacific Studies, University of the South Pacific, Suva, 1977

Krusenstern, A. J. von, *Voyage Round the World in the Years 1803, 1804, 1805 and 1806*, John Murray, London, 1813

Langsdorf, G. von, *Voyages and Travels in Various Parts of the World, During the Years 1803, 1804, 1805, 1806 and 1807*, 2 vols, Henry Colburn, London, 1813

Luke, Sir Harry, *From a South Seas Diary 1938-1942*, Nicholson and Watson, London, 1945

Malinowski, Bronislaw, *Argonauts of the Western Pacific. An Account of the Native Enterprise and Adventures in the Archipelagoes of Melanesian New Guinea*, George Routledge & Sons, London, 1922

Mariners' Museum (Parry, M., et. al.), *A Dictionary of the World's Watercraft. From Aak to Zumbra*, Chatham Publishing, London, 2000

Markham, Sir Clements (ed.), *The Voyages of Pedro Fernandez de Quiros, 1595 to 1607*, 2 vols, Hakluyt Society, Cambridge, 1904

—— *Early Spanish Voyages to the Straits of Magellan*, Hakluyt Society, Cambridge, 1911

Marshall, A. J., *The Black Musketeers*, William Heinemann, London, 1937

Maude, H. E., *Of Islands and Men: Studies in Pacific History*, Studies in Pacific History, Melbourne, 1968

McNab, Robert, *Historical Records of New Zealand*, 2 vols, Government Publication, Wellington, 1908

Miller, Graham, 'Naked Cult in Central West Santo', *Journal of the Polynesian Society* Vol.57/4. 1948

Murray, Rev. A., *Missions in the Western Pacific*, John Snow, London, 1862

Neale, Tom, *An Island to Oneself*, Collins, London, 1966

Paton, James, G., *John G. Paton, Missionary to the New Hebrides: an Autobiography Edited by his Brother Reverend James Paton*, Banner of Truth Trust, London, 1894

Ralston, Caroline, *Grass Huts and Warehouses. Pacific Beach Communities in the Nineteenth Century*, Australian National University Press, Canberra, 1977

Robertson, Rev. H., *Erromanga. The Martyr's Isle*, Hodder & Stoughton, London, 1902

Rodham, M. Critchlow, *Houses Far From Home. British Colonial Space in the New Hebrides*, University of Honolulu Press, Hawaii, 2001

Sharp, N., *Saltwater People. The Waves of Memory*, Allen & Unwin, Sydney, 2002

Shineberg, Dorothy, *They Came for Sandalwood: A Study of the Sandalwood Trade in the South-west Pacific 1830-1865*, Melbourne University Press, Melbourne, 1967

—— 'Guns and Men in Melanesia,' *The Journal of Pacific History* 6, pp.61–82, 1984

Wilkes, Charles, *Narrative of the United States Exploring Expedition During* the Years 1838, 1839, 1840, 1841, 1842, 5 vols, Wiley & Putman, London, 1845

Wilson, Adam, 'Santo's Part in the Pacific War,' *Quarterly Jottings from the New Hebrides*, vol. 212, 1946

Wilson, James, *A Missionary Voyage to the Southern Pacific Ocean, Performed in the Years 1796, 1797, 1798, in the Ship* Duff, *Commanded by Captain James Wilson*, T. Chapman, London, 1799

Wynne, Barry, *The Man Who Refused to Die. Teehu Makimare's 2,000 Mile Drift in an Open Boat Across the South Pacific*, Souvenir Press, London, 1966